KT-104-033

Essentials of Employment Law

Fourth Edition

David Lewis

Institute of Personnel Management

© David Lewis 1983, 1986, 1990, 1994

First published 1983
Second edition 1986
Reprinted 1987
Third edition 1990
Reprinted 1991 and 1992
Fourth edition 1994

All rights reserved. No part of this publication may be reproduced, stored in an information storage and retrieval system, or transmitted in any form or by any means, electronic, mechanical, photocopying, recording or otherwise, without written permission of the Institute of Personnel Management, IPM House, Camp Road, Wimbledon, London SW19 4UX.

British Library Cataloguing in Publication Data

Lewis, David
 Essentials of Employment Law. – 4Rev.ed
 I. Title
 344.1041125024658

 ISBN 0–85292–536–0

The views expressed in this book are the author's own, and may not necessarily reflect those of the IPM.

Phototypeset by Intype, London
and printed in Great Britain by
Short Run Press, Exeter

INSTITUTE OF PERSONNEL MANAGEMENT
IPM House, Camp Road, Wimbledon, London SW19 4UX
Tel: 081–946–9100 Fax: 081–946–2570
Registered office as above. Registered Charity No. 215797
A company limited by guarantee. Registered in England No. 198002

Contents

Preface and acknowledgements

The law is stated as at 4th March 1994. However, the text anticipates the implementation of the maternity provisions contained
in the Trade Union Reform and Employment Rights Act 1993. It
is clear that amendments will be needed to ensure that the hours
thresholds for unfair dismissal and redundancy are compatible
with European law (see page 50). In addition, it is expected that
the following changes will occur later in the year: the laws relating
to Sunday trading will be altered, the limit on compensation in
race discrimination cases will be lifted, the jurisdiction of industrial
tribunals will be extended to certain breach of contract cases and
the Deregulation and Contracting Out Bill will have an impact on
both unfair dismissal and health and safety laws.

I am very grateful to Siobhan Vitelli and all the IPM staff who
contributed to the production of this edition. Thanks also go to
Phil James for his contribution and to my colleagues in the Law
School for their support.

Finally, I would like to dedicate this edition to the memory of
Harry Barnett and Harry Pitkin, both of whom encouraged me in
their different ways.

David Lewis
Middlesex University
March 1994

Abbreviations

ABP	Associated British Ports
AC	Appeal Cases
ACAS	Advisory, Conciliation and Arbitration Service
ACOP	Approved Code of Practice
AER	All England Law Reports
AHA	Area Health Authority
AMRA 1988	Access to Medical Reports Act 1988
APAC	Association of Patternmakers and Allied Crafts
APEX	Association of Professional, Executive, Clerical and Computer Staff
ASTMS	Association of Scientific, Technical and Managerial Staffs
ATGWU	Amalgamated Transport and General Workers Union
AUEW	Amalgamated Union of Engineering Workers
AUT	Association of University Teachers
BC	Borough Council
BFAWU	Bakers, Food and Allied Workers Union
BICC	British Insulated Calendar Cables
BL	British Leyland
BRS	British Road Services
CAC	Central Arbitration Committee
CC	County Council
Ch	Chancery Division
CMLR	Common Market Law Reports
COSHH	Control Of Substances Hazardous to Health Regulations 1988
CRE	Commission for Racial Equality
CSU	Civil Service Union

DC	District Council
DE	Department of Employment
DES	Department of Education and Science
DSS	Department of Social Security
DPA 1984	Data Protection Act 1984
EA 1980	Employment Act 1980
EA 1982	Employment Act 1982
EA 1988	Employment Act 1988
EA 1989	Employment Act 1989
EA 1990	Employment Act 1990
EAT	Employment Appeal Tribunal
EC	European Community
ECA 1972	European Communities Act 1972
ECJ	European Court of Justice
EETPU	Electrical, Electronic, Telecommunication and Plumbing Union
EOC	Equal Opportunities Commission
EPA 1970	Equal Pay Act 1970
EPCA 1978	Employment Protection (Consolidation) Act 1978
EPEA	Electrical Power Engineers Association
EU	European Union
EWC	Expected Week of Confinement
FTUB Regs 1984, 1988	Funds for Trade Union Ballot Regulations 1984, 1988
GCHQ	Government Communications Headquarters
GES	General Engineering Services
GMBATU	General Municipal and Boilermakers Union
GOQ	Genuine Occupational Qualification
HA	Health Authority
HASAWA 1974	Health and Safety at Work, etc. Act 1974
HB	Health Board
HMSO	Her Majesty's Stationery Office
HSC	Health and Safety Commission
HSE	Health and Safety Executive

ICR	Industrial Cases Reports
IPCS	Institute of Professional Civil Servants
IPM	Institute of Personnel Management
IRLB	Industrial Relations Law Bulletin (formerly Industrial Relations Legal Information Bulletin)
IRLR	Industrial Relations Law Reports
IRRR	Industrial Relations Review and Report
IT	Industrial Tribunal
ITR	Industrial Tribunal Reports
ITWF	International Transport Workers Federation
LBC	London Borough Council
LIFO	Last In, First Out
MBC	Metropolitan Borough Council
MDC	Metropolitan District Council
MHSW 1992	Management of Health and Safety at Work Regulations 1992
MLP	Maternity Leave Period
MPP	Maternity Pay Period
MR	Master of the Rolls
NALGO	National and Local Government Officers Association
NATFHE	National Association of Teachers in Further and Higher Education
NATSOPA	National Society of Operative Printers, Graphical and Media Personnel
NCB	National Coal Board
NFU	National Farmers' Union
NGA	National Graphical Association
NUGSAT	National Union of Gold, Silver and Allied Trades
NUJ	National Union of Journalists
NUM	National Union of Mineworkers
NUPE	National Union of Public Employees
NUR	National Union of Railwaymen
NUT	National Union of Teachers

QB	Queen's Bench
RHA	Regional Health Authority
RRA 1976	Race Relations Act 1976
SDA 1975	Sex Discrimination Act 1975
SI	Statutory Instrument
SMP	Statutory Maternity Pay
SOGAT	Society of Graphical and Allied Trades
SRSC Regs 1977	Safety Representatives and Safety Committees Regulations 1977
SSA 1986	Social Security Act 1986
SSA 1989	Social Security Act 1989
SSCBA 1992	Social Security Contributions and Benefits Act 1992
SSHBA 1982	Social Security and Housing Benefits Act 1982
SSP	Statutory Sick Pay
SSP Regs 1982	Statutory Sick Pay (General) Regulations 1982
TGWU	Transport and General Workers' Union
TLR	Times Law Reports
Transfer Regs 1981	Transfer of Undertakings (Protection of Employment) Regulations 1981
TUA 1984	Trade Union Act 1984 (as amended)
TUBIA	Trade Union Ballots and Industrial Action, Code of Practice on, HMSO 1990
TUC	Trades Union Congress
TULRCA	Trade Union and Labour Relations (Consolidation) Act 1992
TURERA 1993	Trade Union Reform and Employment Rights Act 1993
UCATT	Union of Construction and Allied Trades Technicians
UCW	Union of Communication Workers
USDAW	Union of Shop, Distributive and Allied Workers
WLR	Weekly Law Reports
WMC	Working Men's Club

List of cases cited

1 The sources and institutions of employment law

Civil and criminal law

Criminal law is concerned with offences against the state and, apart from private prosecutions, it is the state which enforces this branch of the law. The sanctions typically imposed on convicted persons are fines and imprisonment. Civil law deals with the situations where a private person who has suffered harm brings an action against (i.e. sues) the person who committed the wrongful act which caused the harm. Normally the purpose of suing is to recover damages or compensation. Criminal and civil matters are normally dealt with in separate courts which have their own distinct procedures.

In this book we shall be concentrating largely on civil law but we shall be describing the criminal law in so far as it imposes duties in relation to health and safety and restricts the activities of pickets. In employment law the two most important civil actions are those based on the law of contract and the law of tort. The essential feature of a contract is a binding agreement in which an offer by one person (for example, an employer) is accepted by someone else (for example, a person seeking work). This involves an exchange of promises. Thus, in a contract of employment, there is a promise to pay wages in exchange for a promise to be available for work. As we shall see later, the parties to a contract are not entirely free to negotiate their own terms because Parliament imposes certain restrictions and minimum requirements. The law of tort places a duty on everyone not to behave in a way that is likely to cause harm to others, and in the employment field the tort of negligence has been applied so as to impose a duty on employers to take reasonable care of their employees during the course of their employment. Various torts have also been created by the judiciary in order to impose legal liability for industrial

1

action, for example the tort of interfering with trade or business, but Parliament has intervened to provide immunities in certain circumstances (*see* chapter 20).

Legislation and codes of practice

In this country the most important source of law governing industrial relations is legislation enacted by Parliament. Once a Bill has been passed by both the House of Commons and the House of Lords and received the Royal Assent, it becomes an Act (or statute). It is then referred to (cited) by its name and year, which constitutes its 'short title' (*e.g.* Trade Union Reform and Employment Rights Act 1993). The provisions of an Act may not be brought into operation immediately, for the government may wish to implement it in stages. Nevertheless, once the procedure is completed the legislation is valid. The main provisions of a statute are to be found in its numbered sections, whereas administrative details, repeals and amendments of previous legislation tend to be contained in the schedules at the back. Statutes sometimes give the relevant Secretary of State the power to make rules (regulations) to supplement those laid down in the Act itself. These regulations, which are normally subject to parliamentary approval, are referred to as statutory instruments (SI) and this process of making law is known as delegated or subordinate legislation. Statutory instruments are cited by their name, year and number (*e.g.* the Industrial Tribunal (Constitution and Rules of Procedure) Regulations 1993, SI No 2678.

Since the United Kingdom joined the European Community (EC) in 1973 it has been subject to the Treaty of Rome and to the delegated legislation of both the European Commission and the Council of Ministers. The European Communities Act 1972 (ECA 1972) allows EC laws to take effect in the UK in different ways. First, section 2(1) enables directly effective EC obligations to be enforced as free-standing rights. Thus in *McCarthy's Ltd v Smith*[1] Article 119 (on equal pay) was applied following a reference to the European Court of Justice. However, difficulties have arisen in distinguishing between Directives which can be enforced 'horizontally' (i.e. against private individuals and non-state bodies) and those which are only actionable 'vertically' (i.e. against organs of the state). For example, again on the issue of pay, whereas Directive 75/117 has been treated as having 'horizontal' effect, Directive 76/207 has been regarded as only 'vertically' enforceable. Second, section 2(2) of the ECA 1972 facilitates the introduction of subordinate legislation to achieve compliance with those Community obligations which are not directly enforceable, *e.g.* the Transfer of Undertakings Regulations 1981. Articles 169 and 170 of the Treaty of Rome enable the European Commission to take steps to ensure that the UK complies with its obligation to give effect to Directives. In addition, a person who is not an employee of an organ of the state may be able to obtain damages if a Directive is not implemented.[2] Finally, section 2(4) of the ECA 1972 states that 'any enactment or provision to be passed, other than one contained in this part of the Act, shall be construed and have effect subject to the foregoing provisions of this section'. It was this subsection that was relied on in *Pickstone v Freeman's PLC*[3] when the House of Lords observed that national legislation should be construed in a way which is consistent with the objects of the Treaty, the provisions of any relevant Directives and the rulings of the European Court of Justice. In relation to the interpretation of Directives, this principle applies whether the national legislation came after or preceded the particular Directive.[4]

A relatively recent innovation in the field of employment law has been the issuance of Codes of Practice. The primary function of these codes is to educate managers and workers by publicizing the practices and procedures which the government believes are conducive to good industrial relations. Under section 199 of the Trade Union and Labour Relations (Consolidation) Act 1992 (TULRCA 1992) the Advisory, Conciliation and Arbitration Service (ACAS) has a general power to issue codes 'containing such practical guidance as [ACAS] thinks fit for the purpose of promoting the improvement of industrial relations'. Following representations by interested parties ACAS submits a draft code to the Secretary of State for approval before it is laid before Parliament. At the time of writing ACAS Codes of Practice exist on the following topics: *Disciplinary Practice and Procedures in Employment; Disclosure of Information to Trade Unions for Collective Bargaining Purposes*; and *Time Off for Trade Union Duties and Activities.* The Equal Opportunities Commission (EOC) and the Commission for Racial Equality (CRE) have also issued codes of the same standing as those of ACAS and by virtue of section 16 of the Health and Safety at Work Act 1974 (HASAWA 1974) the Health and Safety Commission (HSC) has the power to approve Codes of Practice provided it obtains the consent of the Secretary of State on each occasion. Finally, sections 203–6 TULRCA 1992 entitles the Secretary of State to issue codes, but before publishing a draft he or she is obliged to consult ACAS. However, no such duty exists if a code is merely being revised to bring it into conformity with subsequent statutory provisions.[5] Although emerging by different means, all these codes have the same legal standing, i.e. nobody can be sued or prosecuted for breaching a code, but in any proceedings before a tribunal, court (if the code was issued under TULRCA 1992 or HASAWA 1974) or the Central Arbitration Committee (CAC) a failure to adhere to a recommendation 'shall be taken into account'.

The common law and the court hierarchy

The feature which distinguishes the English legal system from non-common law systems is that in this country judicial decisions have been built up to form a series of binding precedents. This is known as the case-law method. In practice this means that tribunals and judges are bound by the decisions of judges in higher courts. Thus industrial tribunals, which are at the bottom of the English court hierarchy, are required to follow the decisions of the Employment Appeal Tribunal (EAT or Appeal Tribunal), Court of Appeal and the Appeal Committee of the House of Lords, although they are not bound by other industrial tribunal decisions. The Employment Appeal Tribunal is bound by the decisions of the Court of Appeal and the House of Lords and normally follows its own previous decisions. The Court of Appeal has a civil and criminal division and, while both are bound by the House of Lords' decisions, only the civil division is constrained by its own previous decisions. The House of Lords has stated that it will regard its own earlier decisions as binding unless in the circumstances of a particular case it is thought just to depart from them. Of course all English courts must abide by the decisions of the European Court of Justice.

What constitutes the binding element of a judicial decision is for a judge or tribunal in a subsequent case to determine. Theoretically what has to be followed is the legal principle or principles which are relied on in reaching the decision in the earlier case. In practice judges and tribunals have a certain amount of discretion, for they can take a broad or narrow view of the principles which are binding upon them. If they do not like the principles that have emerged, they can refuse to apply them so long as they are prepared to conclude that the facts of the case before them are sufficiently different from the facts in the previous decision. Not surprisingly, this technique is known as 'distinguishing'. Thus, while it is correct to argue that the doctrine of precedent imports an element of certainty, it is wrong to assume that there is no scope for innovation in the lower courts. In addition to interpreting the law, the judiciary can and does make law.

The court structure in England and Wales is shown in diagrammatic form in Figure 1. Most proceedings involving individual employment rights are commenced at industrial tribunals and appeals against an industrial tribunal decision can normally only be heard by the EAT if there has been an error of law. An error of law occurs where a tribunal has misdirected itself as to the applicable law, where there is no evidence to support a particular finding of fact or where the tribunal has reached a perverse conclusion, *i.e.* one which cannot be justified on the evidence presented.[6] Further appeals can be made on a point of law to the Court of Appeal and the House of Lords, but only if permission is granted by either the body which made the decision or the court which would hear the appeal. Other civil actions can be started in the County Court or High Court (*see* page 140). Appeals on a point of law from a decision made by either court can be lodged with the Court of Appeal and, if permission is granted, further appeal lies to the House of Lords. There is also a 'leapfrog procedure' which enables an appeal from a decision of the High Court to go directly to the House of Lords so long as all the parties involved give their consent.

Criminal proceedings are normally commenced in magistrates' courts, for example if pickets are charged with obstructing police officers in the execution of their duty. The defence can launch an appeal on fact which goes to the Crown Court but it is also possible for either party to appeal on a point of law to the Divisional Court of the Queen's Bench and then on to the House of Lords.

CIVIL COURT STRUCTURE

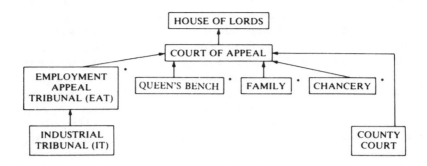

CRIMINAL COURT STRUCTURE

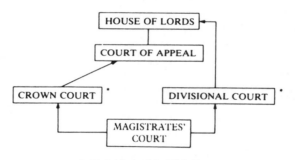

* All divisions of the High Court

Figure 1

Prosecutions for indictable offences, for example under section 33 of HASAWA 1974, are dealt with in the Crown Court and appeals on a point of law go to the Court of Appeal and the House of Lords in the usual way.

The key institutions

Industrial tribunals

Industrial tribunals were first established under the Industrial Training Act 1964 but their jurisdiction has now been extended to cover applications relating to the matters listed in appendix 1. The Central Office of Industrial Tribunals for England and Wales is situated in Bury St Edmunds and for Scotland in Glasgow. In addition there are 14 regional offices each with their own secretariat. The President of these tribunals is a barrister or solicitor of seven year's standing who is appointed by the Lord Chancellor for a five-year term. Normally tribunal cases are heard by legally qualified chairpersons and two other people who are known as lay members.[7] Tribunal appointments are for five years initially and, whereas the chairpersons are appointed by the Lord Chancellor and are subject to the same qualification requirements as the President, the lay members are appointed by the Secretary of State for Employment. The lay members are drawn from two panels; one is formed as a result of nominations made by employer organizations and the other consists of nominees from organizations of workers. Two important points should be noted in relation to the composition of industrial tribunals. First, while lay members are expected to have specialist knowledge of industrial relations they are not supposed to act as representatives of their nominating organizations. Secondly, women and racial minorities are significantly under-represented as both chairpersons and lay members, a fact which causes concern in the light of the tribunals' role in enforcing anti-discrimination legislation.

Hearings at industrial tribunals are relatively informal.[8] The parties, known as applicants and respondents, may represent themselves or be represented by a legal practitioner, a trade union official, a representative from an employers' association or any other person. In practice employers tend to be legally represented more often than employees, one reason being the unavailability of legal aid at present. (Applicants may be able to obtain advice and assistance in preparing their case under the legal aid scheme.) Personnel managers should give very serious thought to the question of representation, since the manager who understands how the shop floor operates and is familiar with the types of argument that may be raised by the disciplinary process may prove more effective than a lawyer from outside. Apart from appeals against improvement or prohibition notices issued under HASAWA 1974, costs are not normally awarded unless either party is deemed to have acted frivolously, vexatiously, abusively, disruptively, or

otherwise unreasonably in bringing or conducting the proceedings.[9]

Tribunal decisions can be challenged either by review or appeal.
The power of review, which enables a tribunal to rehear the whole
or part of a case and set aside or vary the original decision, may
be exercised only on one of the following grounds:

(i)   the decision was wrongly made as a result of error on the
       part of tribunal staff
(ii)   a party did not receive notice of the proceedings
(iii) the decision was made in the absence of a person entitled
       to be heard
(iv)   new evidence has become available since the making of the
       decision and its existence could not have been reasonably
       known of or foreseen
(v)   the interests of justice require a review.[10]

Applications for review must be made within 14 days of the tribunal decision being entered on the register which is kept by the
Secretary of the tribunals. The review may be heard by the tribunal
responsible for the original decision or by a differently constituted
one. An appeal to the Employment Appeal Tribunal can normally
only be made on a point of law and must be lodged within 42
days of the decision or order being sent to the appellant.[11]

The Employment Appeal Tribunal (EAT)

The EAT, which was established in 1976, has a central office in
London but can sit anywhere in England, Wales or Scotland. It
consists of High Court judges nominated by the Lord Chancellor
(one of whom serves as President) and a panel of lay members
who are appointed on the joint recommendation of the Lord
Chancellor and the Secretary of State. This panel consists of nominees from employers' and workers' organizations. Appeals are
heard by a judge and either two or four laypersons, all of whom
have equal voting rights. However, a judge can sit alone where
the appeal arises from proceedings before an industrial tribunal
consisting of the chair alone.

Parties can be represented by whomsoever they please and costs
will only be awarded where the proceedings are deemed to have
been unnecessary, improper, or vexatious or where there has been

unreasonable conduct in bringing or conducting the proceedings.[12] Apart from appeals on points of law this body can hear appeals on fact from a decision of the Certification Officer under section 2 TULRCA 1992 (entry on the list of trade unions), and section 6 TULRCA 1992 (certificates of independence). The EAT has the same review powers as industrial tribunals. Finally, the Appeal Tribunal may adjourn proceedings where there is a reasonable prospect of a conciliated settlement being reached.[13]

The Advisory, Conciliation and Arbitration Service (ACAS)

ACAS has been in existence since 1974. Its work is directed by a council consisting of a chairperson and nine members appointed by the Secretary of State. Three members are appointed after consultation with trade unions, three following consultation with employers' organizations and the remainder are independent. The Service is divided into nine regions which perform most of the day to day work, for example, handling direct enquiries from the public. Although ACAS is financed by the Government, section 147(3) TULRCA 1992 states that it shall not be 'subject to directions of any kind from any Minister of the Crown as to the manner in which it is to exercise its functions'.

ACAS is charged with the general duty of promoting the improvement of industrial relations, in particular, by exercising its functions in relation to the settlement of trade disputes.[14] It also has specific functions which merit separate consideration:

(i) Advice
ACAS may, on request or on its own initiative, provide advice to employers, their associations, workers and trade unions on any matter concerned with or affecting industrial relations.[15] In practice the forms of advice range from telephone inquiries to in-depth projects, diagnostic surveys and training exercises. In 1992 787 in-depth exercises were carried out and 4964 advisory visits were made.

(ii) Conciliation
Where a trade dispute exists or is likely to arise ACAS may, on request or of its own volition, offer assistance to the parties with a view to bringing about a settlement. This may be achieved by

conciliation or other means, for example the appointment of an independent person to render assistance. Before attempting to conciliate in collective trade disputes, ACAS is required to 'have regard to the desirability of encouraging the parties to a dispute to use any appropriate agreed procedures'.[16] According to its Annual Report for 1992, in 85 per cent of the cases where it provided collective conciliation a settlement was achieved or progress was made towards a settlement. Pay and other terms and conditions of employment were the most frequent issues in the disputes conciliated (41 per cent) and 51 per cent of requests for assistance came from both parties jointly.

In addition to collective matters ACAS has the task of conciliating in industrial tribunal cases other than claims for redundancy payments.[17] Particular officers have been designated and are known as 'Conciliation Officers (Tribunals)'. When a complaint is presented to an industrial tribunal a copy of it will be sent to one of these officers who has the duty to promote a settlement without the matter having to go to a hearing. Conciliation officers can intervene if requested to do so by the parties or where they believe they could act with a reasonable prospect of success. At the instigation of either party the officer may act before a complaint has been presented in respect of a matter which could be the subject of tribunal proceedings. (For the conciliation officer's particular duty in unfair dismissal cases, *see* chapter 14.) So as not to undermine the conciliation process it is stipulated that anything communicated to an officer in connection with the performance of her or his functions shall not be admissible in evidence in any proceedings before an industrial tribunal without the consent of the person who communicated it. The ACAS report for 1992 reveals that 32 per cent of tribunal applications reached a hearing although the rate of settlement, withdrawal and abandonment varies according to the particular jurisdiction. In 1992, of the 72,166 cases received for conciliation about 61 per cent were concerned with unfair dismissal, 12 per cent were concerned with discrimination, 23 per cent were under the Wages Act 1986 and 4 per cent involved other employment protection provisions.

(iii)   Arbitration
At the request of one party but with the consent of all the parties to a collective dispute (or potential dispute), ACAS may appoint

an arbitrator or arbitration panel from outside the Service or refer the matter to be heard by the Central Arbitration Committee. In performing this function ACAS is obliged to consider whether the dispute could be resolved by conciliation, and arbitration is not to be offered unless agreed procedures for the negotiation and settlement of disputes have been exhausted (save where there is a special reason which justifies arbitration as an alternative to those procedures).[18] CAC awards can only be published with the consent of all parties involved. According to the ACAS report for 1992, 33 per cent of the 162 cases referred to arbitration and mediation involved disputes over pay and terms and conditions of employment and 35 per cent were concerned with discipline and dismissal. 145 cases went to a single arbitrator, seven to boards of arbitration and seven to a single mediator. There were no references to the CAC in 1992.

(iv) Inquiry

ACAS may inquire into any question relating to industrial relations generally, in a particular industry or in a particular undertaking. Any advice or findings which emerge may be published so long as the views of all concerned parties have been taken into account.[19]

(v) Other duties

Apart from the general power to issue codes of practice (*see* page 3) the only remaining duty is to offer conciliation where a recognized union has lodged a complaint that an employer has failed to disclose information which it requires for collective bargaining purposes (*see* chapter 16).

The Central Arbitration Committee (CAC)

The CAC consists of a chairperson, deputy chairpersons and other members all of whom are appointed by the Secretary of State after consultation with ACAS. The members must have experience as employer or worker representatives, while the deputy chairpersons tend to be lawyers or academic experts in industrial relations. Like ACAS, the CAC is not subject to directions from a Minister. Apart from receiving requests to arbitrate directly from parties to a dispute, the CAC receives arbitration requests from ACAS (*see* above). Additionally the CAC is required to make determinations under sections 183–5 TULRCA 1992 (dealing with complaints arising from a failure to disclose information). CAC awards are published and take effect as part of the contracts of employees covered by the award. Unless it can be shown that the CAC exceeded its jurisdiction,[20] breached the rules of natural justice or committed an error of law,[21] no court can overturn its decisions.

According to the CAC annual report for 1992, 28 references were received. Of the 26 cases completed, 12 were withdrawn after an informal meeting was held, 12 resulted in a settlement without action being taken by the CAC and there were two formal awards.

The Certification Officer

The Certification Officer is also appointed by the Secretary of State after consultation with ACAS and is required to produce an annual report for them. He or she is responsible for maintaining a list of trade unions and employers' associations and if an application is submitted has to determine whether or not a listed union qualifies for a certificate of independence. If the application is rejected the union can appeal to the EAT on a point of law or fact. The Certification Officer also handles disputes which arise from trade union amalgamations and mergers and the administration of union political funds. However, under these jurisdictions an appeal is only possible if a point of law is involved. The Certification Officer is responsible for administering the scheme for providing payment towards expenditure incurred by independent trade unions in respect of designated ballots and may hear complaints that the provisions of chapter IV TULRCA 1992 have been infringed (*see* chapter 19). On union elections the Certification Officer can determine the procedure to be followed on any application or complaint received.[22] Finally under the Trade Union Reform and Employment Rights Act 1993 (TURERA 1993) the Certification Officer can direct a trade union to produce documents relating to its financial affairs. Where it appears that there is impropriety the Certification Officer can appoint inspectors to investigate (*see* chapter 19).[23]

The Commissioner for the Rights of Trade Union Members

This person is empowered to offer assistance to union members who are thinking of bringing legal proceedings against their unions for breach of the rules or specified statutory duties.[24] This assistance may include the making of arrangements for bearing the costs of advice or assistance by a solicitor or barrister and representation in proceedings. Although the Commissioner will normally have a wide discretion, when assistance is sought with a complaint about union elections or political fund ballots, it must be granted if the Certification Officer has made a declaration and the Commissioner thinks that the application has a reasonable prospect of success.[25] However, assistance cannot be provided for an application to the Certification Officer.

The Commissioner for Protection Against Unlawful Industrial Action

This person can also make arrangements for legal advice and representation. However, the facility is currently available only in relation to proceedings brought in respect of unlawful industrial action by a trade union. In deciding whether to grant assistance the Commissioner may have regard to:

(i)   whether the case is so complex that it is unreasonable to expect the applicant to deal with it unaided; and

(ii) whether the case involves a matter of substantial public interest or concern.[26]

Notes

1   [1980] IRLR 208.
2   See *Francovich v Republic of Italy* [1992] IRLR 84.
3   [1988] IRLR 357. See now *R v Secretary of State ex parte EOC* (1994) TLR 4/3/94.
4   See *Marleasing SA v Comercial Internacional de Alimentacion SA* [1992] 1 CMLR 305.
5   See section 205 TULRCA 1992.
6   *British Telecom v Sheridan* [1990] IRLR 27.
7   Section 128 of the Employment Protection (Consolidation) Act 1978

(EPCA 1978) provides that certain claims can be heard by a tribunal chair sitting alone.

8   On tribunal practice and procedure *see* specialist texts listed in the bibliography.

9   Rule 12 Schedule 1 Industrial Tribunal (Constitution and Rules of Procedure) Regulations 1993 SI No 2678.

10 Rule 11 Schedule 1 Industrial Tribunal (Constitution and Rules of Procedure) Regulations 1993 SI No 2678.

11 Rule 3 EAT Rules 1993 SI No 2854.

12 Rule 34 EAT Rules 1993. Section 14 TURERA 1993 allows the EAT to make a 'restriction of proceedings' order against a vexatious litigant in certain circumstances.

13 Rule 36 EAT Rules 1993.

14 Section 209 TULRCA 1992. On fees for the exercise of ACAS's functions see section 251A TULRCA 1992.

15 Section 213 TULRCA 1992.

16 Section 210(3) TULRCA 1992.

17 See sections 133–4 EPCA 1978.

18 See section 212(3) TULRCA 1992.

19 See section 214 TULRCA 1992.

20 See *R v CAC ex parte Hy-Mac Ltd* [1979] IRLR 461.

21 See *R v CAC ex parte BTP Tioxide* [1985] IRLR 61.

22 See section 256 TULRCA 1992.

23 See section 37A-E TULRCA 1992.

24 See section 109 TULRCA 1992.

25 See section 110 TULRCA 1992.

26 See section 235B TULRCA 1992.

2 Formation of the contract of employment (1) The sources of contractual terms

Apart from apprentices and merchant seamen who can only be employed under written deeds and articles respectively, contracts of employment may be oral or in writing. A contract of employment is like any other contract in the sense that it is subject to the general principles of law. In theory this means that the parties are free to negotiate the terms and conditions that suit them so long as they remain within the constraints imposed by statute and the common law. In practice, however, about half the workforce do not negotiate on an individual basis, but are engaged on such terms and conditions as are laid down in currently operative collective agreements.

One aspect of the common law which has been relied on, particularly in unfair dismissal cases, is the principle that courts will not enforce an illegal contract. Thus, if employees receive additional payments which are not taxed, they may be debarred from exercising statutory rights on the ground that they were not employed under valid contracts of employment.[1] However, an employee's dishonesty against an employer does not render the contract illegal in the same way.[2]

Whether the employee is affected by the illegal performance of the contract by the employer depends on whether the employee was a party to or knew of the employer's illegality.[3] In *Coral Leisure Ltd v Barnet*[4] the EAT ruled that a distinction had to be drawn between cases in which there was a contractual obligation to do an unlawful act, and cases where contractual obligations were capable of being performed lawfully and were initially intended to be so performed, but which had, in fact, been performed by unlawful means. The doing of an unlawful act by a party does not, of itself, preclude the further enforcement of that contract. Thus in *Hewcastle Catering v Ahmed*[5] the employee's involvement in a VAT fraud devised by the employer, and from which only the employer benefited, did not preclude a claim of unfair dismissal. According to the Court of Appeal, the general principle that a contract is unenforceable on grounds of illegality applies if in all the circumstances the court would appear to encourage illegal conduct. However, the defence of illegality will not succeed where the employer's conduct in participating in the illegal contract is so reprehensible in comparison with that of the employee that it would be wrong to allow the employer to rely on it.

Although a contract of employment can be entered into quite informally, because of the consequences of having an employee on the books (*see* chapter 4) a considerable degree of formality is desirable. Indeed, if practical as well as legal difficulties are to be avoided, great care should be taken to ensure that all the relevant terms and conditions are understood at the time employment commences.

Express terms and statutory statements

Express terms are those which are expressly stated to form part of the contract and they are binding irrespective of whether they differ from those contained in a job advertisement.[6] Apart from statutorily implied terms, which cannot be undermined, express terms normally take precedence over all other sources, *i.e.* common law implied terms and custom and practice. Not later than two months after the start of employment of a person working eight hours a week or more, and whose employment continues for a month or more, the employer must supply written particulars of key terms of employment.[7] The reasoning behind this is clear: if employees receive written statements of the main terms of employment, disputes over the nature and scope of their contracts will be minimized.

The following information must be given to employees individually, although in relation to the matters mentioned in (vi)-(viii) and (xiv) below it is sufficient to make the information reasonably accessible to them by means of a document to which they are referred and which they are given reasonable opportunities of reading in the course of their employment.[8]

(i)   the identity of the parties

(ii)   the date on which the employee's period of continuous employment began (taking into account any employment with a previous employer which counts towards that period). This is designed to clarify the position of employees who have been involved in a takeover or transfer of the business, since if continuity is not preserved employees who are qualified will be entitled to redundancy payments from their previous employer (*see* chapter 13).

According to Regulation 5(1) of the Transfer of Undertaking (Protection of Employment) Regulations 1981 (Transfer Regulations), where there is a transfer of an undertaking employees who are transferred are to be treated as if they had originally made contracts with the transferee employer. However, Regulation 5(2) only passes liability in respect of 'persons employed in the undertaking transferred' and Regulation 5(3) provides that this is only to include 'persons so employed immediately before the transfer including where the transfer is effected by a series of two or more transactions, a person employed before any of those transactions'.[8A] In order to ensure compliance with Directive 77/187 the House of Lords has held that Regulation 5(3) must be read as if there were inserted after the phrase 'immediately before transfer' the words 'or would have been so employed if he had not been unfairly dismissed in the circumstances described in Regulation 8(1)'[9] (*see* pages 164–5). Thus where employees have been unfairly dismissed before a transfer for a reason connected with that transfer, they are deemed to be employed in the undertaking immediately before the transfer and their employment is statutorily continued with the transferee. However, if the reason for dismissal is not connected with the transfer, Regulation 5(1) will only apply if a contract of employment exists at the very moment of transfer.[10]

Finally, it should be noted that there is no implied right enabling an employee to restrain a proposed transfer.[11] If an employee refuses to transfer he or she will be treated as having resigned, and continuity of service will be broken.[12] (On the scope of the Transfer Regulations generally *see* pages 201–3.)

(iii)   the scale or rate of remuneration, or the method of calculating remuneration, and the intervals at which remuneration is paid. The word 'remuneration' is not defined in the statute and ought to be regarded as including all financial benefits.

(iv)   any terms and conditions relating to hours of work and normal working hours. The concept of normal working hours is crucial (*see* chapter 15) so in order to avoid confusion, employers should specify whether or not overtime is mandatory, *i.e.* forms part of the normal working hours. Working hours are usually a matter for the parties to determine although some special provisions exist in relation to women and young persons (*see* page 54).[13]

(v)   any terms and conditions relating to holidays and holiday pay. It is remarkable in the 1990s that there is no general statutory right to any holiday. Nevertheless employees are entitled to be paid if holidays are taken in accordance with the terms of their employment during their period of notice.[14]

(vi)   any terms and conditions relating to incapacity for work owing to sickness or injury, including any provision for sick pay (*see* page 29 and chapter 8)

(vii)   any terms and conditions relating to pensions and pension schemes and a note stating whether a contracting-out certificate is in force under Part 3 of the Pension Schemes Act 1993.

Although this book does not generally address the complex issues of pension entitlement, two matters will be mentioned here. First, where it is a contractual term that employees are entitled to benefits under a pension scheme, employers must discharge their functions under such a scheme in good faith and, so far as it is within their power, procure the benefits to which the employees are entitled.[15] Second, anything not relating to old age, invalidity or survivors' benefits that is included in a pension scheme will be protected where the Transfer Regulations apply (*see* page 201).[16]

(viii)   the length of notice which the employee is entitled to receive and obliged to give (*see* chapter 10)

(ix)   the title of the job or a brief description of the employee's work. If, in the interests of flexibility, a job description is widely drawn, it should be pointed out to employees that the ambit of their contractual obligations may be wider than the particular duties upon which they are normally engaged.[17]

(x)   where the employment is temporary, the period for which it is expected to continue or, if it is for a fixed term, the date when it is to end;

(xi)   the place of work or, if the employee is required or permitted to work at various places, an indication of that fact and the employer's address;

(xii)   any collective agreements which directly affect the terms and conditions of employment, including, where the employer is not a party, the person by whom they were made;

(xiii)   where the employee is required to work outside the UK for more than a month: (a) the period of work outside the UK, (b) the currency in which payment will be made, (c) any additional pay and benefits to be provided by reason of the work being outside the UK, (d) any terms and conditions relating to the employee's return to the UK.

(xiv)   the name or description of the person to whom employees can apply if they are dissatisfied with any disciplinary decision or seek to redress a grievance. The statement must indicate the manner in which any such application should be made and should explain the procedural steps which will be set in motion. Three points should be noted here. First, this requirement does not apply in relation to disciplinary matters if the employer has less than twenty employees.[18] Second, EPCA 1978 does not state that employers must have disciplinary rules, although the *Code of Practice on Disciplinary Practice and Procedures* emphasizes their desirability (*see* chapter 12). Finally, rules, disciplinary decisions, grievances and procedures relating to health and safety at work are exempted because separate rules and procedures are thought to be appropriate in this area and should be referred to in the

information provided by employers under section 2
HASAWA 1974 (*see* chapter 7).

If there are no particulars to be entered under any of the above
headings, that fact must be mentioned in the written statement. It
should also be noted that information relating to items (iv), (vi)-
(viii), (x) and (xii)-(xiv) may be given in instalments within the
two-month period.

Changes cannot be made to a contract of employment without
the consent of the employee but, where there is a change in any
of the details required by section 1, written notification must be
given to the employee within one month.[19] The nature of the
changes must be set out in full, although the employer may refer
to other documents for the same matters and in the same manner
as for the original provision of particulars. There is no provision
for the changes to be notified in instalments.

It is important to understand that the statement issued does not
constitute a contract or even conclusive evidence of its terms, but
is merely the employer's version of what has been agreed.[20]
Indeed, in *Robertson v British Gas*[21] the Court of Appeal decided
that a statutory statement could not even be used as an aid to the
interpretation of the contract. If agreement has not been reached
in a key area management may choose to include in that statement
what it considers to be reasonable arrangements. Technically the
statement will be inaccurate (because the terms were on offer
rather than agreed at the time they were issued) but if the
employee accepts the arrangements or acquiesces in them, *i.e.* by
not challenging them, the employer's proposals may be deemed
to have contractual effect. However, the EAT has suggested that a
distinction might be drawn between a matter which has immediate
practical application and one which does not. In *Jones v Associated
Tunnelling Co.*[22] it was thought that it would be asking too much
of ordinary employees to require them to object to erroneous
statements of terms which had no immediate practical impact on
them. The law does not oblige employees to sign the written
particulars or even acknowledge their receipt but if they do confirm that what has been issued is an accurate summary of the main
employment terms, the particulars may be treated by the courts
as having contractual status.[23]

Where an employee is given a complete but incorrect statement, *i.e.* some of the particulars are wrong in that they do not reproduce what was agreed between the parties, the employee can complain to an industrial tribunal which has the power to confirm, amend or replace the particulars. If there is no written statement or an incomplete one is issued the tribunal must determine what the missing particulars are.[24] According to the Court of Appeal,[25] the particulars required under (i), (ii), (iii), (viii) and (ix) above are 'mandatory' terms in that actual particulars must be given under those headings. On the other hand, the particulars required under (iv)-(vii) were viewed as 'non-mandatory' in the sense that no particulars need to be inserted if none have been agreed. As regards 'non-mandatory' terms, the Court of Appeal held that an industrial tribunal could not invent a term if nothing had been agreed by the parties. However, where a 'mandatory' term was omitted from a statement a tribunal would probably have to imply one. When the tribunal has decided what particulars should have been included the employer is deemed to have provided the employee with a statement containing those particulars.

Under section 8 EPCA 1978 employers who have 20 or more employees must give an itemized pay statement to those whose contract normally involves eight hours per week or more. The statement must contain the following particulars:

(i)   the gross amount of wages or salary
(ii) the amount of any variable or fixed deductions and the purposes for which they are made (on the legality of such deductions *see* pages 29–30)
(iii) the net wages or salary payable and, where the net amount is paid in different ways, the amount and method of payment of each part payment.

Such a statement need not contain separate particulars of a fixed deduction, *e.g.* of union dues, if it specifies the total amount of fixed deductions and each year the employer provides a standing statement of fixed deductions which describes the amount of each deduction, its purpose and the intervals at which it is made. If no pay statement is issued, an employee may refer the matter to an industrial tribunal to determine what particulars ought to have been included. Where a tribunal finds that an employer failed to provide such a statement or the statement does not contain the required particulars, the tribunal must make a declaration to that effect. Additionally, where it finds that any unnotified deductions have been made during the 13 weeks preceding the application, it may order the employer to pay compensation to the employee. This cannot exceed the total amount of unnotified deductions. Thus, unlike the provisions relating to the enforcement of section 1 EPCA 1978 statements, there is here a penal aspect to the discretion which tribunals have to exercise.

Collective agreements

Terms may be derived from collective agreements as well as being individually negotiated. Such agreements tend to be classed as being either of a procedural or substantive nature. A procedure agreement aims to govern the relationship between the signatories (employers and trade unions) by establishing methods of handling disputes, whereas a substantive agreement is intended to regulate the terms and conditions of employment of those who are covered by it. Although it is possible to conclude a collective agreement which is legally enforceable (*see* pages 247–8) this is not normally the wish of either party. By what mechanism then do individual employees derive the legal right to claim the terms and conditions which have been negotiated on their behalf? The answer lies in the process of incorporation, for by this device collectively agreed terms become legally binding as part of the individual contract of employment.[26]

The simplest way of ensuring that substantive terms are incorporated into an employee's contract is by an express provision to this effect. Thus, workers may be employed on the basis of 'the national agreements for the time being in force'. More commonly collective agreements will be expressly incorporated because they are referred to in a section 1 EPCA 1978 statement of particulars. In relation to the matters specified on page 16, EPCA 1978 permits employers to refer to 'some document which the employee has reasonable opportunity of reading, etc.' and this document may be a copy of the currently operative collective agreement. Equally, it is possible for terms to be incorporated from a collective agreement by implication, although this is less desirable because of the uncertainties involved.[27] This can occur when employees have specific knowledge of the collective agreement and there is conduct which demonstrates that they accept the agreement and are willing to work under it. While this might be relatively straightforward in the case of union members, difficulties can arise in establishing the legal position of non-members. If such employees have habitually accepted and abided by the terms negotiated by the union, an implication arises that they will be bound by future agreements. However, if at any stage non-members declare that they are no longer willing to be bound by such agreements that implication is no longer valid.[28]

It is normally quite easy to decide which terms of a collective agreement are appropriate for incorporation into an individual contract of employment: it is the substantive terms (*e.g.* on wages, hours, etc.) rather than the procedural ones.[29] However, difficulties have been experienced in relation to no-strike clauses. An undertaking by the union not to call a strike before relevant procedures have been exhausted imposes an obligation on the union alone, but the following clause is clearly capable of being incorporated into individual contracts of employment: 'employees will not engage in a strike or other industrial action until the grievance procedure has been exhausted'. The situation has been clarified by section 180 TULRCA 1992 which provides that no-strike clauses are only binding if the collective agreement:

(i)   is in writing and contains a provision stating that the clause may be incorporated into a contract of employment
(ii) is reasonably accessible to the employees concerned
(iii) is concluded by an independent trade union

and if

(iv) the individual contract of employment expressly or impliedly incorporates the no-strike clause.

Such clauses can be useful in drawing an employee's attention to the illegality of industrial action but strictly speaking they are unnecessary since most forms of industrial action are likely to breach an obligation imposed on all employees by the common law, *i.e.* the duty not to impede the employer's business (*see* pages 37–8).

Works rules

The essential difference between collective agreements and works rules lies, not so much in their subject matter, but in the fact that the contents of the latter are unilaterally determined by the employer. While both can be expressly or impliedly incorporated into individual contracts of employment (using the mechanisms described in the previous section) works rules offer one great advantage to the employer: whereas a collective agreement can only be altered with the consent of the parties to it, management can lawfully change the content of works rules at any time. A refusal to adhere to the revised rules would amount to a breach of contract (*i.e.* a failure to obey lawful and reasonable orders) even if there had been no advance warning or consultation with the employees affected. Thus, a contractual term to the effect that employees must abide by 'the currently operative works rules' affords management the maximum degree of flexibility.[30] Nevertheless, the dismissal of an employee for failing to comply with revised works rules will not necessarily be fair since it will depend on what an industrial tribunal regards as being 'reasonable in all the circumstances' (*see* chapter 12).

Custom and practice

In the days when written contracts of employment were less common and written statements of particulars were not required by statute, custom and practice played an important part in helping to identify the contractual terms. Today custom and practice is not such an important source of law, although it may still be invoked occasionally to fill gaps in the employment relationship. To do so a custom or practice must be definite, reasonable and generally applied in the area or trade in question. If these criteria are met the fact that the particular employee against whom the custom is applied is ignorant of its existence appears to be of no consequence.[31] The major drawback of custom and practice is its uncertain legal effect and therefore its unreliability. After what period of time can it be said that a non-union member who has always worked in accordance with current collective agreements is bound to accept future agreements? If a custom and practice is useful to management, it is logical that efforts should be made to convert it into an express term of the contract. This may not always be possible either because of the imprecise nature of the custom or because unions might oppose such a move as being contrary to the interests of their members. It almost goes without saying that a union will be in a better position to modify a custom or practice if it has not become embodied in a contract of employment. Finally, it should be noted that there may still be a place for custom and practice as an aid to interpreting a contractual term, *e.g.* the meaning of 'reasonable overtime' at a particular workplace.

Terms implied by statute

Terms and conditions awarded by the CAC under section 185 TULRCA 1992 (on disclosure of information) operate as part of the contract of employment of each worker affected. However, the terms and conditions imposed may be superseded or varied by a collective agreement between the employer and the union 'for the time being representing the employee' or an express or implied agreement between the employer and the employee so far as that agreement effects an improvement in the terms and conditions awarded by the CAC.

Another example of a term implied by statute is the equality clause inserted by virtue of section 1 EPA 1970 (*see* pages 70–1).

Terms implied by the common law

There are two distinct types of common law implied terms. First, where there is a gap in the contract of employment it is possible to imply a term if a court can be persuaded that it is necessary to do so in the circumstances of the particular case (implied terms of fact). Secondly, there are terms which are regarded by the courts as being inherent in all contracts of employment (implied terms of law). This section will outline the mechanism for establishing implied terms of fact and the next chapter will examine the major obligations which are automatically imposed on the parties to a contract of employment.

It is a basic principle that a contractual term can only be implied if it is consistent with the express terms of the contract. However, despite the increased use of written contracts and statements, it is not unusual for the parties to discover that they have failed to provide for a particular contingency. If there is a dispute over something which is not expressly dealt with in the contract of employment, a court or tribunal may be asked to insert a term to cover the point at issue. The party wishing to reply on an implied term must satisfy a court either that such a term was so obvious that the parties did not think it necessary to state it expressly (the 'officious bystander' test) or that such a term was necessary to give 'business efficacy' to the relationship.[32]

Notes

1   See *Tomlinson v Dick Evans* [1977] IRLR 77 and *Hyland v J Barker Ltd* [1989] IRLR 403.
2   *Broaders v Kalkare Ltd* [1990] IRLR 421.
3   See *Salvesen v Simons* [1994] IRLR 52.
4   [1981] IRLR 204.
5   [1991] IRLR 473. See also *Annandale Engineering v Samson* [1994] IRLR 59.
6   See *Deeley v British Rail Engineering Ltd* [1980] IRLR 147.
7   Sections 1–3 EPCA 1978.
8   See sections 1 and 2(3) EPCA 1978.
8A See *Longden v Kennedy International Ltd* (1994) TLR 14/2/94.
9   See *Litster v Forth Dry Dock* [1989] IRLR 161.
10 See *Secretary of State v Spence* [1985] IRLR 248.
11 See *Newns v British Airways* [1992] IRLR 575.
12 See Regulation 5(4A)(4B) Transfer Regulations (as amended).
13 The Sex Discrimination Act 1986 removed the major restrictions on women's working hours. On hours of work generally see ACAS Advisory Booklet No. 13.
14 See paragraph 2(1) of Schedule 3 EPCA 1978. On entitlement to accrued holiday pay on termination of employment see *Morley v Heritage PLC* [1993] IRLR 400.
15 See *Mihlenstedt v Barclays Bank* [1989] IRLR 522.
16 See *Glitz v Watford Electrical Co.* [1978] IRLR 89.
17 See Regulation 7 Transfer Regulations (as amended).
18 See section 3(3) EPCA 1978.
19 Section 4 EPCA 1978.
20 See *System Floors (UK) Ltd v Daniel* [1981] 475.
21 [1983] IRLR 302.

22 [1981] IRLR 477.
23 See *Gascol Conversions v Mercer* [1974] IRLR 155.
24 Section 11 EPCA 1978.
25 *Eagland v British Telecom PLC* [1992] IRLR 323.
26 See *Gibbons v Associated British Ports* [1985] IRLR 376.
27 See *Hamilton v Futura Floors* [1990] IRLR 478.
28 See *Singh v British Steel* [1974] IRLR 131 (IT).
29 On the enforceability of a redeployment and redundancy agreement see *Marley v Forward Trust Ltd* [1986] IRLR 369. On the unenforceability of a recognition agreement see *NCB v NUM* [1986] IRLR 439.
30 See *Cadoux v Central Regional Council* [1986] IRLR 131.
31 See *Sagar v Ridehalgh* [1931] Ch 310.
32 See *United Bank v Akhtar* [1989] IRLR 507.

3 Formation of the contract of employment (2) Implied terms of law

In the previous chapter we looked at the different ways in which contractual terms may come into existence and observed that certain terms would be implied into all contracts of employment. We must now examine the major obligations which are imposed by law on both parties. Some of these are based on long-established common law principles, while others are of relatively recent origin having emerged as a result of legislative intervention, such as unfair dismissal.

Duties of the employer

To pay wages

This is the most basic obligation of employers and is normally dealt with by an express term. However, in certain circumstances the law does not leave the parties entirely free to determine the amount of remuneration payable, *e.g.* where there is a legally enforced pay policy or if an equality clause operates. One major issue is whether an employer is required to pay wages if there is no work for the employee to do. The general rule is that wages must be paid if an employee is available for work[1] but everything will depend on whether there is an express or implied term of fact in the contract which deals with the matter. Thus, an express term to the effect that 'no payment shall be made during a period of lay-off' will eliminate the possibility of a contractual claim being brought in such a situation. (*see* chapter 9 on the right to a guarantee or redundancy payment). The question of what wages are owed to employees who only partly perform their contracts is dealt with on pages 139–40.

Another problem area is whether an employer is *contractually* required to pay wages when an employee is absent from work owing to sickness. The correct approach here is to look at all the facts and circumstances to see whether a term is to be implied that wages should or should not be paid. Such a term may be implied from the custom or practice in the industry or from the knowledge of the parties at the time the contract was made. The nature of the contract will have to be taken into account and, on occasions, it will be permissible to look at what the parties did during the period of the contract. Only if all the factors and circumstances do not indicate what the contractual term is will it be assumed that wages should be paid during sickness. If such a term is implied it is likely to provide for the deduction of sums received under social security legislation.[2] In *Howman & Sons v Blyth*[3] it was held that the reasonable term to be implied as to duration in an industry where the normal practice is to give sick pay for a limited period only is the term normally applicable in the industry. The EAT did not accept that where there is an obligation to make payments during sickness, then in the absence of an express term to the contrary, sick pay is owed so long as the employment continues. The *statutory* duty on an employer to make payments during sickness is dealt with in chapter 8.

According to the Wages Act 1986, a deduction from wages or payment to the employer from a worker is unlawful unless it is required by statute, for example PAYE or social security contributions, or the worker has agreed to it.[4] The worker must give oral or written consent to the deduction before it is made[5] and where the agreement constitutes a term of the contract of employment it must be in writing and drawn to the employee's attention (or its effect must have been notified to the worker in writing).[6] To satisfy the requirements of the Act there must be a document which clearly states that a deduction is to be made from the employee's wages and that the employee agrees to it.[7] Thus, if a tribunal is not persuaded on the evidence that a deduction was authorized by a provision of the employee's contract, the individual is entitled to be paid the money deducted. According to the EAT, the Wages Act contemplates that where there is a dispute as to the justification for a deduction it is the industrial tribunal's task to resolve it.[8] However, this Act has not given tribunals jurisdiction to determine whether a deduction by reason of industrial action was contractually authorized.[9]

Written agreements under which employers pay a proportion of wages to third parties are not affected by this act, although in the circumstances specified on page 269 it will be unlawful to deduct union subscriptions. In retail employment deductions or payments made to an employer in relation to stock or cash shortages are subject to a limit of one-tenth of gross pay, except for the final payment of wages.[10]

At the time of writing only one case on unlawful deductions has been heard by the House of Lords. In *Delaney v Staples*[11] it was held that a payment in lieu is not wages within the meaning of the 1986 Act if it relates to a period after termination of employment. According to the House of Lords, the Act requires wages to be construed as payments in respect of the rendering of services during employment. Thus the only payments in lieu covered by the legislation are those in respect of 'garden leave', since these can be viewed as wages owed under a subsisting contract of employment. In the same case the Court of Appeal accepted that non-payment of wages constitutes a deduction for these purposes, as does the withholding of commission and holiday pay.[12] Indeed, the withholding of commission may amount to an unlawful deduction even where it is discretionary so long as commission was normally expected by the employee.[13]

A complaint that there has been an unauthorized deduction must normally be lodged with an industrial tribunal within three months of the deduction being made.[14] If it is well founded the tribunal must make a declaration to that effect and must order the reimbursement of the amount of the deduction or payment to the extent that it exceeded what should lawfully have been deducted or received by the employer.[15] It should be noted that after such an order has been made the employer is prevented from recovering that money by any other means.[16] The only method of contracting out of the requirements of this Act is if an agreement is reached following action taken by an ACAS officer or there is a valid compromise agreement (*see* page 210).

Finally, it should be noted that employers may be entitled to restitution of overpayments made to an employee owing to a mistake of fact but *not* a mistake of law.[17] Indeed, employees may commit theft if they fail to notify the employer of an accidental overpayment.[18] The Wages Act makes specific provision for the recovery of overpayments.[19]

To provide work

Employers are generally not obliged to provide work and most employees who receive their full contractual remuneration cannot complain if they are left idle. Nevertheless, in certain circumstances the failure to provide work may amount to a breach of contract. First, if a person's earnings depend on work being provided. Thus employees who are paid by results or commission or receive shift premiums must be given the opportunity to work, since the payment of basic wages alone would deprive them of a substantial part of what they had bargained for – the opportunity to earn more. Secondly, where the lack of work could lead to a loss of publicity or affect the reputation of an employee. Indeed, in one tribunal case it was held that the higher a person is in the management structure, the more important it is for work to be given when it is available.[20] Thirdly, special attention has been focused on the position of employees who may need practice in order to preserve their skills. The Court of Appeal has suggested that such employees should be given the opportunity of performing work when it is available.[21] In terms of future developments, it seems likely that courts and tribunals will be increasingly sympathetic to the notion that there is an implied term in contracts of employment that employers should provide work.[22] (On 'garden leave' *see* page 39)

To co-operate with the employee

Originally this duty amounted to little more than an obligation not to impede the employees in the performance of their contracts. However, one of the effects of the unfair dismissal provisions has been that the courts have displayed a greater willingness to accept that employers have a positive duty to ensure that the purposes of the contract are achieved. Thus it has been frequently stated that employers must not destroy the mutual trust and confidence upon which co-operation is built. Although each case depends on its particular set of facts, it may be interesting to note that employers have been held to be in breach of contract in the following situations: where an applicant for transfer had not been dealt with fairly,[23] where an employer's discretion under a mobility clause was exercised in a way which made it impossible for the employee to comply with a contractual obligation to move,[24] where there was a failure to investigate a genuine safety grievance,[25] where there was a false accusation of theft on the basis of flimsy evidence,[26] and finally where an employer has persistently attempted to vary an employee's conditions of service.[27] Similarly it has been suggested that this duty might require those who employ large numbers to permit reasonable time off in an emergency[28] and should also inhibit employers from issuing unjustified warnings which are not designed to improve performance but to dishearten employees and drive them out.[29]

Finally, the House of Lords has accepted that in certain circumstances it will be necessary to imply an obligation on the employer to take reasonable steps to bring a contractual term to the employee's attention. Such a duty will arise when:

(i)   the contractual terms have not been negotiated with individuals but result from collective bargaining or are otherwise incorporated by reference
(ii) a particular term makes available to employees a valuable right contingent upon action being taken by them to avail themselves of its benefit
(iii) employees cannot in all the circumstances reasonably be expected to be aware of the term unless it is drawn to their attention.[30]

To take reasonable care of the employee

In addition to this duty implied by law, there are a number of key statutes in the area of health and safety. We shall be looking at legislation in chapter 7, although it is important to note at this stage that a person who is injured in the course of employment in a factory may be able to bring an action for damages based either on the common law duty or breach of the Factories Act 1961 or other regulations.

Recognizing that employers cannot guarantee that no employee will be injured at work, the standard of care which the law demands is that which 'an ordinary prudent employer would take in all the circumstances'.[31] Generally speaking, if a job has risks to health and safety which are not common knowledge but of which an employer knows or ought to know, and against which she or he cannot guard by taking precautions, then the employer should tell anyone to whom employment is offered what those risks are if, on the information then available, knowledge of those risks would be likely to affect the decision of a sensible prospective employee about accepting the offer.[32] Thus the common law accepts that employers should only be held liable if they fail to safeguard against something which was reasonably foreseeable.[33] It should also be observed that the general duty of care does not extend to taking all reasonable steps to protect the economic welfare of employees, whether by insuring them against special risks known to the employer or by advising them of those risks so that they can obtain appropriate cover. Thus, in the absence of a contractual term to the contrary, the employer's duty is limited to the protection of the employee against physical harm or disease.[34]

Employers are entitled to follow recognized practices in their industry, unless they are obviously unsafe, but must make arrangements to ensure that they keep abreast of current developments, *e.g.* by joining an employers' association. Once an employer knows of a source of danger, or could have been expected to know of it, it is necessary to take all reasonable steps to protect employees from risks which have hitherto been unforseeable.[35] The duty is to assess the likelihood of injury and to weigh the risk against the cost and inconvenience of taking effective precautions to eliminate it. Employers owe a single personal duty of care to each of their employees, having proper regard to the employee's skill and experience, etc. Thus even if the employer delegates this duty to another person who is reasonably believed to be competent to perform it, the employer will remain personally liable for injuries to an employee caused by that other person's negligence.[36] Similarly, where an employee's labour is subcontracted, the employer's duty of care is still owed.[37]

Having considered some general issues, it may be useful to subdivide this duty into the following headings:

Safe premises

The case of *Latimer v AEC Ltd*[38] provides a suitable illustration of what is required of employers in this connection. Owing to exceptionally heavy rainfall, a factory was flooded. A layer of oil and grease was left on the floor which the employers attempted to cover with sawdust. However, this was not spread across all of the factory floor and the employee slipped in an area which was uncovered. It was held by the House of Lords that the employers had taken reasonable precautions and they could not be expected to close down their factory in order to avoid what was a fairly small risk of injury.[39] More recently it has been acknowledged that in certain circumstances UK-based employers may have to satisfy themselves as to the safety of overseas sites. According to the Court of Appeal, the employer's duty to take all reasonable steps to ensure the safety of employees applies whether the premises where the employee is required to work are occupied by the employer or by a third party.[40]

Safe plant, equipment and tools
If employers know that a tool or piece of machinery could be a source of danger it is incumbent upon them to take reasonable precautions to safeguard employees. Where tools or equipment are purchased from a reputable supplier and employers have no reason to suspect that they are defective they cannot be held liable at common law. If in these circumstances an employee were to sustain an injury as a result of a defect, he or she would be obliged to sue the person responsible under the general law of negligence in order to recover damages. Since proving negligence in these circumstances would be virtually impossible, the Employers' Liability (Defective Equipment) Act 1969 was passed to assist such employees. According to section 1 of this Act if

> an employee suffers personal injury in the course of his employ-
> ment in consequence of a defect in equipment provided by his
> employer for the purposes of the employer's business and the
> defect is attributable wholly or partly *to the fault of a third party*
> (whether identified or not), the injury shall be deemed to be
> also attributable to negligence on the part of the employer.
> (author's emphasis in *italic*)[41]

Thus, employees must still be able to show that someone was at fault in order to claim from their employer. (Any damages paid out by the employer can be recovered from the third party whose fault it was.) In the same year the Employers' Liability (Compulsory Insurance) Act was passed to ensure that all employers were able to meet personal injury claims from their employees.[42]

Safe system of work
Under this heading are included all the matters which relate to the manner in which the work is performed: job design, working methods, the provision of protective clothing, training and supervision. In one case it was argued that, following a wages snatch, the employer had been negligent in not hiring an outside firm of security specialists to collect wages. However, the Court of Appeal held that no more could be expected of an employer who had provided proper instruction in ways of reducing the risk of injury.[43] If safety rules and procedures exist employees must be informed as to their content and, if safety clothing or equipment is required, it must be readily available.[44] Clearly the more dangerous the task or workplace situation the greater is the need for precautions to be taken, but how far must an employer go to ensure that safety devices are properly utilized?

In *Crouch v British Rail Engineering*[45] the Court of Appeal decided that where an employee is regularly performing tasks which involve a reasonably foreseeable risk to the eyes, the employer has the duty to actually put goggles into the employee's hands. Similarly, in *Pape v Cumbria County Council*[46] the High Court ruled that an employer has a duty to warn cleaners of the dangers of handling chemical cleaning materials with unprotected hands and to instruct them as to the need to wear gloves at all times. It would seem that the circumstances that have to be considered in ascertaining the extent of the duty of care include: the risk of injury; the gravity of any injury which might result; the difficulty of providing protective equipment or clothing; the availability of that equipment or clothing and the distance which the worker might have to go to fetch it; the frequency of occasions on which the employee was likely to need the protective equipment or clothing; and the experience and degree of skill to be expected of the employee. Bearing in mind both this common law duty and the obligations imposed by legislation (*see* chapter 7), managers would be advised to ensure that an unreasonable refusal to follow safety rules or procedures is classed as a breach of discipline which could ultimately lead to dismissal for misconduct.

As regards working hours, the Court of Appeal has held that a doctor who was expressly required to work 40 hours and to be available for a further 48 hours of overtime on average each week had a cause of action when he was required to work so much overtime that it was reasonably foreseeable that his health would be impaired.[47] In this case the relationship between express and implied terms was discussed and the majority were of the opinion that the power conferred on the employer by the express terms of the contract was subject to the implied obligation to safeguard the employee's health. Thus if there is a general contractual term (for example, the duty to take reasonable care of the employee's health) and another term which is precise and detailed (for example, an obligation to work on particular tasks even though they involve an obvious health risk) the ambit of the employer's duty of care will be narrower than it would be were there no such express terms. It is also worth noting that an express term may be rendered ineffective by section 2(1) of the Unfair Contract Terms Act 1977, which provides that 'a person cannot by reference to any contract term . . . exclude or restrict his liability for . . . personal injury resulting from negligence'. Finally, in the subsequent case of *Petch v Commissioners of Customs and Excise*[48] the Court of Appeal suggested that employers have a duty to protect an employee's mental health from the result of overwork or stress.

Competent and safe colleagues

Employers are required to take reasonable steps to ensure that employees do not behave in such a fashion that they are a source of danger to others. This means that employers must engage competent staff, or train recruits to a safe worker level, must instruct their employees in safe working methods and then provide adequate supervision to check that these methods are being adhered to. Practical jokers cannot be tolerated and if they do not respond to warnings, their employment should be terminated in accordance with disciplinary procedures. Such people are a threat to everyone and are unlikely to attract the sympathy of their workmates.

Finally, mention should be made of the Congenital Disabilities (Civil Liability) Act 1976. Under this Act an employer may be liable to a child of an employee who is born disabled as a consequence of a breach of a common law or statutory duty owed to the parent. The child's right to sue in respect of a pre-natal injury exists whether or not the parent suffered any harm and irrespective of whether the employer knew that the foetus existed. However, liability to the child is conditional on the employer being liable in tort to the parent.

Duties of the employee

To co-operate with the employer

We are concerned here with the duty to obey lawful and reasonable orders and the duty not to impede the employer's business. In this context the obligation to carry out lawful orders has two distinct aspects. First, it means that employees are not required to obey an order if to do so would break the law, for example producing false accounts. Secondly, it also means that employees are not obliged to obey orders which fall outside the scope of the contract. This is consistent with the view that (at least in theory) the terms of a contract cannot be unilaterally varied. However, as we will discover later (chapter 12), this does not prevent employees from being fairly dismissed for refusing to follow instructions which are outside their contractual obligations.

As regards the duty not to impede the employer's business, it is clear that going on strike breaches a fundamental term of the contract: the essence of the employment relationship is that the employee is ready and willing to work in exchange for remuneration. However, is there a duty on employees not to engage in industrial action which falls short of a strike? In the leading case of the *Secretary of State v ASLEF*,[49] which involved a work to rule on the railways, the Court of Appeal gave different reasons in reaching the conclusion that such a duty exists. Lord Justice Roskill thought that there is an implied term that employees ought not to obey lawful instructions in such a way as to disrupt the employer's business. Lord Justice Buckley extended the notion of fidelity (*see* below) and proclaimed that 'the employees must serve the employer faithfully with a view to promoting those commercial interests for which he is employed'. Lord Denning chose to focus attention on motive, *i.e.* the wilfulness of the disruption caused, and his formulation leads to the conclusion that all forms of industrial action are likely to be unlawful. More recently the High Court has ruled that it is a professional obligation of teachers to co-operate in running schools and that the failure to cover for absent colleagues amounts to a breach of contract.[50] (On the options open to an employer where an employee only part-performs the contract *see* pages 139–40).

Fidelity

Employees must avoid putting themselves in a position whereby their own interests conflict with the duty they owe their employer or an employer to whom they have been seconded.[51] Thus employees must not accept any reward for their work other than from their employer, *e.g.* a gift or secret commission. However, employees have no contractual duty to disclose their own misconduct and whether there is a duty to report the misconduct of fellow employees depends on the individual contract of employment and the circumstances.[52] There are three particular aspects to this duty which we must now consider: the obligation not to compete with the employer, not to disclose confidential information and the law relating to inventions and copyright.

The obligation not to compete with the employer

Generally the spare time activities of employees are no business of the employer, although an injunction may be granted to prevent employees working for competitors during their spare time if it can be shown that the employer's business would be seriously damaged. However, in *Nova Plastics Ltd v Froggatt*[53] the EAT rejected the argument that there is a general implication that any work for a competitor should be regarded as being a breach of trust or a failure to give loyal service. It should be noted that the intention to set up in competition with the employer is not in itself a breach of the implied duty of loyalty. Unless the employer has reasonable grounds for believing that the employee has committed or is about to commit some wrongful act, dismissal will not be justified (*see* page 174).[54]

Normally ex-employees are entitled to make use of the skills and knowledge which they have acquired and are allowed to compete with a former employer provided they do not rely on confidential information (*see* below). However, this is not the position if there is an express clause in the contract of employment which restrains competition by employees when they leave. Such restraint clauses (restrictive covenants) will only be enforced by the courts if they provide protection against something more than competition alone, if they are shown to be reasonable in the circumstances, and are not contrary to the public interest.[55] Thus where the true skill in a job lies in the make-up of the person performing it, for example their personality, temperament and ability to get on with people, there is no proprietary right which an employer can claim to protect as part of the business.[56]

What about the enforcement of 'garden leave' clauses, *i.e.* clauses which provide that during the period of notice an employee will not be obliged to work but will receive full pay and be prevented from working for anyone else? Such clauses will not be enforced if it appears that the business for which the employee wishes to work before the notice expires has nothing to do with the employer's business. On the other hand where the period during which the employee is not required to work is not excessive and there is a risk of damage to the employer's business, it may be appropriate to restrain the employee from taking other employment during the notice period, either under a specific clause or as a breach of the duty of fidelity.[57] However, the wrongful dismissal of an employee (*see* pages 145–6) will prevent the employer from relying on a restrictive covenant.[58]

Finally, one effect of Regulation 5 of the Transfer Regulations (*see* page 201) is that the transferee may benefit from a restrictive covenant in contracts of employment made with the transferor. Thus an employee may be restrained from doing or seeking to do business with anyone who had dealt with the transferor during the period stipulated in the original contract.[59]

The obligation not to disclose confidential information
The following principles have been enunciated by the Court of Appeal.[60] First, an individual's obligations are to be determined by the contract of employment and, in the absence of any express term, the employee's obligations in respect of the use and disclosure of information are the subject of implied terms. Second, while the individual remains in employment the obligations are included in the implied term which imposes a duty of fidelity on the employee. The extent of this duty varies according to the nature of the contract and would be broken if an employee copied a

list of the employer's customers for use after the employment ended, or deliberately memorized such a list.[61] Third, the implied term which imposes an obligation on the employee as to his or her conduct after the employment has terminated is more restricted than that imposed by the duty of fidelity. The obligation not to use or disclose information might cover secret processes of manufacture or designs, or any other information of a sufficiently high degree of confidentiality as to amount to a trade secret. Thus the names of customers and the goods they buy may be a trade secret.[62] However, this obligation does not extend to information which is only 'confidential' in the sense that any unauthorized disclosure to a third party while the employment subsisted would be a breach of the duty of fidelity. Fourth, in order to determine whether any particular item of information falls within the implied term thus preventing its use or disclosure after the employment has ceased, it is necessary to consider all the circumstances of the case. Among the matters to which attention must be paid are:

(i)   the nature of employment. A high obligation of confidentiality might be imposed if the employment was such that confidential material was habitually handled

(ii) the nature of the information. Information will only be protected if it can be classed as a trade secret or as material which in all the circumstances is of such a highly confidential nature as to require the same protection as a trade secret[63]

(iii) whether the employer impressed on the employee the confidentiality of the information. However, an employer cannot prevent the use or disclosure of information merely by telling the employee that it is confidential.

(iv) whether relevant information could be easily isolated from other information which the employee was free to use or disclose. The fact that the alleged confidential information was part of a package and that the remainder of the package was not confidential might throw light on whether the information in question was really a trade secret.

In practice it can be very difficult to differentiate between use and abuse of the knowledge which an ex-employee possesses, for example of the former employer's customers. Thus employers should be advised to draft express restraint clauses which set precise limits on the future employment of key workers. Such clauses must be carefully worded, since it is a court's duty to give effect to covenants as they are expressed rather than to correct errors or supply omissions.[64] Since breaches will be relatively easy to identify, enforcing such clauses should be a fairly simple process. Indeed, the mere presence of a restraint clause can be valuable as a reminder to the employee that disclosure of confidential information will not be condoned. The employer who relies solely on the implied term is at a serious disadvantage because an employee can only be stopped from disclosing confidential information once the plaintiff employer has proved that such information has already been divulged. The aggrieved employer may also have a remedy against a third party to whom the employee has passed trade secrets or confidential information.[65]

Four further points need to be considered. First, in an appropriate case a court has power to grant injunctions against ex-employees to restrain them from fulfilling contracts already concluded with third parties.[66] Second, a court will not grant an injunction preventing an employee from disclosing confidential information about a company to a regulatory authority, for example, the Inland Revenue.[67] Third, despite the statutory provisions on disclosure of information (*see* chapter 16), an employee has no implied right to disclose confidential information to a trade union even if it is thought to be essential for the purpose of collective bargaining. Finally, the Data Protection Act 1984 now imposes additional constraints on an employee's ability to disclose information (*see* chapter 17).

The law governing inventions and copyright

Since section 39(1) of the Patents Act 1977 came into force an invention belongs to an employer if:

(i) it was made in the course of the employee's normal duties or those specifically assigned to him or her, and the circumstances in either case were such that an invention might reasonably be expected to result from the carrying out of those duties; or

(ii) it was made in the course of the employee's duties and, at the time of making the invention, because of the nature of the duties and the particular responsibilities arising from them there was a special obligation to further the interests of the employer's undertaking.

In all other circumstances the invention belongs to the employee notwithstanding any contractual term to the contrary. This section was considered in *Reiss Engineering v Harris* [68] where the Patents Court held that for these purposes employees' 'normal duties' are those which they are actually employed to do. Section 39(1)a was interpreted as referring to an invention which achieves or contributes to achieving whatever was the aim or object to which the employee's efforts in carrying out his or her duties were directed, *i.e.* an invention similar to that made but not necessarily the precise invention as that actually made. The extent and nature of the 'special obligation' in section 39(1)b will depend on the status of the employee and the attendant responsibilities and duties of that status.

Even if the invention belongs to the employer, an employee can apply to the Patents Court or Controller of Patents for an award of compensation. This may be granted if the patent is of outstanding benefit (in money or money's worth) to the employer and it is just to make an award. The burden of proof lies on the employee to show that the employer has derived benefit from the patented invention. Where inventions belong to employees and their interests have been assigned to the employer, they are still entitled to seek compensation if they can show that the financial benefit they have derived is inadequate in relation to the benefit derived by the employer from the patent and it is just that additional compensation should be paid. However, no compensation can be paid if, at the time the invention is made, there is in force a 'relevant collective agreement' (an agreement between a trade union to which the employee belongs and the employer or an association to which the employer belongs) which provides for the payment of compensation for inventions made by the employee. It is anticipated that collective agreements will improve upon the statutory rights, yet there appears to be nothing to prevent employers and unions negotiating less favourable compensation schemes.

According to section 11 of the Copyright, Designs and Patents Act 1988, where a literary, dramatic, musical or artistic work is made by an employee in the course of employment, the employer is the first owner of any copyright subject to any agreement to the contrary.

To take reasonable care

Employees must exercise reasonable skill and care in the performance of their contracts.[69] If they do not do so, apart from any
disciplinary action that may be taken against them, there is an
implied duty to indemnify the employer in respect of the consequences of their negligence.[70] In theory, therefore, if by virtue of
the doctrine of vicarious liability (*see* pages 47–8) an employer is
required to pay damages to an injured third party the amount
paid out could be recovered by suing the negligent employee. In
practice, such embarrassing litigation is avoided because it is the
employer's insurance company which actually pays the damages.

Notes

1 See *R v Liverpool City Corporation* [1985] IRLR 501.
2 See *Mears v Safecar Security* [1982] IRLR 183.
3 [1983] IRLR 139.
4 For these purposes 'wages' is defined in section 7 and 'worker' is
   defined in section 8.
5 See *Discount Tobacco v Williamson* [1993] IRLR 327.
6 Section 1 Wages Act 1986.
7 See *Potter v Hunt Contracts Ltd* [1992] IRLR 108.
8 See *Fairfield Ltd v Skinner* [1993] IRLR 3.
9 See *Sunderland Polytechnic v Evans* [1993] ICR 196.
10 See section 2 Wages Act 1986.
11 [1992] IRLR 191.
12 [1991] IRLR 112.
13 See *Kent Management Services v Butterfield* [1992] IRLR 394.
14 'or, within such further period as the tribunal considers reasonable
   in a case where it is satisfied that it was not reasonably practicable
   for the complaint to be presented within three months', section
   5 Wages Act 1986. This 'escape clause' applies to other statutory
   jurisdictions and throughout the rest of the book will be referred to
   as the 'time limit escape clause'.
15 On the relationship with section 8 EPCA (itemized pay statements)
   see section 6(2).
16 Section 5 Wages Act 1986.
17 See *Avon County Council v Howlett* [1983] 1 AER 1073.
18 See *Attorney General's Reference* (No 1 of 1983) [1984] 3 AER 369.

19   See section 1 (5)(a)(i).
20   *Bosworth v A Jowett* [1977] IRLR 374 (IT).
21   *Langston v AUEW* [1974] ICR 180.
22   See *McLory v Post Office* [1992] ICR 758.
23   *Post Office v Roberts* [1980] IRLR 347.
24   *United Bank v Akhtar* [1989] IRLR 507.
25   *BAC v Austin* [1978] IRLR 332.
26   *Robinson v Crompton Parkinson* [1978] IRLR 61.
27   *Woods v WM Car Services* [1982] IRLR 413.
28   *Warner v Barber's Stores* [1978] IRLR 109.
29   *Walker v J. Wedgwood Ltd* [1978] IRLR 105.
30   See *Scally v Southern Health Board* [1991] IRLR 522.
31   *Paris v Stepney Borough Council* [1951] AC 376.
32   See *White v Holbrook Ltd* [1985] IRLR 215.
33   See *Hewett v Brown Ltd* [1992] ICR 530 on the duty owed to an employee's family.
34   See *Reid v Rush & Tompkins PLC* [1989] IRLR 265.
35   See *Baxter v Harland & Wolff* [1990] IRLR 516.
36   See *McDermid v Nash Dredging Ltd* [1987] IRLR 334.
37   See *Morris v Breaveglen Ltd* [1993] IRLR 350.
38   [1953] AC 643.
39   See also *Smith v Scot Bowyers Ltd* [1986] IRLR 315.
40   See *Cook v Square D Ltd* [1992] IRLR 34.
41   On the meaning of 'equipment' see *Knowles v Liverpool City Council* [1993] 1 WLR 1428.
42   See Employers' Liability (Compulsory Insurance) Exemption Regulations 1971 SI No 1933 and Employers' Liability (Compulsory Insurance) General Regulations 1971 SI No 1117 (as amended).
43   *Charlton v Forrest Ink* [1980] IRLR 331.
44   See *Pentney v Anglian Water Authortity* [1983] ICR 463.
45   [1988] IRLR 404.
46   [1991] IRLR 463.
47   *Johnstone v Bloomsbury Health Authority* [1991] IRLR 118.
48   [1993] ICR 789.
49   [1972] QB 443.
50   See *Sim v Rotherham MBC* [1986] IRLR 391.
51   *Macmillan Inc v Bishopsgate Investment* [1993] IRLR 393.
52   See *Sybron Corporation v Rochem Ltd* [1983] 253.
53   [1982] IRLR 146.
54   See *Laughton v Bapp Industrial Ltd* [1986] IRLR 245.
55   See *Office Angels Ltd v Rainer-Thomas* [1991] IRLR 214; *Hanover Insurance Brokers Ltd v Schapiro* [1994] IRLR 82.
56   See *Cantor Fitzgerald Ltd v Wallace* [1992] IRLR 215.
57   See *Provident Group PLC v Hayward* [1989] IRLR 84.
58   See *Living Design Ltd v Davidson* [1994] IRLR 69.
59   See *Morris Angel Ltd v Hollande* [1993] IRLR 169.
60   See *Faccenda Chicken Ltd v Fowler* [1986] IRLR 69.
61   See *Bullivant Ltd v Ellis* [1987] IRLR 491.

62 See *Lansing Linde Ltd v Kerr* [1991] **IRLR** 80.
63 See *Johnson & Bloy Ltd v Fallon* [1987] **IRLR** 499.
64 See *WAC Ltd v Whillock* [1990] **IRLR** 23.
65 See *Sun Printers Ltd v Westminster Press Ltd* [1982] **IRLR** 92.
66   See *PSM International v McKechnie* [1992] **IRLR** 279.
67 See *Re a Company's Application* [1989] **IRLR** 477.
68 [1985] **IRLR** 232.
69 See also section 7 HASAWA 1974 (chapter 7).
70 See *Janata Bank v Ahmed* [1981] **IRLR** 457.

4 Recruitment and selection

At the beginning of this chapter we raise some of the policy issues which will have to be considered by the personnel department.[1] First, is it preferable to hire employed or self-employed persons? Secondly, if employees are engaged should they have indefinite or fixed-term contracts? Thirdly, is there any advantage in employing workers on a temporary or part-time basis? Fourthly, is it necessary to impose a probationary period on new recruits? The latter part of the chapter deals with some of the legislative constraints which impinge upon the process of recruitment and selection. The law relating to refusal of employment on union grounds, the employment of disabled persons, rehabilitated offenders, and women and young persons is outlined here but sex and race discrimination are discussed in the following chapter.

Some policy considerations

Employees or independent contractors?

Perhaps the most fundamental decision to be made is whether workers are to be hired under contracts of service (*i.e.* employees) or contracts for service (*i.e.* independent contractors). Although some statutes apply to all workers, for example the Sex Discrimination Act 1975 (SDA 1975),[2] there are still significant legal differences drawn between employed and self-employed persons. Employees gain the benefit of a number of statutory employment rights and are subject to the unwritten general obligations implied in all contracts of employment (*see* chapter 3). When employed as opposed to self-employed persons are engaged employers are required by statute to deduct tax under Schedule E and social security contributions. In addition, employers are obliged to insure against personal injury claims brought by employees.[3] Perhaps the most significant difference at common law is that the doctrine of vicarious liability applies to employees but not to the self-employed, although in exceptional circumstances employers will be liable for the tortious acts of their independent contractors, *e.g.* if they authorize the commission of the wrongful act or have a responsibility which cannot, by law, be delegated to someone else.

The essence of the doctrine of vicarious liability is that employers are held liable to third parties for the civil wrongs committed by employees in the course of their employment. Determining what is 'in the course of employment' has caused immense difficulties over the years but the position today appears to be as follows. Clearly employees act 'in the course of employment' where they carry out acts which are authorized by the employer. Similarly, where their actions are so closely connected with the employment as to be incidental to it, although prohibited and unauthorized by the employer, employees act 'in the course of employment'. However, if an employee's action is so outside the scope of employment as to be 'alien and wholly distinguishable from it' the employer is not liable.[4]

As regards travelling in the course of employment, the House of Lords has laid down the following six propositions:

(i) employees travelling from their ordinary residence to their regular place of work, whatever the means of transport and even if it provided by the employer, are not normally acting in the course of employment. However, if they are contractually obliged to use the employer's transport, they will normally, in the absence of an express condition to the contrary, be regarded as acting in the course of employment while doing so

(ii) travelling in the employer's time between workplaces could be in the course of employment

(iii) receipt of wages, although not the receipt of a travelling allowance, would indicate that the employee was travelling in the course of employment. The fact that an employee may have discretion as to the mode and time of travelling would not take the journey out of the course of employment

(iv) employees travelling in their employer's time from their ordinary residence to a workplace other than their regular

workplace or in the course of a peripatetic occupation or to
the scene of an emergency would be acting in the course
of employment

(v)   a deviation from or interruption to a journey undertaken in
the course of employment, unless the deviation or
interruption was merely incidental to the journey, would for
the time being take the employee out of the course of
employment

(vi) return journeys are to be treated on the same footing as
outward journeys.

These propositions are not intended to exhaustively define when
travelling time is in the course of employment and are subject to
any express arrangements between employer and employee.[5]

Before an employer can be held vicariously liable some nexus
has to be established between the employee's wrongful act and
the circumstances of employment. Thus a contractor engaged to
clean offices (including telephones) was not vicariously liable when
an employee dishonestly used the phones for his own purposes.[6]
Employees remain personally liable for their own acts and theoretically may be required to reimburse the employer for any damages paid out as a result of their failure to take care (*see* chapter
3). It should also be noted that in some cases the criminal law
regards an employee's act as being that of the employer, in which
case the latter will be responsible for the wrongs committed by
the former.

Additionally, a company might be liable as a substitute employer
for the negligence of employees not directly employed by them if
it can be shown that the substitute employer had sufficient power
of control and supervision properly to be regarded as the effective
employer at the critical time.[7]

Given all the consequences of having an employee on the books,
is it always possible to discern whether a contract is a contract of
service or a contract for services? Unfortunately the answer must
be in the negative, for the courts have ruled that the intention of
the parties cannot be the sole determinant of contractual status;
otherwise it would be too easy to contract out of employment
protection legislation. It is the operation of the contract in practice
that is crucial rather than its appearance. According to the Court
of Appeal[8] tribunals have to consider: 'all aspects of the relation-

ship, no single feature being in itself decisive and each of which may vary in weight and direction, and having given such balance to the factors as seems appropriate to determine whether the person was carrying on business on his own account'. The fact that workers pay their own tax and national insurance cannot be conclusive in determining employment status[9] and the cases show that people who perform work at home may be classed as employees so long as there is an element of continuing mutual contractual obligation.[10] Unless the relationship is dependent solely upon the true construction of a written contract, whether a person is engaged under a contract of employment is a question of fact for a court or tribunal to determine.[11] Although individuals engaged under special employment schemes may not be categorized as employees they are to be treated as such for certain purposes.[12]

Occasionally an organization may ask an agency to provide staff and if the worker engaged by the client organization is under a personal obligation to perform the work, a contract of employment may exist. However, if the agency does not undertake to send a specific person then the person supplied is unlikely to be an employee. If the client organization pays the agency for the labour provided and the latter pays the worker, then a contract of employment could only exist between the agency and the worker concerned.

Fixed-term or indefinite contract?

Assuming that a decision has been taken that the organization will engage employees, another matter for consideration is whether to hire for a fixed term or for an indefinite period. From the employer's point of view the main advantage of the fixed-term contract is that if it is for two years or more it is possible to remove an employee's right to claim unfair dismissal or redundancy while retaining the right to give notice.[13] However, if there is no written clause, the expiry of a fixed-term contract without its renewal on the same terms amounts to a dismissal in law (*see* chapter 11).

Temporary or part-time employees?

Temporary employees have exactly the same statutory rights as other employees so long as they possess any necessary qualifying period of service and work the required number of hours. The only two exceptions to this proposition arise where an individual is employed on a temporary basis as a replacement for a woman on maternity leave or to replace someone absent from work under the statutory provisions relating to medical suspension (*see* chapters 6 and 8 respectively). Part-time employment is only indirectly defined by statute and the statutory provisions are frequently at variance with the lines drawn in practice by employers and trade unions. Schedule 13 of EPCA 1978 provides that any person who is employed under a contract of employment for more than 16 hours per week or who has been continuously employed for the previous five years under a contract for more than eight hours per week is entitled to the full range of statutory protections. However, in March 1994 the House of Lords declared that these thresholds were incompatible with European Law.[13A] It remains to be seen how the Government will react to this decision. (On discrimination against part-timers *see* page 60 and 66.)

Should a probationary period be imposed?

We will see in chapter 11 that (save in exceptional circumstances) only those who have been continuously employed for two years can claim that they have been unfairly dismissed. In a sense this requirement serves to impose a probationary period but many employers will regard two years as excessive for the purpose of establishing whether a person's appointment should be confirmed. Often a much shorter period will be deemed appropriate, some employers preferring to make an assessment within four weeks so as to avoid having to give statutory notice to terminate the contract (*see* chapter 10). The great advantage of operating a probationary period is that new recruits are made aware that they are on trial and therefore must establish their suitability.

General legislative constraints

At common law, employers have the right to decide what policies to adopt in relation to recruitment but this position has now been altered by a series of legislative interventions designed to protect certain categories of job applicant. In this section we consider the major statutory provisions, apart from the legislation on sex and race discrimination, which have a bearing on the process of selection for employment.[14]

Discrimination on the grounds of union membership or non-membership

Section 137 of TULRCA 1992 makes it unlawful to refuse employment to people because (a) they are or are not members of a trade union, or (b) they refuse to accept a requirement that they become a member or cease to be a member or a requirement that they suffer deductions if they fail to join.[15] People are deemed to have been refused employment with an employer if that employer:

(i)   refuses or deliberately omits to entertain the application or enquiry, or

(ii) causes the applicant to withdraw or cease to pursue the application or enquiry, or

(iii) refuses or deliberately omits to offer employment, or

(iv) makes an offer of employment the terms of which are such as no reasonable employer who wished to fill the post would offer and which is not accepted, or

(v) makes an offer of employment but withdraws it or causes the applicant not to accept it.

Where a person is offered a job subject to the condition that they become or cease to become a union member and they refuse the offer on the grounds that they are unwilling to accept the condition, they are to be treated as having been refused employment for that reason. As regards job advertisements,[16] if an advertisement indicates, or might reasonably be understood as indicating, that employment is only open to people who are or are not union members, or that there is a requirement applying to the post of the sort mentioned in (b) above, then if people who do not meet the relevant condition are refused employment it will be conclusively presumed that this was because they failed to satisfy the condition. Where it is the practice for trade unions to supply job applicants, non-members who are refused employment are deemed to have been so refused on account of their non-membership.

Section 138 makes it unlawful for an agency which finds employment for workers or supplies employers with workers to refuse its services to people because they are or are not union members or are unwilling to accept a condition or requirement of the type mentioned in (b) above. The provisions relating to advertisements also apply to such agencies.

A complaint about the infringement of these provisions must be presented to an industrial tribunal within three months of the date of the conduct complained about, unless the 'time limit escape clause' applies.[17]

Under section 139 TULRCA 1992 the date of the conduct complained of will be:

(i)   in the case of an actual refusal, the date of the refusal
(ii)   where there was a deliberate omission to offer employment or deal with an application or enquiry, the end of the period within which it was reasonable to except the employer to act
(iii) in the case of conduct causing the applicant to withdraw or cease to pursue an application, the date of that conduct
(iv)   in a case where an offer was made but withdrawn, the date when it was withdrawn
(v)   in a case where an offer was made but not accepted, the date the offer was made.

Provision is made for conciliation but if a complaint is upheld the tribunal must make a declaration to that effect and may make such of the following remedies as it considers just and equitable:[18]

(i)   an order obliging the respondent to pay compensation, which is to be assessed on the same basis as damages for breach of statutory duty and may include damages for injury to feelings
(ii)   a recommendation that the respondent takes such action as the tribunal thinks practicable in order to obviate or reduce the effect on the complainant of the conduct to which the

claim relates. If such a recommendation is not complied with any award of compensation can be increased although the total award cannot exceed the amount stipulated in section 75 EPCA 1978 (£11,000 in 1993).

Finally, it should be noted that a trade union may be joined as a defendant in tribunal proceedings where an employer or agency maintains that it was induced to act in the manner complained of by union pressure.[19] If compensation is awarded the union may be ordered to pay all or part of it. Appeals against tribunal decisions go to the EAT if a point of law is involved.

The Disabled Persons (Employment) Acts 1944 and 1958

Under these Acts organizations with more than 20 employees must ensure that at least 3 per cent of their labour force consists of registered disabled people. In addition handicapped persons must be given preference for certain jobs, for example car park or lift attendants. Exceptions are allowed if the employment of a handicapped person might be hazardous and special permission can be obtained if it proves impossible to meet the quota because either the work is unsuitable or no suitable disabled person has applied. It is a criminal offence to breach the provisions of these Acts although there have been very few prosecutions in practice.

As a result of the Companies (Directors' Report, Employment of Disabled Persons) Regulations 1980 the annual directors' report of companies which employ on average more than 250 people must include a statement which outlines the policy the company has applied during the previous financial year in relation to the employment training, career development and promotion of disabled persons.[20]

The Rehabilitation of Offenders Act 1974

The law does not require applicants to disclose facts about themselves which could hinder them in getting jobs (unless their silence amounts to fraud). Thus, if employers believe that certain information is important, they should seek it specifically before the job is offered.

Section 4 of this Act relieves certain rehabilitated persons from the obligation to disclose 'spent' convictions to a prospective employer and makes it unlawful for an employer to deny employment on the grounds that the applicant had a conviction which was 'spent'. It is the policy of the Act that applicants should not be questioned about spent convictions, although if this situation does arise applicants are entitled to deny that they have ever been convicted. However, under an exemption order protection is not afforded to those applying for a whole range of jobs, *e.g.* as a doctor, nurse, teacher, social worker or probation officer.[21] Sentences of over two and a half years' imprisonment never become 'spent', otherwise convictions become 'spent' after periods which are related to the gravity of the sentence imposed. Thus for a sentence of imprisonment of between six months and two and a half years the rehabilitation period is 10 years. Imprisonment for less than six months requires a seven year rehabilitation period and fines or community service orders take five years to become 'spent'. A probation order, conditional discharge or binding over need not be disclosed after a year or until the order expires (whichever is the longer), and absolute discharges can be concealed if six months has elapsed since sentence. Despite the existence of the Act, the courts cannot compel an employer to engage a rehabilitated offender, they can only declare the exclusion of the applicant to be unlawful.

Women and young persons

The Sex Discrimination Act 1986 and the Employment Act 1989 lifted many of the restrictions on the employment of women and young people (those under the age of 18). Nevertheless certain restrictions remain, for example, the prohibition on employing a woman in a factory within four weeks of giving birth and restrictions on the employment of women in processes involving lead and ionizing radiations.[22] Although there is still a prohibition on young persons cleaning machinery, the requirements relating to the hours of work and holidays of such persons have been removed.

Notes

1   See generally ACAS Advisory Booklet No 6, entitled *Recruitment and Selection*, and *The IPM Recruitment Code* 1990.
2   See *Mirror Group Ltd v Gunning* [1986] IRLR 27.
3   Employers' Liability (Compulsory Insurance) Act 1969.
4   See *Aldred v Nacanco Ltd* [1987] IRLR 292. On the employer's liability for torts committed by employees during the course of industrial action see *GES Ltd v Kingston and St Andrew Corporation* [1989] IRLR 35.
5   See *Smith v Stages* [1989] IRLR 177.
6   See *Heasmans v Clarity Cleaning Co.* [1987] IRLR 286.
7   See *Sime v Sutcliffe Catering* [1990] IRLR 228.
8   *O'Kelly v Trusthouse Forte* [1983] IRLR 369. See also *Lee v Chung* [1990] IRLR 236.
9   See *Young & Woods Ltd v West* [1980] IRLR 201.
10   See *McCleod v Hellyer Bros* [1987] IRLR 232.
11   See *Lee v Chung* (note 8 above).
12   See Health and Safety (Training for Employment) Regulations 1990.
13   See sections 143(1–2) EPCA 1978 and *BBC v Dixon* [1979] IRLR 114.
13A See *R v Secretary of State ex parte EOC* (1994) TLR 4/3/94.
14   Age discrimination is not unlawful at the hiring stage but see the IPM's Equal Opportunities Code (section 5) and Statement on Age and Employment.
15   These provisions do not apply if the employee will ordinarily work outside Great Britain.
16   Defined by section 143 TULRCA 1992.
17   See section 139 TULRCA 1992 and chapter 3, note 14.
18   Section 140 TULRCA 1992.
19   Section 142 TULRCA 1992.
20   See generally Department of Employment, *Code of Good Practice on the Employment of Disabled People 1988*, and the IPM Equal Opportunities Code (section 4).
21   Rehabilitation of Offenders Act 1974 (Exemption) Order 1975.
22   Section 61 of the Factory and Workshop Act 1901, section 205 of the Public Health Act 1906, sections 74, 128 and 131 of the Factories Act 1961 and the Ionizing Radiations Regulations 1983.

5 Discrimination against employees on the grounds of sex or race

The Sex Discrimination Act 1975 and the Race Relations Act 1976

It is important to note that the titles of these statutes do not fully reflect the matters that are covered. While the earlier Act also outlaws discrimination against married (but not single) persons on the grounds of marital status, 'racial grounds' are defined as meaning colour, race, nationality, national or ethnic origins.[1] A racial group which is defined by colour may include people of more than one ethnic origin.[2] In *Mandla v Lee*[3] the House of Lords held that 'ethnic origins' meant a group which was a segment of the population distinguished from others by a sufficient combination of shared customs, beliefs, traditions and characteristics derived from a common or presumed common past, even if not drawn from what in biological terms was a common racial stock, in that it was that combination which gave them an historically determined social identity in their own eyes and in the eyes of those outside the group. Although a racial group cannot be defined by language or religion alone[4] it has been accepted that Sikhs, Jews and gypsies all fall within the scope of the Race Relations Act 1976. In *Dawkins v Department of the Environment*[5] it was accepted that Rastafarians are a separate group with identifiable characteristics, but the Court of Appeal concluded that they have not established a separate identity by reference to their ethnic origins and are therefore not protected by the 1976 Act.

Both the Equal Opportunities Commission (EOC) and the Commission for Racial Equality (CRE) have issued Codes of Practice for the purpose of eliminating discrimination in employment.[6] A failure to observe any of the provisions of these codes does not render a person liable to legal proceedings but the Commissions' recommendations are admissible in evidence before industrial tribunals.[7]

Both statutes recognize that discrimination can be either direct or indirect. Direct discrimination occurs where on the grounds of sex, marital status or race a person is treated less favourably than a person of the opposite sex, a single person or person not of the same racial group, would be treated. Section 1(2) RRA 1976 states that segregation on racial grounds amounts to less favourable treatment, although it has been decided that allowing members of a racial group to congregate voluntarily, *e.g.* in a particular department, will not render an employer liable.[8] A person can complain of indirect discrimination where an employer applies a requirement or condition which would apply equally to a person of the opposite sex (single people or persons not of the same racial group) but which is such that the proportion of the applicant's sex (marital status or racial group) who can comply with it is considerably smaller than the proportion of persons of the opposite sex (single people or persons not of the same racial group). The applicant must also show that he or she suffered a detriment as a result of being unable to comply with the requirement or condition. Employers can avoid liability by demonstrating that the requirement or condition is 'justifiable' irrespective of the sex, marital status or race of the person to whom it is applied.[9] Both statutes stipulate that when drawing comparisons the relevant circumstances must be the same or not materially different.[10]

A number of points need to be made about the application of the foregoing definitions. As regards direct discrimination, it would seem that the phrase 'on the grounds of sex' does not refer to the alleged discriminator's reason or motive but to the intention to provide less favourable treatment. According to the House of Lords, the relevant question is 'would the complainant have received the same treatment but for his or her sex?'[11] Words or acts of discouragement can amount to less favourable treatment.[12] The phrase 'on the grounds of' covers cases of harassment and where the reason for the discrimination is a generalized assumption that people of a particular sex, marital status or race possess or lack certain characteristics.[13] In *Showboat Entertainments Ltd v Owens*[14] it was held that section 1(1)a RRA 1976 covers all cases of discrimination on racial grounds whether the racial characteristics in question are those of the person treated less favourably or some other person. Thus the dismissal of an employee because of his refusal to carry out an instruction to exclude blacks from the employer's premises was on racial grounds notwithstanding that the employee was white.

Sexual harassment has been defined as 'unwanted conduct of a sexual nature, or other conduct based on sex affecting the dignity of women and men at work'.[15] It is also worth noting that the industrial tribunal and EAT rules may allow these tribunals to make a 'restricted reporting order' in cases where allegations of sexual misconduct are made. Whether such an order is made is up to the discretion of the tribunal and its effect will be to prohibit the publication or broadcasting of anything likely to lead the public to identify either the person making the allegation or any person affected by it. Unless revoked earlier, an order will lapse when the tribunal promulgates its decision.[16]

In relation to indirect discrimination, the requirement or condition must be mandatory and the failure to comply with it must be an absolute bar. Hence a claim cannot succeed if the criterion complained of was merely one factor which the alleged discriminator had taken into account.[17] The words 'requirement or condition' are of wide import and are capable of including any obligation of service, for example an obligation to work full-time.[18] Indeed, the mere fact that the employer requires workers to perform the jobs they were employed to do may be regarded as 'applying a requirement'.[19] However, in *Brook v London Borough of Haringey*[20] the EAT upheld the industrial tribunal's decision that a requirement to obtain a prescribed number of points by reference to multiple factors in order to avoid redundancy did not amount to a 'condition.'

The courts have interpreted the words 'can comply' to mean 'can in practice comply' rather than physically or theoretically comply. Thus it has been held that an age limit of 28 for recruitment could amount to indirect discrimination against women since they are less likely than men to be available for work below that age owing to child bearing and rearing.[21] However, the expression 'can comply' cannot be equated with 'may wish to comply'; ultimately it is a question of reasonableness with all the surrounding circumstances being considered. In *Clarke v Eley (IMI) Kynoch Ltd*[22] the issue arose whether the words 'can comply' and 'cannot comply' include past opportunities to comply. The EAT decided that the date on which the detriment must be demonstrated was the date the discriminatory conduct operated so as to create the alleged detriment.

As regards the relative proportion of persons who can comply, much will depend on the tribunal's own knowledge and experience and its selection of the appropriate section of the population for comparison. For example, in *Jones v University of Manchester*[23] the Court of Appeal ruled that in finding that the requirement for a career adviser to be a graduate aged between 27 and 35 years had a disproportionate impact on women, the industrial tribunal had erred in restricting the pool for comparison to mature students. According to the Court of Appeal, the appropriate pool was all men and women with the required qualifications not including the requirement complained of, in this case graduates with the necessary experience. In *Greater Manchester Police v Lea*[24] the EAT was keen to avoid a discussion about statistical bases and upheld the industrial tribunal's decision that the proportion of men in the pool who could comply with the condition of not being in receipt of an occupational pension (95.3 per cent) was considerably smaller than the proportion of women (99.4 per cent).

Where a prima facie case of indirect discrimination has been established the employer will have to satisfy the tribunal that the discriminatory requirement or condition was justifiable. This means that an objective balance has to be struck between the discriminatory effect of the requirement or condition and the reasonable needs of the party applying it.[25] Clearly a nexus must be established between the function of the employer and the imposition of the requirement or condition. In addition a tribunal must assess both the quantitative and the qualitative effects of the requirement or condition on those affected by it.[26] However, if an employer requires a Sikh to wear a safety helmet on a construction site and has no reasonable grounds for believing that he would not wear a turban at all times when on the site, the requirement is conclusively presumed to be unjustifiable.[27]

The European Court of Justice has indicated that Article 119 of the Rome Treaty precludes national legislation which has a disproportionate effect on women unless the member state concerned can show that the legislation is justified by objective factors unrelated to any discrimination on the ground of sex.[28] The precise effect of this decision remains to be seen but it is clearly arguable that all payments to employees which are based on statute infringe Article 119 to the extent that they exclude part-timers, for example medical suspension, guarantee and redundancy payments. However, when the Equal Opportunities Commission sought a judicial review of the qualifying thresholds for both unfair dismissal and redundancy payments(*see* pages 149–50), the High Court ruled that the Secretary of State had objectively justified those thresholds on the basis that a reduction in them would adversely affect the opportunities for part-time employment. The Court of Appeal were of the opinion that the EOC was not entitled to bring the proceedings and that the industrial tribunal was the appropriate forum for anyone seeking to enforce their rights under Article 119.[29] Finally, it should be noted that neither sex nor race discrimination can be justified on the basis of customer or union preferences.[30]

It is unlawful to discriminate on the prohibited grounds in the arrangements made for the purpose of determining who should be offered employment, in the terms on which employment is offered or by 'refusing or deliberately omitting' to offer employment.[31] 'Employment' covers engagement under a contract of service or a contract personally to execute any work or labour.[32] According to the Court of Appeal, the legislation contemplates a contract whose dominant purpose is that the party contracting to provide services under it performs personally the work or labour which forms the subject matter of the contract.[33] Both statutes aim to prevent the emergence or continuation of discriminatory practices, *i.e.* conduct which does not, in itself, amount to unlawful discrimination but which in fact results in discriminatory treatment.[34] Thus, if it becomes common knowledge that Asians are unlikely to get jobs with a particular organization because of the stringent English language tests it imposes, it may be possible to establish the existence of a discriminatory practice even though there is no applicant for a post.[35] Advertisements must not indicate or reasonably be understood as indicating an intention to discriminate unlawfully nor should they adopt a job title with a sexual connotation, *e.g.* waiter or stewardess, since this will be taken to indicate a discriminatory intent unless there is an indication to the contrary.[36] The word 'advertisement' is defined to include 'every form of advertisement, whether to the public or not'.[37]

It would seem to follow that personnel managers should ensure that application forms and interviewers only ask questions and insist on minimum qualifications which are relevant to the requirements of the job.[38] Thus a height requirement and certain conditions relating to past experience, *e.g.* having served an apprenticeship, might be difficult to justify under either Act. Clearly word of mouth recruitment is suspect and refusing to employ those who live in a particular geographical area could amount to indirect discrimination if there was a racial imbalance in the population residing there.[39]

Despite what has been stated above, discrimination may be lawful in certain circumstances. The major exception, which is common to both statutes, is where sex or race is a genuine occupational qualification (GOQ). In the case of sex, this occurs where:[40]

(i)   the essential nature of the job demands a particular physiology (excluding physical strength) or for reasons of authenticity in entertainment

(ii)   the job needs to be held by a particular sex to preserve decency or privacy because either it is likely to involve physical contact in circumstances where members of the opposite sex might reasonably object to its being carried out (*e.g.* searching for security purposes) or because people are in a state of undress or are using sanitary facilities. In *Sisley v Britannia Security*[41] it was held that this exclusion covered all matters reasonably incidental to an employee's work and is not confined to cases where the job itself requires the holder to be in a state of undress

(iii)   the nature or location of the employer's establishment makes it impracticable for the job holder to live anywhere other than on the employer's premises and the premises are not equipped with separate sleeping accommodation and sanitary facilities for one sex and it is unreasonable to expect the employer to equip those premises with separate facilities or to provide separate premises (*e.g.* where the employment is on a remote site). The words 'to live in' involve the concept of residence either permanent or temporary and do not cover the situation where the employee is obliged to remain on the premises for a limited period eating or resting[42]

(iv)   the nature of the establishment demands a person of a particular sex because it is an establishment for persons requiring special care or attention and those persons are all of a particular sex and it is reasonable, 'having regard to the essential character of the establishment', that the job should not be held by a person of the opposite sex

(v)   the job holder provides personal services which can most effectively be provided by a person of a particular sex (*e.g.* in a team of social workers)

(vi)   the job is one of two to be held by a married couple

(vii)   the job is likely to involve the holder working or living in a private home and the job needs to be done by a member of one sex because objection might reasonably be taken to allowing someone of the other sex the degree of physical or social contact with a person living in the home or the knowledge of such a person's private affairs, which the job is likely to entail

(viii) the job is likely to involve the performance of duties outside the UK in a country whose laws or customs are such that the duties could not effectively be performed by a woman.

The only GOQs allowed for under the 1976 Act depend on authenticity in the provision of food and drink, in entertainment and modelling, and where the job holder provides personal welfare services which can most effectively be provided by a person of a particular racial group. In relation to personal welfare services the Court of Appeal has ruled that the word 'personal' indicates that the identity of the giver and the recipient of the services is important and appears to contemplate direct contact between the giver and the recipient.[43] Under both Acts GOQs apply even though they relate to only some of the job duties, and unless a duty is so trivial that it ought to be disregarded altogether it is not for tribunals to assess the importance of the duty.[44] However, a GOQ will not provide a defence if the employer already has sufficient employees capable of carrying out those duties and whom it would be reasonable to employ in that way.[45]

The GOQ defence is also unavailable if there is a discriminatory dismissal. In *Timex Corporation v Hodgson*[46] the EAT had to consider whether a GOQ could be used as a defence where a male supervisor had been selected for redundancy on sexual grounds. Rather surprisingly it was held that the employers had discriminated by selecting a woman to do the revised job, and not in dismissing the man. Since the discrimination lay in 'deliberately omitting to offer' or failing to transfer to the revised job the GOQ defence could apply.

Turning our attention to unequal treatment in the course of employment[47] and to discriminatory dismissals, it is unlawful for employers to discriminate:[48]

(i)   (under the RRA 1976) in the terms of employment afforded[49]

(ii) in the way they afford access to opportunities for promotion, transfer or training, or to any other benefits, facilities or services, or by refusing or deliberately omitting to afford access to them

(iii) by dismissing or subjecting the employee to any other detriment.[49A]

However, special arrangements can be made to train persons of a particular sex or racial group if it can be shown that within the previous 12 months only a small minority of that sex or racial group was performing a particular type of work.[50] A refusal to investigate complaints of unfair treatment may amount to a refusal of access to 'any other benefits, facilities or services'.[51]

Under the Social Security Act 1989, which was due to come into force on 1 January 1993, it is unlawful to discriminate on the grounds of sex or marital status:

(i)   in the terms on which employment is offered which relate to how access is given in benefits, facilities or services under an occupational pension scheme

(ii) in the way an employee is given access to such benefits, facilities or services

(iii) by refusing or deliberately omitting to afford an employee access to any such benefits, facilities or services

(iv) by subjecting an employee to any detriment in connection with such a scheme.

However, these principles have been affected by the European Court's judgment in *Barber v Guardian Royal Exchange Group*.[52] This case requires equality in occupational pensions only in relation to benefits payable in respect of periods of employment after 17 May 1990.

Good motive cannot excuse discriminatory behaviour. Thus, despite the Court of Appeal's decision in *Peake*'s case,[53] it is submitted that allowing one sex or racial group to arrive late or leave work early constitutes unlawful discrimination since those not specially favoured have been either denied access to a benefit or have suffered a detriment. The Court of Appeal has subsequently recognized that such arrangements cannot be condoned on the grounds of chivalry or administrative convenience and it is no trifling matter that an employer has introduced a sex-based scheme when the same objective could be achieved in a non-discriminatory fashion. Employers can still insist on certain types of clothing being worn if the rules on clothing apply to all employees and do not have an indirectly discriminatory effect which cannot be justified.[54] Nevertheless, the words 'subjecting . . . to any other detriment' are to be given their broad ordinary meaning, so it is clear that almost any discriminatory conduct by an employer is potentially unlawful.[55]

As regards termination of employment, it is expected that during 1994 it will become automatically unfair to dismiss a woman, irrespective of her hours of work or length of service, if the reason for dismissal is that she is pregnant or if the reason is in any way connected with her pregnancy (*see* pages 83–5). Until this time or the intervention of the ECJ beforehand, it would seem that to dismiss a woman simply because she is pregnant (or to refuse to employ a woman of child-bearing age because she may become pregnant) is unlawful, since child-bearing is a female characteristic. However, where there is no direct application of a gender-based criterion, it is legitimate to draw a comparison between the non-availability of a woman because of pregnancy and the non-availability of a man at the relevant time. Thus in *Webb v EMO Ltd*,[56] where a woman recruited to cover for an employee taking maternity leave was dismissed when it was discovered that she too was pregnant, the House of Lords ruled that it was appropriate for the industrial tribunal to consider whether a hypothetical male hired for the same purpose would have been treated similarly if he had become unavailable at the material time.

Selection for redundancy on the grounds of sex will be unlawful, but supposing a woman was selected for redundancy on the grounds that while she had a longer period of cumulative service she had less continuous service than a man. It could be argued that because women are likely to have shorter periods of continuous service than men, as a consequence of child-bearing and rearing, such a basis for selection constitutes indirect discrimination and would therefore need to be justified.[57] In *Clarke*'s case[58] the EAT decided that redundancy selection criteria which resulted in the selection of part-timers first was unlawful because they had a disproportionate impact on women and could not be justified on the particular facts of the case. Dismissal on the grounds of sex or race cannot be excused simply because there was pressure from other employees.

Originally the SDA 1975 did not apply to provisions in relation to death or retirement, but as a result of the Sex Discrimination Act 1986, the dismissal of a woman on the ground of age when a man of that age in comparable circumstances would not have been dismissed, or vice versa, will be unlawful. However, there is nothing in the SDA 1975 which prevents the employer having a variety of retiring ages for different jobs, provided there is no direct or indirect discrimination based on gender.[59] In *Marshall v Southampton and South West Hampshire AHA*[60] the European Court of Justice held that a policy of dismissing a woman solely because she had attained, or passed, the qualifying age for a state pension constituted discrimination on the ground of sex, contrary to Council Directive No 76/207. Article 5(1) of this Directive prohibits any discrimination on the grounds of sex with regard to working conditions, including conditions governing dismissal, and can now be relied on as against a *state authority* acting in its capacity as an employer. As regards occupational pension schemes, the European Court of Justice has declared that these fall within the scope of Article 119 of the Treaty of Rome and that pensionable age must be the same for men and women.

Section 77 of the SDA 1975 makes a term in a contract or collective agreement void where its inclusion renders the making of the contract unlawful by virtue of this Act or it provides for the doing of an act which would be unlawful under this legislation. This section also applies to the rules of employers, employers' associations, professional or qualifying bodies and trade unions. Employees (or job seekers) can complain to an industrial tribunal that a term of a collective agreement or a works rule is void. However, to do so they must believe that the term or rule may have some effect on them in the future, or that the term provides for the doing of an unlawful discriminatory act which might be done to them, and the collective agreement was made by or on behalf of the employer or an employers' organization to which the employer belongs. It is interesting to note that tribunals have no power to amend the term so as to make it non-discriminatory.[61] Where the victim of the discrimination is a party to the contract the term is unenforceable against that person.

In *Kowalska v Freie und Hansestadt Hamburg*[62] the ECJ declared that Article 119 precludes the application of a provision of a collective agreement under which part-timers are excluded from the benefit of severance pay, when it is clear that a considerably smaller proportion of men than women work part-time, unless the employer shows that the provision is justified by objective factors unrelated to sex discrimination. Where there is indirect discrimination in a collective agreement, members of the group which is disadvantaged must be treated in the same way as other workers in proportion to the hours they work. Similarly it would be unlawful for a collective agreement to provide for the service of full-timers to be fully taken into account for regrading purposes when only half of such service is taken into account in the case of part-timers, and the latter group comprise a considerably smaller percentage of men than women, unless the employer can prove that such a provision is objectively justified.[63]

Any provision of existing legislation is void to the extent that it imposes a requirement to do an act which would amount to sex discrimination. However, it is lawful to discriminate if it is necessary to do so to comply with a requirement of an existing statutory provision whose purpose is to protect women as regards pregnancy or maternity or 'other circumstances' giving rise to risks specifically affecting women.[64] It is also lawful to discriminate if it is necessary to do so to comply with a requirement of Part 1 HASAWA 1974 (*see* chapter 7), or certain other health and safety legislation. For this exception to apply the employer must demonstrate not only that the discriminatory act was necessary to comply with the statutory duty but also that it was done for the purpose of protecting the woman in relation to pregnancy, maternity or other circumstances giving rise to risks specifically affecting women.[65] Two further points should be made at this stage. First, section 2(2) of SDA 1975 prevents men complaining that special treatment has been afforded to women in connection with pregnancy or childbirth. Second, any special treatment given to a Sikh as a consequence of the exemption from the obligation to wear a safety helmet when on a building site will not amount to race discrimination.[66]

If the provisions of the SDA 1975 or RRA 1976 are not complied with both the employing body and named individuals may be sued. Individuals may be liable for instructing or putting pressure on someone to perform an unlawful act and for knowingly aiding another person to do an unlawful act.[67] Employers are liable for the acts of employees in the course of employment, whether or not they were done with the employer's knowledge or approval, unless it can be proved that the employer 'took such steps as were reasonably practicable to prevent the employee from doing that act'.[68] Hence it is not sufficient to adopt an equal opportunities policy, it is also necessary to check that such a policy has been communicated to all staff, has been understood and implemented. Additionally, employers should ensure that informal practices do not develop which could lead to an act of unlawful discrimination.[69]

Both statutes permit individuals to bring complaints before an industrial tribunal within three months of an 'act complained of' occurring. For these purposes an act which extends over a period, for example the refusal of a mortgage subsidy, is to be treated as done at the end of that period.[70] Over the years the courts have struggled to distinguish a continuing act from a one-off act with a continuing consequence. Thus the following have been held to constitute continuing acts: an employer's failure to implement promised remedial measures[71] and a requirement to work on less favourable pension terms.[72] Although in *Sougrin v Haringey Health Authority*[73] the Court of Appeal thought that the placing of a black nurse at a lower grade than a white colleague and the rejection of her appeal was not a continuing act, it is difficult to see why the appeal itself could not constitute a separate 'act complained of'.[74] According to the EAT, in determining when the 'act complained of was done' the question is whether the cause of action had crystallized on the relevant date, not whether the complainant felt that he or she had suffered discrimination on

that date.[75] Out of time claims can be heard if it is just and
equitable to do so[76] and in this respect the strength of the
employee's complaint may be a factor.[77]

Only the Equal Opportunities Commission or the Commission
for Racial Equality can commence proceedings where there has
been discriminatory advertising, a discriminatory practice, or
where there have been instructions or pressure to discriminate.[78]
However, there is nothing to prevent an individual complaining
that an advertisement led to discrimination in the arrangements
made for determining who should be offered employment.[79]

It is recognized that obtaining information can be particularly
difficult where discrimination is alleged and so Questions and
Replies Orders were passed in 1975 (sex) and 1977 (race) to
assist applicants in this respect. Although special forms are not
necessary, an aggrieved person's questions and any reply by the
employer are admissible in evidence. If there is a failure to reply
within a reasonable period or an 'evasive or equivocal' response
is received the inference may be drawn that an unlawful act has
been committed.[80] Thus, where an employer failed to answer all
but one of nine questions asked by an unsuccessful job applicant,
the reply was regarded as evasive and the inference drawn that the
applicant had suffered unlawful discrimination in the selection
arrangements.[81] Again the House of Lords has ruled that the
contents of documents must be disclosed if such 'discovery' (a
technical legal term) is necessary to dispose fairly of the proceedings.[82] In this context 'fair disposal' means a disposal of the proceedings which is fair to the applicant.[83] However, a tribunal is
not empowered to order an employer to disclose information
which is not available at the time.[84]

Both Acts allow the Commissions to devote resources to assisting actual or prospective complainants[85] and, if they think it desirable, they can instigate formal investigations of anyone believed to
be discriminating unlawfully.[85] However the Commissions cannot
embark on a 'named person' investigation in the absence of any
belief that the person named might have committed an unlawful
act.[87] The Commissions also have the power to require the production of documents, to make recommendations and, if necessary,
to issue non-discrimination notices.[88] As a last resort either body
may seek a county court injunction to prohibit discriminatory acts.

In relation to the burden of proof, it is worth referring to the principles and guidelines set out by the Court of Appeal in *King v GB–China Centre*:[89]

(i)   it is unusual to find direct evidence of discrimination
(ii) therefore the outcome of a case will usually depend on what inferences it is proper to draw from the facts found by the tribunal
(iii) a finding of discrimination and of a difference in race (or sex) will often point to the possibility of discrimination. In such circumstances it will be for the employer to explain. If no explanation is offered or the tribunal considers the explanation to be unsatisfactory it will be legitimate to infer that the discrimination was on racial (or sexual) grounds
(iv) it is unnecessary and unhelpful to introduce the concept of a shifting evidential burden of proof. Tribunals should reach a conclusion on the balance of probabilities, bearing in mind both the difficulties which face a person who complains of unlawful discrimination and the fact that it is for the complainant to prove his or her case.

Action taken prior to the legislation coming into force can be taken into account, as can evidence of events subsequent to the alleged act of discrimination if it is logically probative of a relevant fact.[90]

If no settlement is reached[91] and the complaint is held to be well founded, three possible remedies are available.[92] First, the tribunal can make a declaration of the complainant's rights. Second, it can require the respondent to pay compensation. In the light of the European Court's decision in *Marshall v Southampton and South West Hampshire AHA (No. 2)*[93] that compensation must enable loss and harm actually sustained to be made good in full, the Government has removed the upper limit in compensation for sex discrimination.[94] Both statutes currently provide that in cases of indirect discrimination no compensation can be awarded if the employer shows that there was no intention to discriminate.[95] It remains to be seen whether these provisions can survive the pressure generated by the *Marshall* decision. What is clear is that a claim for hurt feelings is almost inevitable in discrimination cases[96] and that exemplary damages are unavailable.[97] Third, there may be a recommendation that the employer takes action within a specified period designed to reduce the effect of the discrimination which has taken place, such as removing an age barrier to recruitment.[98]

Finally, both the SDA 1975 and RRA 1976 outlaw the victimization of people simply because they have given evidence in connection with proceedings, have brought proceedings or intend to do so against someone (*e.g.* some other employer) under the Equal Pay Act 1970, the SDA 1975, the RRA 1976 or Schedule 5 of the Social Security Act 1989.[99] However, the Court of Appeal has insisted that for the necessary causal link to be established the employer's motive for inflicting the less favourable treatment must be consciously connected with the anti-discrimination legislation.[100]

The Equal Pay Act 1970 (as amended)

According to the Equal Pay Act 1970 an equality clause operates when a person is employed on 'like work', work rated as equivalent or work of equal value to that of a person of the opposite sex in the same employment.[101] For these purposes men and women are to be treated as in the same employment if they are employed at the same establishment or at establishments in Great Britain which observe common terms and conditions of employment.[102] According to the EAT, in deciding whether men and women are in the same employment, the first test is to ensure that the applicant and the comparator are typical of their respective groups. Second, common terms and conditions must be observed in relation to the comparator's class at his or her establishment and that same class at the applicant's establishment. In determining whether terms and conditions are common, two factors are particularly relevant: their derivation and the influence of geography.[103]

The effect of the equality clause is that any term in a person's contract (whether concerned with pay or not) which is less favourable than in the contract of a person of the opposite sex is modified so as to be not less favourable. Thus in *Hayward v Cammell Laird*[104] the House of Lords held that a woman is entitled to have the same term as to basic pay as male comparators irrespective of whether she was as favourably treated as the men when the whole of the benefits of their contracts were taken into account. It should also be noted that paragraph 2 of Article 119 states that 'pay' means 'the ordinary basic minimum wage or salary and any other consideration, whether in cash or in kind, which the worker receives, directly or indirectly, in respect of his employment from his employer'. According to the ECJ, a benefit is pay if the worker is entitled to receive it from his or her employer by reason of the existence of the employment relationship. Thus Article 119 covers not only occupational retirement and survivors' pensions,[105] travel concessions on retirement, and statutory and contractual severance payments but also paid leave or overtime for participation in training courses given by an employer under a statutory scheme.[106] Section 6 of the EPA 1970 (as amended) provides that an equality clause does not operate where there are terms affording special treatment to women in connection with pregnancy or childbirth.

What is 'like work'? This concept focuses on the job rather than the person performing it. Once a person has shown that her or his work is of the same or broadly similar nature as that of a person of the opposite sex, unless the employer can prove that any differences are of practical importance in relation to terms and conditions of employment, that person is to be regarded as employed on 'like work'.[107] In comparing work, a broad approach should be taken and attention must be paid to the frequency with which any differences occur in practice as well as their nature and extent. Trivial differences or 'differences not likely in the real world to be reflected in terms and conditions of employment' are not to be taken into account.[108] Similarly, tribunals are required to investigate the actual work done rather than rely on theoretical contractual obligations. The performance of supervisory duties may constitute 'things done' of practical importance[109] but the time at which the work is done would seem to be irrelevant. In *Dugdale v Kraft Foods*[110] the men and women were employed on broadly similar work but only men worked the night shift. It was held that the hours at which the work was performed did not prevent equal basic rates being afforded since the men could be compensated for the night shift by an additional payment. Thus an equality clause will not result in equal pay if persons of one sex are remunerated for something which persons of the other sex do not do.[111] However, it is not permissible to ignore part of the work which a person actually performs on the ground that his or her pay includes an additional element in respect of that work,[112] although there might be an exception where part of the work is, in effect, a separate and distinct job. Finally, in determining whether differences are of practical importance a useful guide is whether the differences are such as to put the two employments in different categories or grades in an evaluation study.[113]

What is 'work rated as equivalent'? According to section 1(5) EPA 1970, a person's work will only be regarded as rated as equivalent to that of a person of the opposite sex if it has been given equal value under a properly conducted job evaluation scheme. In determining whether two jobs have equal value it is necessary to have regard to the full results of a job evaluation scheme, including the allocation to grade or scale at the end of the evaluation process. Thus in *Springboard Trust v Robson*[114] it was accepted that the applicant was employed on work rated as equivalent notwithstanding that the comparator's job scored different points, where the result of converting the points to grades provided for under the evaluation scheme was that the jobs were to be treated as in the same grade.

A valid job evaluation exercise will evaluate the job and not the person performing it, and if evaluation studies are to be relied on they must be analytical in the sense of dividing a physical or abstract whole into its constituent parts. It is clearly insufficient that bench mark jobs have been evaluated on a factor demand basis if the jobs of the applicant and comparators were not.[115] Employers are not prevented from using physical effort as a criterion if the tasks involved objectively require a certain level of physical strength, so long as the evaluation system as a whole precludes all sex discrimination by taking into account other criteria.[116] If the work has been rated as equivalent a complainant does not have to show that the employees concerned have actually been paid in accordance with the evaluation scheme.[117]

An equal value claim can be brought even though a person of the opposite sex is performing like work or work rated as equivalent (perhaps a 'token' male). In order to promote the objectives of Article 119 the House of Lords has ruled that an equal value claim can be pursued so long as the applicant's comparator is not engaged on like work or work rated as equivalent.[118] However, where work has been given different ratings under a job evaluation study an equal value claim cannot proceed unless a tribunal is satisfied that there are reasonable grounds for determining that the study was made 'on a system which discriminates on the grounds of sex.'[119] Section 2A(3) states that there is discrimination on the grounds of sex for these purposes where a 'difference, or coincidence, between values set by that system on different grounds under the same or different headings is not justifiable irrespective of the sex of the person on whom those demands are made'. This would appear to cover both direct and indirect discrimination.

Where a woman, for example, can show that she is employed on like work or work rated as equivalent, an employer can still defeat a claim for equal pay by proving on the balance of probabilities that the variation is 'genuinely due to a material difference (other than the difference of sex) between her case and his'.[120] However, if there is an equal value claim the employer need only show that a variation is genuinely due to a material factor. In this context 'material' means significant and relevant. Initially, it was thought that the material difference defence related to the personal circumstances of the employee rather than to the job, whereas the material factor defence allowed employees to be distinguished on the basis of extrinsic factors, *e.g.* market forces. However, it now seems that both defences require the employer to demonstrate objectively justified grounds for different treatment. Thus where statistics disclose an appreciable difference in pay between two groups of workers who do work of equal value – one group comprising largely women and the other comprising largely men – the onus of proof would shift to the employer. According to the ECJ, the employer cannot rely on the fact that rates of pay have been set by collective bargaining even if the bargaining process is untainted by sex discrimination. In the same case the ECJ acknowledged that market forces cannot constitute a complete defence where they account only for part of the difference in pay.[121]

The objectively justified grounds need not be solely economic and could include administrative efficiency in appropriate cases.[122] It is worth noting that the following have been regarded as genuine material differences: the method of entering employment;[123] working in a different part of the country;[124] responsibility allowances;[125] financial constraints;[126] longer service; better academic qualifications; higher productivity. It is clearly insufficient to show that the reason the applicant was paid less was an understandable error.[127]

In *Jenkins v Kingsgate Clothing Ltd (No 2)*[128] the question of whether a female 'part-timer' was entitled to the same hourly rate as a 'full-time' man was referred to the ECJ. This court decided that a difference in pay between full and part-time workers does not amount to discrimination prohibited by Article 119 unless it is in reality merely an indirect way of reducing the level of pay of part-timers on the ground that that group of workers is composed exclusively or predominantly of one sex. Having received no clear guidance from the European Court the EAT chose to construe the EPA 1970 as requiring any difference in pay to be objectively justified. Thus employers now bear the burden of proving that a variation in remuneration is in fact reasonably necessary in order to achieve some objective other than an objective related to the sex of the worker (on the treatment of part-timers by collective agreements *see* page 66).

More recently, in the *Danfoss* case[129] Equal Pay Directive 75/117 was interpreted as meaning that where employees do not understand how the criteria for pay increments are applied, if a woman establishes that the average pay of females is lower than that of men, the burden of proof is on the employer to show that the pay system is not discriminatory. Thus where vocational training or flexibility operate to the disadvantage of women the employer will have to justify their application. According to the European Court of Justice, vocational training can be justified as a criterion if the employer shows that such training is important for the performance of specific work tasks. Similarly, in so far as flexibility refers to adaptability to variable work schedules rather than to the quality of the work, it can be justified by demonstrating that such adaptability is of importance for the performance of specific job duties. As regards seniority, the ECJ has acknowledged that its objectivity depends on all the circumstances, notably on the relationship between the nature of the duties performed and the experience afforded by their performance after a certain number of working hours.[130]

One device that needs to be scrutinized as a result of the EPA 1970 is that of 'red circling'; that is, the practice of drawing a circle round the names of those within a protected group. Such action may be perfectly lawful, *e.g.* where employees accept lower-paid work in a redundancy situation, but if the underlying reason for different treatment is sex-based it cannot be accepted as a defence.[131] Employers have to justify the inclusion of every employee in a red circled group and must prove that at the time of admission to the circle the more favourable terms were related to a consideration other than sex.[132] Again if a person's wages are protected on a transfer, perhaps because of age or illness, tribunals must be satisfied that this was not merely because of sex or that the new job was not one which was open only to one sex. The prolonged maintenance of a red circle may not only be contrary to industrial relations practice but may in all the circumstances give rise to a doubt as to whether the employers have discharged the statutory burden of proof imposed on them by section 1(3) EPA 1970.

Where there is a dispute as to the effect of an equality clause, both the employee and the employer can apply to an industrial tribunal. Under the EPA 1970 complaints must be brought within six months of the termination of employment, yet no time limit is stipulated for a free-standing claim under Article 119. In order to provide some certainty the EAT has indicated that a period of three to six months would be reasonable for bringing claims directly under European law.[133] The employee may claim arrears of pay or damages but a tribunal cannot make an award in respect of any employment earlier than two years before the date on which the proceedings were instituted.[134] Complainants must identify a comparable person of the opposite sex and cannot launch an application without any sort of prima facie case.[135] Although a comparison cannot be made with a hypothetical person, the ECJ has decided that Article 119 allows a complainant to compare herself or himself with a previous job incumbent.[136]

Where an equal value claim is lodged the industrial tribunals must allow the parties to apply for an adjournment in order to reach a settlement.[137] A tribunal can only reach a decision if it is satisfied that there are reasonable grounds for determining that the work is of equal value and a report has been received from a member of the panel of independent experts.[138] An industrial tribunal is not entitled to require an expert's report before deciding whether there were reasonable grounds.[139] However, it is entitled to hear evidence of a job evaluation scheme undertaken by the employer after the commencement of proceedings, provided it relates to facts and circumstances existing at the time the proceedings were initiated. Indeed, it is open to an employer to utilize such a scheme as evidence at any stage up to the final hearing.[140] The employer can ask the tribunal to hear the material factor defence before the expert is required to prepare the report but this issue can be raised again after the report has been submitted.[141] A minimum period of six weeks is allowed for the preparation of the report and the parties have an opportunity to make representations before it is drawn up.[142] No method for comparing jobs is stipulated although it is envisaged that this will involve evaluating factors such as effort, skill and decision.

While there is a presumption in favour of admitting the report it can be challenged on the following grounds:[143]

(i)   the expert failed to follow the designated procedure
(ii)   the expert's conclusion was not reasonably reached
(iii) for 'some other material reasons' (excluding simple
       disagreement with the expert's conclusion or reasoning)
       the report is unsatisfactory.

The expert may be obliged to attend the tribunal hearing as a witness and may be required to explain any matter contained in the report.[144] Indeed, the tribunal is entitled to take into account the expert's oral evidence in deciding whether to admit the report.[145] If the tribunal rejects the report it must commission another. Each party is entitled to call one witness to give evidence on the equal value question but a tribunal has no power to require a complainant to be interviewed by an expert appointed by the employer.[146] The tribunal can only hear factual evidence relating to a conclusion in the report if it relates to the genuine material factor defence or a party has failed to provide information or produce documents for the expert.[147] Finally, it should be remembered that the decision as to whether an equal value claim succeeds is that of the tribunal and not the expert. The current attitude of the EAT is that an independent expert appointed by a tribunal has no greater standing than an expert called by either side.[148]

Notes

1 Section 3(1) Race Relations Act 1976.
2 See section 2(2) RRA 1976 and *London Borough of Lambeth v CRE* [1990] IRLR 231.
3 [1983] IRLR 209.
4 See *Gwynedd v Jones* [1986] ICR 833; *Nyazi v Rymans Ltd* (1988) IRLIB 367; *Seide v Gillette Industries* [1980] IRLR 427. On nationality see *Orphanos v Queen Mary College* [1985] 2 AER 233. On national origins see *Tejani v Superintendent Registrar of Peterborough* [1986] IRLR 502.
5 [1993] IRLR 284.
6 *EOC Code*, HMSO 1985; *CRE Code*, CRE, 1984. See also IPM *Equal Opportunities Code* and sections 7 and 8 Local Government and Housing Act 1989 on the appointment of local authority staff.
7 Section 56A(10) SDA 1975, section 47(10) RRA 1976.
8 See *FTAT v Modgill* [1980] IRLR 142.
9 Section 1(1) of both Acts.
10 Section 5(3) SDA 1975, section 3(4) RRA 1976.
11 See *James v Eastleigh BC* [1990] IRLR 288.
12 See *Tower Hamlets LBC v Rabin* [1989 ICR 693.
13 See *Coleman v Skyrail Oceanic Ltd* [1981] IRLR 398, *Hurley v Mustoe* [1981] IRLR 208 and EOC Code paragraph 13(a).
14 [1984] IRLR 7.
15 European Commission Code of Practice on measure to combat sexual harassment. See also the IPM Statement on harassment at work and *Porcelli v Strathclyde Regional Council* [1986] IRLR 134.
16 Sections 40–1 TURERA 1993.
17 See *Meer v Tower Hamlets LBC* [1988] IRLR 399.
18 See *Holmes v Home Office* [1984] IRLR 299.
19 See *Briggs v North Eastern Education and Library Board* [1990] IRLR 181.
20 [1992] IRLR 478.
21 *Price v Civil Service Commission* [1978] IRLR 3. Compare *Kidd v DRG ·Ltd* [1985] IRLR 190 and see EOC Code, paragraphs 13(c) and 43.
22 [1982] IRLR 482.
23 [1993] IRLR 218.
24 [1990] IRLR 372. See also *McCausland v Dungannon DC* [1993] IRLR 583.
25 See *Hampson v DES* [1989] IRLR 69.
26 *Jones v University of Manchester* [1993] IRLR 218.
27 Section 12 Employment Act 1989.
28 See *Rinner-Kuhn v FWW Spezial Gebaudereinigung* [1989] IRLR 494.

29   *R v Secretary of State ex parte EOC* [1993] IRLR 10. See page 50
     for the House of Lords' decision in this case.
30   Section 40 SDA 1975 and section 31 RRA 1976 deal with induce-
     ment or attempted inducement to perform an unlawful act.
31   Section 6(1) SDA 1975 and section 4(1) RRA 1976. See *Brennan
     v Dewhurst Ltd* [1983] IRLR 357.
32   See section 82(1) SDA 1975, section 78(1) RRA 1976. On employ-
     ment outside Great Britain see section 10 SDA 1975, section 8
     RRA 1976, *Haughton v Olau Line* [1985] ICR 711 and *Deria v
     General Council of British Shipping* [1986] IRLR 108.
33   See *Mirror Group Ltd v Gunning* [1986] IRLR 27.
34   Section 37 SDA 1975 and section 28 RRA 1976.
35   On language qualifications see *Raval v DHSS* [1985] IRLR 370;
     on language training see CRE Code 1.26–7.
36   Section 38 SDA 1975 and section 29 RRA 1976.
37   Section 82(1) SDA 1975, section 78(1) RRA 1976.
38   See EOC Code, paragraph 23, CRE Code 1.13–14 and IPM
     Recruitment Code.
39   See EOC Code, paragraph 19; CRE Code 1.6, 1.10.
40   Section 7 SDA 1975 (as amended).
41   [1983] IRLR 404.
42   See *Sisley v Britannia Security* (note 41).
43   See *Lambeth LBC v CRE* (note 2).
44   See *Tottenham Green Under-fives v Marshall* (No 2) [1991] IRLR
     161.
45   See *Etam PLC v Rowan* [1989] IRLR 150.
46   [1981] IRLR 530.
47   Section 9 SDA 1975 and section 7 RRA 1976 outlaw discrimi-
     nation against contract workers.
48   Section 6(2) SDA 1975, section 4(2) RRA 1976. See also EOC
     Code paragraphs 25, 28, 32 and CRE Code paragraphs 1.16–17,
     1.20–1.
49   Section 4(2)a RRA 1976. In relation to sex the EPA 1970 deals
     with discrimination in contractual matters.
49A Protection is limited to events occuring during the subsistence
     of the employment relationship. See *Nagarajan v Agnew* [1994]
     IRLR 61.
50   Section 47 SDA 1975 and section 37 RRA 1976. On positive action
     see EOC Code, paragraph 42, CRE Code paragraphs 1.44–5.
51   See *Eke v Commissioners of Customs and Excise* [1981] IRLR
     384, EOC Code paragraph 31 and CRE Code paragraph 1.22.
52   [1990] IRLR 240.
53   *Peake v Automotive Products Ltd* [1977] IRLR 365.
54   See *Burrett v West Birmingham Health Authority* [1994] IRLR 7
     and CRE Code paragraph 1.24.
55   See *Barclays Bank PLC v Kapur* [1991] IRLR 136.
56   [1993] IRLR 27.
57   See *Brook v London Borough of Haringey* [1992] IRLR 478.

58   See note 22.
59   See *Bullock v Alice Ottley School* [1992] IRLR 564.
60   [1986] IRLR 140.
61   Section 6 SDA 1986 (as amended).
62   [1990] IRLR 447.
63   *Nimz v Freie and Hansestadt Hamburg* [1991] IRLR 222.
64   Section 51(1)(2) SDA 1975 (as amended). Compare section 41
      RRA 1976, and see *Hampson v DES* [1990] 3 WLR 42.
65   See also section 4 and schedule 1 EA 1989.
66   See sections 11, 12 EA 1989.
67   Sections 30–40, 42 SDA 1975 and sections 30–1, 33 RRA 1976.
      See *CRE v Imperial Society of Teachers of Dancing* [1983] IRLR
      315.
68   Section 41 SDA 1975 and section 32 RRA 1976. See *Balgobin v
      LB of Tower Hamlets* [1987] IRLR 401.
69   See EOC Code, paragraphs 33–40, CRE Code paragraphs 1.33–43.
70   See *Calder v Finlay Ltd* [1989] IRLR 55.
71   *Littlewoods PLC v Traynor* [1993] IRLR 54.
72   *Barclays Bank PLC v Kapur* [1991] IRLR 136.
73   [1992] IRLR 416.
74   See *Adekeye v Post Office* [1993] IRLR 324.
75   See *Clarke v Hampshire Electro-Plating Ltd* [1991] IRLR 491.
76   Section 76 SDA 1975 and section 68 RRA 1976. See *Berry v
      Ravensbourne NHS Trust* [1993] ICR 871.
77   See *Foster v South Glamorgan HA* [1988] IRLR 277.
78   Section 72(4) SDA 1975 and section 63(4) RRA 1976.
79   See *Brindley v Tayside Health Board* [1976] IRLR 364 (IT).
80   Section 74 SDA 1975 and section 65 RRA 1976.
81   See *Virdee v ECC Quarries* [1978] IRLR 295.
82   See *Nasse v Science Research Council* [1979] IRLR 465.
83   See *British Library v Palyza* [1984] IRLR 307.
84   See *Carrington v Helix Ltd* [1990] IRLR 6.
85   Section 75 SDA 1975 and section 66 RRA 1976.
86   Sections 57–8 SDA 1975 and sections 48–9 RRA 1976.
87   See *Re Prestige PLC* [1984] IRLR 166.
88   Sections 59–60, 67 SDA 1975 and sections 50–1, 58 RRA 1976.
      See *R v CRE ex parte Westminster CC* [1985] IRLR 426.
89   [1991] IRLR 513.
90   See *Eke*'s case (note 51) and *Chattopadhyay v Headmaster of
      Holloway School* [1981] IRLR 487.
91   On conciliation see *Livingstone v Hepworth Refractories* [1992]
      IRLR 63 and page 209.
92   Section 65 SDA 1975 and section 56 RRA 1976.
93   [1993] IRLR 445.
94   See Sex Discrimination and Equal Pay (Remedies) Regulations
      1993 SI 2798, which give tribunals discretion to include interest
      on sums awarded. The upper limit in race cases is likely to be
      removed in 1994.

95   Section 66(3) SDA 1975 and section 57(3) RRA 1976.
96   See *Murray v Powertech Ltd* [1992] IRLR 257.
97   See *Deane v London Borough of Ealing* [1993] IRLR 209.
98   See *Noone v North West Thames RHA* [1988] IRLR 530.
99   Section 4 SDA 1975, section 2 RRA 1976 and schedule 5 paragraph 14(1) SSA 1989.
100   See *Aziz v Trinity Taxis* [1988] IRLR 206.
101   Section 1(2) (as amended). On work of greater value see *Murphy v Bord Telecom Eireann* [1988] IRLR 267.
102   See section 1(6).
103   *British Coal v Smith* [1993] IRLR 308. See also *Leverton v Clwyd CC* [1989] IRLR 28.
104   [1988] IRLR 257.
105   See *Ten Oever v Stichting Berits Pensioen Funds* [1993] IRLR 601. On inequality in bridging pensions see *Bird's Eye Ltd v Roberts* [1994] IRLR 29. On discrimination in actuarial factors see *Neath v Hugh Steeper Ltd* [1994] IRLR 91.
106   See *Botel's* Case [1992] IRLR 423.
107   Section 1(4) EPA 1970.
108   See *Capper Pass Ltd v Lawton* [1976] IRLR 366.
109   See *Eaton v Nuttall* [1977] IRLR 71.
110   [1976] IRLR 368.
111   See *Thomas v NCB* [1987] IRLR 451. See also *Calder v Rowntree Mackintosh* [1993] IRLR 212.
112   See *Maidment v Cooper & Co* [1978] IRLR 462.
113   See *British Leyland v Powell* [1978] IRLR 57.
114   [1992] IRLR 261.
115   See *Bromley v Quick Ltd* [1988] IRLR 249.
116   See *Rummler v Dato-Druck GmbH* [1987] IRLR 32. On job evaluation generally see the ACAS Advisory Booklet entitled *Job Evaluation: an Introduction* and EOC Document *Job Schemes Free of Sex Bias*.
117   See *O'Brien v Sim-Chem Ltd* [1980] IRLR 373.
118   See *Pickstone v Freemans PLC* [1988] IRLR 357.
119   Section 2A(1–2) EPA 1970.
120   See *Financial Times v Byrne* (No 2) [1992] IRLR 163.
121   *Enderby v Frenchay Health Authority* [1993] IRLR 591.
122   See *Rainey v Greater Glasgow HB* [1987] IRLR 26.
123   *Rainey v Greater Glasgow HB* (see note 122).
124   See *NAAFI v Varley* [1976] IRLR 408.
125   See *Avon and Somerset Police Authority v Emery* [1981] ICR 229.
126   *Beneviste v University of Southampton* [1989] IRLR 122.
127   See *McPherson v Rathgael Centre* [1991] IRLR 206.
128   [1981] IRLR 388.
129   [1989] IRLR 532.
130   See *Nimz v Freie und Hansestadt Hamburg* [1991] IRLR 222.
131   See *Snoxell v Vauxhall Motors* [1977] IRLR 123.
132   See *Methuen v Cow Industrial Polymers* [1980] IRLR 289.

133 See *Rankin v British Coal* [1993] IRLR 69.
134 Section 2(4) EPA 1970. No time constraint is imposed by Article 119. On the power to award interest on arrears of remuneration see Sex Discrimination and Equal Pay (Remedies) Regulations 1993.
135 See *Clwyd CC v Leverton* [1985] IRLR 197.
136 See *McCarthy's Ltd v Smith* [1980] IRLR 210.
137 Rule 13 Schedule 2 Industrial Tribunal (Constitution and Rules of Procedure) Regulations 1993 SI No 2687.
138 Section 2A (1)(4) EPA 1970. See *Dennehy v Sealink Ltd* [1987] IRLR 120.
139 See *Sheffield MDC v Siberry* [1989] ICR 208.
140 *Dibro Ltd v Hore* [1990] IRLR 129.
141 Rule 9 Schedule 2 Industrial Tribunal Regulations 1993 (see note 137).
142 Rule 8A Schedule 2 Industrial Tribunal Regulations 1993 (see note 137).
143 See note 142 and *Tennant's Textiles v Todd* [1989] IRLR 3.
144 See note 142.
145 See *Aldridge v British Telecom* [1990] IRLR 10.
146 See *Lloyds Bank v Fox* [1989] IRLR 103.
147 See note 142.
148 See *Dibro Ltd v Hore* (note 139).

6 Maternity rights

Time off for antenatal care

Irrespective of the length of service or the number of hours she works a pregnant woman who, on the advice of a registered medical practitioner, midwife or health visitor, has made an appointment to receive antenatal care, has the right not to be unreasonably refused time off during working hours to enable her to keep the appointment. Apart from the first appointment, the woman may be required to produce a medical certificate and some documentary evidence of the appointment for the employer's inspection. A woman who is permitted such time off is entitled to be paid for her absence at the appropriate hourly rate.[1]

If time off is refused or the employer has failed to pay the whole or part of any amount to which she feels she is entitled a woman can complain to an industrial tribunal. Unless the 'time limit escape clause' applies her claim must be presented within three months of the date of the appointment concerned.[2] Where a tribunal finds that the complaint is well founded it must make a declaration to that effect, and if time off has been unreasonably refused, the employer will be ordered to pay a sum equal to what she would have been entitled to had the time off not been refused. If the complaint is that the employer failed to pay the amount to which she was entitled, the employer must pay the amount which the tribunal finds due to her. However, any contractual remuneration paid to a woman in respect of a period of time off under this section goes towards discharging any statutory liability to pay that arises, and conversely, any payment made as a result of this section goes towards discharging any contractual liability to pay for the period of time off.[3]

Suspension from work on maternity grounds

It is anticipated that from October 1994 sections 45–7 EPCA 1978 (as amended) will give rights to female employees who are suspended from work on maternity grounds under a relevant provision[4] of any enactment or statutory instrument, or a code of practice issued or approved under HASAWA 1974. A woman is to be treated as suspended on maternity grounds if the reason for the suspension is that she is pregnant, has recently given birth or is breastfeeding.

If an employer has suitable alternative work available for a woman who would otherwise be suspended on maternity grounds, the employee must be offered that work before any suspension occurs. Alternative work will be suitable if it is both suitable in relation to the employee and appropriate for her to do in the circumstances. The terms and conditions applicable must not be substantially less favourable than those which apply to her normal work. An industrial tribunal may award compensation to a woman if her employer fails to offer suitable alternative employment.[5]

A woman who is suspended on maternity grounds is entitled to be paid by her employer during the suspension. However, this right is lost if she unreasonably refuses an offer of suitable alternative work. The remuneration payable is a week's wage for each week of suspension and *pro rata* for any part of a week of entitlement. Any contractual remuneration paid goes towards discharging the employer's liability. Conversely, any suspension payment goes towards discharging any contractual obligation the employer may have. Where an employer fails to pay all or any of the amount due, an industrial tribunal will order the employer to pay the remuneration owed.[6]

Dismissal on the grounds of pregnancy or maternity

Where a woman is qualified to bring a claim of unfair dismissal[7] it is unfair to dismiss her because she is pregnant or because of any other reason connected with her pregnancy unless the employer can prove that at the effective date of termination (*see* chapter 11) she was, as a result of her pregnancy, incapable of adequately doing the work she was employed to do or that she could not continue to do her work without contravention (either by her or the employer) of a duty or restriction imposed by statute.[8] In *Brown v Stockton-on-Tees BC*[9] the House of Lords concluded that a woman who was selected for redundancy because she would require maternity leave was unfairly dismissed in that her dismissal was for a reason connected with her pregnancy. Similarly, it will be unfair to dismiss on the grounds that the employer can only find a permanent rather than a temporary replacement for a woman who is taking maternity leave.[10] Clearly a miscarriage is connected with pregnancy, but if the employer does not know of the pregnancy it is impossible to hold that it was the reason for dismissal.[11]

Even if employers can rely on either of the defences outlined above, they are still obliged to offer the woman any suitable available vacancy that exists before or on the date her original contract terminates. The burden of proof is on the employer to show that an offer to re-engage was made in accordance with this section or that there was no suitable available vacancy.[12] Any new contract must fulfil the following three requirements:

(i) it must take effect immediately on the ending of the previous contract
(ii) the work must be suitable and appropriate for her to do in the circumstances
(iii) the terms and conditions must not be substantially less favourable than the corresponding provisions in the previous contract.

It would seem, therefore, that an employer is not bound to modify or alter a pregnant woman's existing job, nor to create another job for her.

Whether or not a suitable vacancy existed, a tribunal must still be satisfied that the employer behaved reasonably in dismissing.[13] Thus if a woman cannot be retrained in her original job and there is no suitable available vacancy, an employer would be advised to ascertain whether another employee would be prepared to exchange duties on a temporary basis.

It is anticipated that from October 1994 it will be automatically unfair to dismiss a woman, irrespective of her hours of work or length of service, if:

(i)   the reason or principal reason for dismissal is that she is pregnant or is any other reason connected with her pregnancy

(ii)   she is dismissed during her maternity leave period (MLP) and the reason or principal reason for dismissal is that she has given birth or any other reason connected with her having given birth

(iii)   she is dismissed for a reason mentioned in (ii) above within four weeks of her MLP ending, if during her MLP she submitted a medical certificate stating that she would be incapable of work after the end of that period by reason of disease or bodily or mental disablement, and, at the time of dismissal, that incapability continued and the certificate remained current

(iv)   she is dismissed after the end of her MLP and the reason or principal reason for dismissal is that she took, or availed herself of the benefits of, maternity leave

(v)   the reason or principal reason for dismissal is a requirement or recommendation referred to in section 45(1) (suspension on maternity grounds)

(vi)   she is dismissed during the MLP and the principal reason for dismissal is that she is redundant and the employer has not offered her any suitable alternative vacancy

(vii)   redundancy is the reason or principal reason for dismissal but the employee is selected for dismissal while other employees in similar positions are not, and the reason for selection is one of those set out in (i)-(v) above.[14]

Where an employee is dismissed while she is pregnant or during her MLP, she is entitled to written reasons for her dismissal. This right does not depend on any qualifying period of service and the woman does not need to request the reasons (*see* pages 162–3).[15]

The right to maternity leave

Section 45 EPCA 1978 gives a woman who has been absent from work wholly or partly because of pregnancy the right to return to work with her original employer (or, where appropriate, a successor) at any time before the end of 29 weeks, beginning with the week in which the confinement occurs. A woman is entitled to return to the job in which she was employed under the original contract of employment and on terms and conditions not less favourable than those which would have applied had she not been absent. 'Job' is defined as 'the nature of the work she is employed to do in accordance with her contract and the capacity and the place in which she is so employed'.[16] It follows that, unless contractual provision is made, women do not have the right to return to precisely the same post, doing exactly the same work, in the same department or for the same boss.

The phrase 'terms and conditions not less favourable' means that as regards seniority, pension rights and other similar rights the period of employment prior to a woman's absence is deemed to be continuous with her employment following that absence. On the other hand, if a woman returns to work in accordance with these provisions, the period of maternity leave counts for statutory purposes.[17] As regards employment-related benefit schemes,[18] the Social Security Act 1989 protects women against unfair maternity provisions. Thus during any period of maternity absence when an employee is in receipt of statutory or contractual maternity pay, a woman must be treated as if she was working normally (and receiving the remuneration she was likely to be paid for doing so) in determining her continuity of membership, accrual of rights and benefits payable to or in respect of her. At the same time a woman can only be required to pay contributions on the amount of statutory or contractual maternity pay actually paid to her in respect of that period.[19]

To exercise the right to return to work it is necessary for the woman to remain in employment (whether or not she is at work) until immediately before the eleventh week prior to the expected week of confinement and at this point to have two years' continuous service. If so requested the woman has to produce a certificate from a registered medical practitioner or certified midwife which states the expected week of confinement.[20] She must also inform her employer in writing of three things at least 21 days before her absence begins:[21]

(i) that she will be absent from work wholly or partly because of pregnancy
(ii) that she intends to return to work with the employer

(ii)   the expected week of confinement or the date of
       confinement if it has occurred.

The fact that a woman has not made up her mind as to whether
she wants to return to work is not something which makes it not
reasonably practicable to serve the notice.[22] However, if a woman
has been dismissed on the grounds stated in section 60(1)(a) or
(b) EPCA 1978, but would otherwise have been qualified to claim,
she will still be entitled to return if she notifies her employer in
writing before, or as soon as reasonably practicable after the
dismissal takes effect, that she intends to return to work.

Forty-nine days after the expected week of confinement (or the
date of confinement) an employer may despatch a written request
asking the woman for written confirmation that she intends to
return to work, and unless this confirmation is given within 14
days[23] of receiving the request the woman will lose her entitlement
to return. The request must be accompanied by a written statement
which explains the consequences of failing to confirm her intention
to return. Nevertheless, at the end of the day the employer has
no statutory redress against a woman who has indicated that she
intends to return to work yet does not do so.

Before returning, a woman must give three weeks' written
notice and the day on which she proposes to return is known as
the 'notified date'. The employer can postpone the return for up
to four weeks if reasons are given and the woman can postpone
her return for a maximum of four weeks if she supplies a medical
certificate which states that she is incapable of work on the day
she was due to resume work, or, where no day of return had been
notified, at the end of the 29 week period. However, the woman's
right of postponement can be exercised only once.[24] Where it is
unreasonable to expect a woman to return on the notified date
because there is an interruption of work (whether owing to industrial action or some other reason) she may instead return when
normal working resumes. The same applies if there is an interruption of work but no day of return has been notified. In these
circumstances a woman may be away from work for a period in
excess of 33 weeks beginning with the actual week of confinement.[25]

According to section 56 EPCA 1978, where a woman is entitled
to return to work but she is not permitted to do so, then she is to

be treated as if she had been continuously employed until the notified day of return and as if she had been dismissed on that day for the reason she was not allowed to return. A failure to give the requisite notice of return will preclude the employee from claiming unfair dismissal.[26] Nevertheless, where a woman does not exercise her statutory rights the failure to allow her to return will amount to a dismissal if it can be shown that her contract was not terminated when her absence began but had subsisted throughout.[27]

In assessing the fairness or otherwise of the dismissal the reason for dismissal must be considered in isolation from the fact of her absence.[28] However, this provision does not apply if the employer can show that either of the following sets of circumstances existed. First, that immediately before her absence began, her employer together with any associated employer[29] employed less than six persons and it was not reasonably practicable for the employer to permit the woman to return to work in accordance with section 45(1) EPCA 1978 or for the employer (or an associated employer) to offer alternative employment satisfying the following conditions. These are that the work to be done is both suitable and appropriate for her to do in the circumstances and that the provisions of the contract as to the capacity and place in which she is to be employed and as to the other terms and conditions of employment are not substantially less favourable to her than if she had returned to work in accordance with section 45(1) EPCA 1978.[30] Secondly, section 56 EPCA 1978 does not apply if, irrespective of the size of the organization, it was not reasonably practicable to permit the woman to return to work in accordance with section 45(1) EPCA 1978, and the employer (or any associated employer) offered employment under a contract satisfying the conditions specified above in relation to alternative employment, and this offer was accepted or unreasonably refused.

If it is not practicable to permit a woman to return to work because of redundancy, she is entitled, where there is a suitable available vacancy, to be offered alternative employment under a new contract of employment. In *Community Task Force v Rimmer*[31] the EAT held that a vacancy may be 'available' for these purposes even though it is impossible for economic reasons to offer it. The work done under the new contract must be both suitable and appropriate for her to do in the circumstances and the contractual provisions as to the capacity and place in which she is to be employed and as to the other terms and conditions must be not substantially less favourable than if she had returned to work in accordance with section 45(1) EPCA 1978. If no offer of alternative employment is forthcoming, then the dismissal (which by virtue of section 56 EPCA 1978 is treated as taking place) will be unfair.[32]

Where the employer has engaged a replacement for the absent woman, provided that person has been informed in writing that his or her employment will be terminated on the woman's return to work, the dismissal of the replacement will be regarded as having been for a substantial reason (*see* chapter 12). This does not mean that such a dismissal will always be fair since a tribunal will have to be satisfied that it was reasonable to dismiss in the circumstances. Thus it might be unfair to dismiss if the employer had a vacancy which the replacement could have filled. This possibility is somewhat remote now that the qualifying period for claiming unfair dismissal has been raised to two years.

It is anticipated that as from October 1994 section 23 of TURERA 1993 will be in effect. This grants a general right of maternity leave to all female employees irrespective of their length of service or working hours. Under the new scheme the MLP begins on the date the woman notifies to her employer as the date on which she intends her MLP to begin. This cannot be before the beginning of the eleventh week before the expected week of childbirth. However, if a woman is absent from work wholly or partly because of the pregnancy or childbirth on an earlier date (which falls after the beginning of the sixth week before the expected week of childbirth) the MLP starts on the first date of that absence. If the employee gives birth before her MLP would have begun, the MLP commences at the date of birth.[33] The MLP lasts for 14 weeks or until the birth of the child, if later. However, there are two exceptions to this. First, if the woman is prohibited by law from working for a period after the birth, the MLP must last at least until the end of that period (see page 83 on suspension on maternity grounds). Second, if the woman is dismissed during the MLP, the MLP terminates at the time of dismissal.[34] While she is absent from work during her MLP a woman has the terms and conditions of employment (except for remuneration) to which she would have been entitled if she had not been absent and had not been pregnant or given birth.[35]

In order to get the benefit of these maternity leave rights a woman must fulfil the following notification requirements:

(i)　at least 21 days before her MLP begins (or as soon as reasonably practicable afterwards) she must give her employer a written notice stating that she is pregnant. She must also indicate the expected week of childbirth or, if the baby has been born, the birth date[36]

(ii)　if the employer requests one, the woman must supply a certificate from a registered medical practitioner or midwife which states the expected week of childbirth[37]

(iii)　she must give her employer at least 21 days' notice (or as soon as reasonably practicable afterwards) of the date on which she intends the MLP to commence. Where an employee's MLP has been triggered by a pregnancy-related absence (*see* page 89) before the notified leave date or before such a date has been notified, the woman must notify the employer as soon as is reasonably practicable that she is absent for that reason. Similarly, where the employee gives birth before the notified leave date or before notice of that date has been given, she must inform the employer of the birth as soon as is reasonably practicable. These notices must be in writing if her employer so requests.[38]

Where a woman wishes to return to work before the end of her MLP, she must give the employer at least seven days' notice of her intended date of return. If she returns before the end of the MLP without giving such notice the employer can postpone her return to a date that will provide seven days' notice of her return. However, the employer cannot delay the employee's return to a date after the end of the MLP.[39] If during a woman's MLP it is not practicable by reason of redundancy for her to continue to be employed under her existing contract of employment, she is entitled to be offered any alternative work which is suitable and appropriate for her to do in the circumstances. The offer must be made before the end of the original contract and the alternative employment may be with her employer, a successor or an associated employer. The new contract must take effect immediately and be in terms and conditions which are not substantially less favourable than those in the original contract.[40]

Sections 39–44 EPCA 1978 (as amended by TURERA 1993) preserve the existing right of women who meet the current requirements to return to work at any time up to 29 weeks after the beginning of the week in which they gave birth (*see* page 85). However, the notification rules are amended to reflect the changes made by TURERA 1993. Thus, to qualify for the right to return, a woman must give the employer written notice of her pregnancy and must state that she intends to return to work. The employer may request, in writing, that the woman confirms that she will return to work and the request must include a warning about the consequences of failing to reply. Such a request cannot be made earlier than 21 days before the end of the MLP and the woman's response must be given within 14 days of receiving the request (or as soon as reasonably practicable afterwards).[41]

Statutory maternity pay

An employee who gives her employer at least 21 days' notice[42] that she is going to be absent from work wholly or partly because of pregnancy or confinement may be entitled to statutory maternity pay (SMP).[43] This notice must be in writing if so requested. To qualify for SMP a woman must also:

(i)   have at least 26 weeks' continuous employment with the same employer ending with 'the week immediately preceding the 14th week before the expected week of confinement' (EWC). Thus the 15th week before the EWC is known as the qualifying week for these purposes. A woman who has worked for less than 26 weeks for her employer may be able to claim state maternity allowance if she satisfies the contribution requirements
(ii)   for the eight weeks immediately preceding the qualifying week have had normal (*i.e.* gross average) weekly earnings at or above the lower earnings limit for national insurance contributions (£56 at the time of writing)[44]
(iii) have reached the eleventh week before the EWC or have been confined.[45]

SMP is available for a maximum of 18 weeks. It is not normally payable for a week in which the woman works and the maternity pay period (MPP) is not extended to take account of such weeks.[46] Payment may begin 11 weeks before the EWC but cannot commence later than six weeks before the EWC. This creates a core period of 13 weeks' absence at this date. SMP is only payable for complete weeks and women who have two years' continuous service at the qualifying week are entitled to receive 9/10th of their normal weekly earnings for the first six weeks. Those who have between six months' and two years' service are eligible only for the lower (flat) rate (£47.95 in 1993).[47] SMP should be paid on the normal pay day and the 'set off' formula applies.[48] Employers will be reimbursed for the payments they make through deductions from their national insurance remittances. In addition, compensation is available for the national insurance contributions that employers must pay on SMP.[49]

In respect of a period before the request is made a woman can ask her employer for a written statement of one or more of the following:

(i) the weeks in which the employer regards himself or herself as liable to pay SMP
(ii) the reasons why she or he does not so regard other weeks in that period
(iii) the amount of weekly SMP to which the woman is entitled.

To the extent that this request is reasonable an employer or former employer must comply with it in a reasonable time.[50] Currently, records must be kept for at least three years after the relevant tax year.[51]

Where there is a dispute an employee or Department of Social Security officer can refer the matter to an Adjudication Officer and appeals are processed through Social Security Appeal Tribunals and Social Security Commissioners.[52] Some decisions (for example, on employment status or length of continuous service) are reserved for the Secretary of State and the parties may be required to provide the information which is required for such a determination.[53] Ultimately, if an employer refuses to pay or is insolvent the employee can recover from the Secretary of State.[54]

The issue of pay during the MLP (which comes into force after October 1994) has not been resolved at the time of writing. The

'Pregnant Workers' Directive 92/85 provides for the 'maintenance of a payment to, and/or entitlement to an adequate allowance for' women on maternity leave. Although the Directive permits member states to impose eligibility conditions on the right to maternity pay, these cannot include a service requirement of more than 52 weeks' employment immediately prior to the expected date of confinement.

Notes

1 See section 31A(5) EPCA 1978.
2 Section 31A(7) EPCA 1978 and chapter 3 note 14.
3 Section 31A(10) EPCA 1978. This is known as a 'set-off formula' and throughout the rest of the book similar statutory provisions will be referred to in this way.
4 A 'relevant provision' is one that is specified as such by the Secretary of State: section 45(3) EPCA 1978.
5 Section 46 EPCA 1978.
6 Section 47 EPCA 1978.
7 *See* page 64 on the possibility of claiming sex discrimination.
8 Section 60(1) EPCA 1978. See *Grimsby Carpet Company v Bedford* [1987] IRLR 438.
9 [1988] IRLR 263.
10 See *Clayton v Vigers* [1990] IRLR 177.
11 See *Del Monte v Mundon* [1980] IRLR 224.
12 Section 60(4) EPCA 1978.
13 See section 57(3) EPCA 1978 and chapter 12.
14 Sections 59 and 60 EPCA 1978.
15 Section 53(2A) EPCA 1978.
16 Section 153(1) EPCA 1978.
17 Schedule 13 paragraph 10 EPCA 1978.
18 Defined in SSA 1989 schedule 5 paragraph 7(a).
19 SSA 1989 schedule 5 paragraph 5.
20 Section 53(5) EPCA 1978.
21 'or, if that is not reasonably practicable, as soon as is reasonably practicable': Section 33(3)C EPCA 1978. In future such phraseology will be referred to as the 'reasonably practicable' safeguard.
22 See *Mallinson v Nu-Swift International Ltd* [1988] IRLR 537.
23 The 'reasonably practicable' safeguard applies here (see note 21).
24 Section 47(4) EPCA 1978. See *Kelly v Liverpool Maritime Ltd* [1988] IRLR 310.
25 Section 47(5)(6) 1978.
26 See *Institute of Motor Industry v Harvey* [1992] IRLR 343.
27 See *Lucas v Norton Ltd* [1984] IRLR 86.

28 See schedule 2 paragraph 2(1) EPCA 1978.
29 See chapter 15 on the definition of an 'associated employer'.
30 Section 56A(3) EPCA 1978.
31 [1986] IRLR 203.
32 Schedule 2 paragraph 2(2) EPCA 1978.
33 Section 34 EPCA 1978 (as amended by TURERA 1993).
34 Section 35 EPCA 1978 (as amended).
35 Section 33(1) EPCA 1978 (as amended).
36 Section 37(1) EPCA 1978 (as amended).
37 Section 37(2) EPCA 1978 (as amended).
38 Section 36 EPCA 1978 (as amended).
39 Section 37A EPCA 1978 (as amended).
40 Section 38 EPCA 1978 (as amended).
41 Section 40 EPCA 1978 (as amended).
42 Unless it is not reasonably practicable, in which case the notice must be given as soon as is reasonably practicable: section 164(4) SSCBA 1992.
43 On evidence of pregnancy and the expected week of confinement see SMP (Medical Evidence) Regulations 1987 SI 235.
44 Section 164(2) SSCBA 1992.
45 Regulation 3 of the SMP (General) Regulations 1986. SI No. 1960 deals with dismissals 'solely or mainly for the purpose of avoiding liability for SMP'.
46 Section 165 and regulation 2 of the SMP (General) Regulations (as amended).
47 Section 166 SSCBA 1992.
48 See note 3 above and schedule 13 SSCBA 1992.
49 Section 167 SSCBA 1992 and SMP (Compensation of Employers) Regulations 1987 SI 91 (as amended).
50 Section 15(2) Social Security Administration Act 1992.
51 Regulation 26 SMP (General) Regulations (as amended). On penalties for non-compliance see regulation 32.
52 Section 20 Social Security Administration Act 1992.
53 Regulation 25 SMP (General) Regulations (as amended).
54 Regulation 7 SMP (General) Regulations (as amended).

7 Health and safety at work

We have previously looked at the common law obligations of employer and employee in relation to health and safety and in this chapter we will examine their rights and duties under the Health and Safety at Work etc. Act (HASAWA) 1974 and other legislation. Although much of the previous legislation remains in existence, for example the Factories Act 1961 and the Offices, Shops and Railway Premises Act 1963, it is intended that the older statutes will be replaced by new regulations and approved codes of practice which will be designed to maintain or improve standards of health, safety and welfare.[1]

A fundamental feature of HASAWA 1974 and the Management of Health and Safety at Work Regulations 1992 (MHSW 1992)[2] is that they apply to people rather than premises and, with certain exceptions, all employed persons are covered. They also seek to protect persons other than those at work against risks to their health and safety arising out of or in connection with, work activities. While a breach of HASAWA 1974 or regulations issued under it amounts to a criminal offence, civil liability only arises if there is failure to comply with regulations.[3] However, according to section 11 of the Civil Evidence Act 1968, a conviction for a criminal offence is admissible in civil proceedings as evidence that the person so convicted committed the offence. Thus, a conviction may become relevant to the issue of civil liability. A failure to observe any provision of an approved code of practice does not of itself render a person liable to any civil or criminal proceedings, but such a code is admissible in evidence and proof of a failure to meet its requirements will be sufficient to establish a contravention of a statutory provision unless a court is satisfied that the provision was complied with in some other way.[4]

The employer's general duties towards employees

The fundamental feature of MHSW Regulations is the duty imposed on all employers and the self-employed to conduct a risk assessment. This assessment must be both suitable and sufficient and must consider the risk to the health and safety of all employees and other persons arising from the conduct of the undertaking. The purpose of the assessment is to identify the measures which need to be taken to ensure compliance with the relevant statutory provisions. These provisions are specified in the approved Code of Practice (ACOP) and include the general duties under HASAWA 1974 (*see* below). The risk assessment must be reviewed if there is reason to suspect that it is no longer valid or there has been a significant change in the matters to which it relates. Where the employer has five or more employees the significant findings of the assessment must be recorded.[5]

Regulation 4 requires employers to give effect to appropriate arrangements for the effective planning, organization, control, monitoring and review of the measures they need to take as a result of the risk assessment. Again, such arrangements must be recorded if the employer has five or more employees. Regulation 5 obliges employers to provide appropriate health surveillance for their employees.

Under Regulation 6 employers must appoint one or more 'competent persons' to assist them in implementing the measures they need to comply with the relevant statutory provisions. The number of people appointed, the time available for them to fulfil their functions and the means at their disposal must be adequate having regard to the size of the undertaking and the risks to which employees are exposed. A 'competent person' is defined as someone who has sufficient training and experience or knowledge to enable him or her to assist properly in the undertaking.[6]

Regulation 7 obliges employers to establish appropriate procedures to be followed in the event of 'serious and imminent danger to persons at work in his undertaking'. Employers must nominate a sufficient number of competent persons to implement these procedures and to ensure that employees are unable to enter dangerous areas without having received adequate health and safety instruction. It is made clear that this Regulation requires both the provision of information and procedures which enable employees to leave their work immediately in the event of danger.[7]

Turning to HASAWA 1974, according to section 2(1), 'it shall be the duty of every employer to ensure, so far as is reasonably practicable, the health, safety and welfare at work of all his employees'. The matters to which this duty extends include:[8]

(i) the provision and maintenance of plant[9] and systems of work that are, so far as is reasonably practicable, safe and without risks to health[10]

(ii) arrangements for ensuring, so far as is reasonably practicable, safety and absence of risks to health in connection with the use, handling, storage and transport of articles and substances[11]

(iii) the provision of such information, instruction, training and supervision as is necessary to ensure, so far as is reasonably practicable, the health and safety at work of employees

(iv) so far as is reasonably practicable as regards any place of work under the employer's control, the maintenance of it in a condition which is safe and without risks to health and the provision and maintenance of means of access to and egress from it that are safe and without such risks

(v) the provision and maintenance of a working environment for his employees that is, so far as is reasonably practicable, safe, without risks to health, and adequate as regards facilities and arrangements for their welfare at work.[12]

It could be argued that the above duties merely enact the employer's common law obligations. While this is largely true, the extent to which detailed requirements are spelt out is of considerable consequence. The words 'reasonably practicable' do not mean that the employer must do everything that is physically possible to safeguard employees, only that the risks be weighed against the trouble and expense of eliminating or reducing them.[13] Employers are to be judged according to the knowledge they had or ought to have had at the time, and in any legal proceedings the accused has to prove that it was not reasonably practicable to do more than was in fact done.[14] The existence of a universal practice is evidence which goes to the question whether any other method was reasonably practicable but it does not necessarily discharge the onus on the employer.[15]

Some further points might be made in connection with these important subsections. In relation to safe plant, the High Court has ruled that section 2 is breached if an employer makes unsafe plant available even if it has not been used or is not being used. The statutory duty arises when the plant is provided.[16] As regards the duty to provide information, the Health and Safety Information for Employees Regulations[17] obliges employers to display a poster or distribute leaflets informing their employees in general terms about the requirements of health and safety law. This information must be kept up to date and where a poster is displayed it must be in a reasonably accessible place and positioned so that it can be easily read. Regulation 8 of MHSW Regulations 1992 requires employers to provide employees with comprehensible and relevant information on the risks to which they are exposed and the measures which the employer has taken in accordance with the risk assessment that has been conducted (*see* page 96). Information must also be given on the procedures to be taken in cases of serious and imminent danger. Regulation 7 of the Safety Representatives and Safety Committees Regulations 1977 (SRSC Regs) obliges employers to make available to safety representatives information within their knowledge which is necessary to enable representatives to fulfil their functions.[18] In addition, inspectors are obliged, in circumstances in which it is necessary to do so for the purpose of assisting in keeping employees adequately informed about health, safety and welfare matters, to give employees or their representatives factual information relating to an employer's premises and information with respect to any action which they have taken or propose to take in connection with those premises. Such information must be conveyed to the employer and inspectors can also give a written statement of their observations to anyone likely to be a party to any civil proceedings arising out of any accident, etc.[19]

The words 'instruction' and 'training' suggest that employees should be taught to understand the duties imposed by legislation. Indeed, Regulation 11 of MHSW 1992 stipulates that, in entrusting tasks to their employees, employers must taken into account their capabilities in relation to health and safety. In particular, employers have a duty to ensure that their employees are provided with adequate health and safety training when recruited or if they are exposed to new or increased risks. As regards supervision, it would seem to follow that if the employer's efforts do not persuade an employee to adopt safe working practices disciplinary or other action may have to be taken. Finally, although 'welfare at work' is not defined by HASAWA 1974 it is presumed to cover matters which were the subject of earlier legislation, *e.g.* washing and toilet facilities, drinking water, etc.[20]

Except where less than five employees are employed at any one time in an undertaking,[21] every employer must:

> Prepare and as often as may be appropriate revise a written statement of his general policy with respect to the health and safety at work of his employees, and the organization and arrangements for the time being in force for carrying out that policy, and to bring the statement and any revision of it to the notice of all of his employees.[22]

The Act does not give any further indication as to what the statement should contain but advice and guidance notes, which are not legally enforceable, are available from the Health and Safety Executive.[23] Clearly it is intended that employers will seek solutions to their own particular safety problems and it will not be sufficient simply to adopt a model scheme drawn up by some other body. As an absolute minimum the safety policy should deal with the various responsibilities of all employees, from the board of directors down to the shop floor. Indeed, the statement may be used as evidence if a prosecution is launched under section 37 HASAWA 1974 (*see* page 113). It should also deal with general safety precautions, mechanisms for dealing with special hazards, routine inspections, emergency procedures, training and arrangements for consulting the workforce.

In industrial relations terms it is obviously desirable to reach agreement with trade unions on the contents of the written statement but this is not a legal requirement. No guidance is given as to how the statement should be brought to the notice of employees, although ideally a copy should be supplied to each person. Special precautions may need to be taken in relation to those who have language difficulties. Finally, it should be noted that Schedule 7 Part IV of the Companies Act 1985 enables regulations to be made which provide that directors' reports 'contain such information as may be so prescribed about the arrangements in force in that year for securing the health, safety and welfare at work of employees of the company and its subsidiaries and for protecting other persons against risks to health or safety arising out of or in connection with the activities at work of those employees'.

Safety representatives and safety committees

Section 2(4) HASAWA 1974 provides for the appointment by recognized trade unions of safety representatives from among the employees.[24] Where such representatives are appointed, employers have a duty to consult them with a view to the making and maintenance of arrangements which will enable the employer and employees to co-operate effectively in promoting and developing measures to ensure the health and safety at work of the employees, and in checking the effectiveness of such measures.[25] In particular, employers must consult safety representatives in good time with regard to:

(i)   the introduction of any measure which may substantially affect the health and safety of the employees represented
(ii)   the arrangements for appointing or nominating competent persons in accordance with regulations 6(1) and 7(1)b of MHSW 1992
(iii) any health and safety information that the employer must provide to the employees represented
(iv)   the planning and organization of any health and safety training the employer is required to provide for the employees represented
(v)   the health and safety consequences for the employees represented of the planning and introduction of new technologies.[26]

Safety representatives may be elected or appointed where there is no recognized trade union but they will not have the rights afforded by HASAWA 1974 or the SRSC Regulations. These regulations stipulate that if an employer has received written notification from a recognized independent trade union of the names of the people appointed as safety representatives, such persons have the functions set out in Regulation 4 of SRSC Regs (below). So far as is reasonably practicable, safety representatives will either have been employed by their employer throughout the preceding two years or have had at least two years' experience in similar employment.[27] Employees cease to be safety representatives for the purpose of these regulations when:

(i)   the trade union which appointed them notifies the employer in writing that their appointment has been terminated
(ii) they cease to be employed at the workplace[28]
(iii) they resign.

Theoretically there is no limit to the number of safety representatives who can be appointed but guidance notes published with the regulations suggest appropriate criteria for assessment.[29]

Apart from representing employees (not simply trade union members) in consultation with the employer under section 2(6) HASAWA 1974, safety representatives are given the following functions by Regulation 4(1) SRSC Regs:

(i)   to investigate potential hazards and dangerous occurrences at the workplace (whether or not they are drawn to their attention by the employees they represent) and to examine the causes of accidents at the workplace
(ii)   to investigate complaints by any employee they represent relating to that employee's health, safety or welfare at work
(iii) to make representations to the employer on general matters affecting the health, safety or welfare at work of the employees at the workplace
(v)   to carry out inspections in accordance with Regulation 5, 6 and 7 SRSC Regs
(vi)   to represent the employees they are appointed to represent in consultation at the workplace with inspectors from the enforcing authorities
(vii) to receive information from inspectors in accordance with section 28(8) of HASAWA 1974 (*see* page 98)
(viii) to attend meetings of safety committees where they attend in their capacity as safety representatives in connection with any of the above functions.

Two points should be noted. First, none of these functions imposes a duty on safety representatives, although they will be liable for the actions they take as ordinary employees (*see* pages 104–5). Second, employers must provide such facilities and assistance as safety representatives may reasonably require for carrying out these functions and those imposed by the MHSW Regulations 1992.

According to Regulation 4(2) SRSC Regs, a safety representative is entitled to such time off with normal or average pay[30] during working hours as is necessary to perform the functions outlined above and to undergo such training in aspects of those functions as may be reasonable in all the circumstances, having regard to the provisions of the approved Code of Practice.[31] Thus in *White v Pressed Steel Fisher*[32] the EAT held that if employers provide an adequate in-plant course it is not necessarily reasonable for them to be required to grant paid time off for safety representatives to attend a union course. The Code recommends that as soon as possible after their appointment safety representatives should be permitted time off with pay for basic training approved by the TUC or the independent union which appointed the representatives. Further training, similarly approved, should be undertaken where the safety representative has special responsibilities or where such training is necessary to meet changes in circumstances or relevant legislation. Aggrieved safety representatives can complain to an industrial tribunal that their employer has failed to permit them to take time off or that they have not been paid in accordance with the Regulations. If the complaint is well founded, the tribunal must make a declaration and may make an award of compensation.[33]

By virtue of Regulation 5 SRSC Regs, safety representatives are entitled to inspect the workplace at least every three months, but they must give reasonable notice in writing of their intention to do so. Of course inspections may take place more frequently if the employer agrees. Additional inspections may be made if there has been a substantial change in the conditions of work or new information has been published by the HSC or HSE relevant to the hazards of the workplace. Inspections may also be conducted where there has been a notifiable accident or dangerous occurrence or a notifiable disease contracted[34] for the purpose of determining the cause. The employer must provide reasonable facilities and assistance for the purpose of carrying out an inspection, including facilities for independent investigation by the representatives and private discussion with the employees. However, there is nothing to prevent the employers or their representatives from being present during an inspection.

Where at least two safety representatives submit a written request the employers must establish a safety committee, but before doing so they must consult the safety representatives who made the request and the representatives of recognized trade unions. Such a committee must be formed within three months of the request being made, and a notice must be posted stating the composition of the committee and the workplaces covered.[35] Under section 2(7) HASAWA 1974 the function of safety committees is to keep under review the measures taken to ensure the health and safety at work of employees.

It should be noted that the Code of Practice advises employers, recognized unions and safety representatives to make full and proper use of existing industrial relations machinery to reach the degree of agreement necessary to achieve the purpose of the SRSC Regulations and to resolve any differences. However, where an employee suffers a detriment as a result of the health and safety activities listed on page 164, a complaint may be brought under section 57A (if the individual was dismissed) or section 22A EPCA 1978. The remedies available for infringement of section 22A mirror those available for action short of dismissal on trade union grounds (*see* pages 272–3)

Other general duties

Section 3 HASAWA 1974 imposes a duty on employers and self-employed persons to conduct their undertakings in such a way as to ensure, so far as is reasonably practicable, that persons not in their employment who may be affected thereby are not exposed to risks to their health and safety. More specifically, Regulation 10 of the MHSW Regulations 1992 obliges employers and self-employed people to supply any person working in their undertaking who is not their employee with comprehensible information and instruction on any risks which arise out of the conduct of the undertaking. It is clear that the word 'risk' should be given its ordinary meaning of denoting the possibility of danger rather than actual danger.[36] Like section 2, section 3 cannot be regarded as applicable only when an undertaking is in the process of actively being carried on. Thus, when machinery belonging to a cleaning company was left at a store which the company was under a contract to clean, and the company had agreed that employees of the store could use the machine, the company was in breach of section 3 when, because of a fault in a cable, one of the store's employees was electrocuted while using one of the company's machines.[37]

Section 4 HASAWA 1974 provides that a person who has control of non-domestic premises used as a place of work must take such measures as are reasonably practicable to ensure that the means of access and egress and any plant or substance in the premises is safe and without risks to health. According to the House of Lords, once it is proved:

(i)   that premises made available for use by others are unsafe and constitute a risk to health
(ii)   that the employer had a degree of control over those premises, and
(iii) that, having regard to the employer's degree of control and knowledge of the likely use, it would have been reasonable to take measures to ensure that the premises were safe,

the employer must demonstrate that, weighing the risk to health against the means (including cost) of eliminating it, it was not reasonably practicable to take those measures. However, if the premises are not a reasonably foreseeable cause of danger to people using them in circumstances which might reasonably be expected to occur, it is not reasonable to require further measures to be taken.[38]

Section 5 HASAWA 1974 obliges every person having control of prescribed premises[39] to use the best practicable means for preventing the emission into the atmosphere of noxious or offensive substances and for rendering harmless and inoffensive such substances as may be emitted. It should be noted that the duty to use the best practicable means imposes a higher standard than in any of the preceding sections.

Section 7 of HASAWA 1974 imposes two general duties on employees while they are at work:[40]

(i)   to take reasonable care of the health and safety of themselves and of others who may be affected by their acts or omissions
(ii)   as regards any duty imposed on employers or any other

person by any of the relevant statutory provisions, to co-operate with them so far as is necessary to enable that duty to be performed.

Clearly it could be argued that employees who refuse to wear protective clothing or fail to observe safety procedures are in breach of their statutory duty.[41] In addition, the employee may not be entitled to damages for any injury suffered as a result of the failure to use safety equipment. Section 8 HASAWA states that nobody should intentionally or recklessly interfere with or misuse anything provided in the interests of health, safety or welfare in pursuance of any of the relevant statutory provisions.

The following additional obligations are placed on employees by the MHSW Regulations:

(i) to use anything provided by employers under their statutory duties in accordance with any training and instructions received

(ii) to inform employers of any work situation which could reasonably be considered to represent a serious and immediate danger to health or safety, and of any shortcomings in the employer's protection arrangements which have not previously been reported.[42]

Finally, an employer is not allowed to charge an employee in respect of anything done or provided in pursuance of any specific requirement of any relevant statutory provision.[43] Thus if employers are compelled by regulations to supply safety spectacles (for example, under the Protection of Eyes Regulations 1974) they cannot charge for them, but where there is no specific requirement employees may be asked to pay for protective clothing or equipment.

Articles and substances for use at work

Articles

A person who designs, manufactures, imports or supplies any article for use at work[44] or any article of fairground equipment has the duty:

(i)   to ensure, so far as is reasonably practicable, that the article is so designed and constructed that it will be safe and without risks to health at all times when it is being set, used, cleared or maintained by a person at work. According to section 6(10) HASAWA 1974, in determining whether this duty has been performed, regard shall be had to any relevant information or advice which has been provided to any person by the person by whom the article has been designed, manufactured, imported or supplied. However, where a person designs, manufactures, imports or supplies an article for another on the basis of a written undertaking by that other that specified steps will be taken to ensure, so far as is reasonably practicable, that the article will be safe and without risks to health when properly used, the undertaking relieves the designer, etc. from this duty to such extent as is reasonable having regard to the terms of the undertaking

(ii)   to carry out, or arrange for the carrying out of, such testing and examination as may be necessary for performing the above duty. This does not require the repetition of any tests, etc. which have been carried out by others in so far as it is reasonable to rely on their result[45]

(iii)   to take such steps as are necessary to secure that persons supplied with the article are provided with adequate information about the use for which the article has been designed and tested, and about any conditions necessary to ensure that it will be safe and without risks to health at all such times as were mentioned in (i) above and when it is being dismantled or disposed of

(iv)   to take such steps as are necessary to secure, so far as is reasonably practicable, that persons so supplied are provided with all such revisions of information provided to them by virtue of the preceding paragraph as are necessary by reason of its becoming known that anything gives rise to a serious risk to health and safety.

Additionally, manufacturers and designers have the duty to carry out or arrange for the carrying out of any necessary research with a view to the discovery and, so far as is reasonably practicable, the elimination or minimization of any risks to health and safety to which the design or article may give rise.[46] It is also the duty of anyone who erects or installs any article for use at work to ensure, so far as is reasonably practicable, that nothing about the way in which it has been erected or installed makes it unsafe or a risk to health when properly used.[47] Finally, manufacturers, designers, importers and suppliers of plant and equipment likely to cause exposure to noise levels of 85 dB(A) or above must provide purchasers with adequate information on the noise generated by the plant or equipment.[48]

Substances

Manufactures, importers or suppliers of any substance for use at work[49] are obliged

(i)   to ensure, so far as is reasonably practicable, that the substance is safe and without risks to health at all times when it is being used, handled, processed, stored or transported by a person at work or in premises to which section 4 HASAWA 1974 applies

(ii) to carry out or arrange for the carrying out of such testing and examination as may be necessary for the performance of the above duty

(iii) to take such steps as are necessary to secure that persons supplied by that person with the substance are provided with adequate information about any risks to health or safety to which the inherent properties of the substance may give rise, about the results of any relevant tests which have been carried out on or in connection with the substance and about any conditions necessary to ensure that the substance will be safe and without risks to health at all such times as are mentioned in (i) above and when the substance is being disposed of, and

(iv) to take such steps as are necessary to secure, so far as is reasonably practicable, that persons so supplied are provided with all such revisions of information provided to them by virtue of (iii) above as are necessary by reason of its becoming known that anything gives rise to a serious risk to health or safety.[50]

Manufacturers also have to conduct any necessary research with a view to the discovery and, so far as is reasonably practicable, the elimination or minimization of any risks to health and safety to which the substance may give rise.[51] The above duties of designers, manufacturers, importers and suppliers only extend to things done in the course of a trade, business or other undertaking (whether for profit or not) and to matters within that person's control.[52]

The Control of Substances Hazardous to Health (COSHH) Regulations 1988[53] apply to all workplaces where substances hazardous to health are produced, stored, used or manufactured. Employers are obliged to adopt principles of good occupational hygiene in dealing with such substances and to this end there are four Approved Codes of Practice and the HSE has produced a number of guidance notes and advisory leaflets. Failure to adhere to the Regulations is a criminal offence but in any proceedings it is a defence for a person to prove that he or she took 'all reasonable precautions and exercised all due diligence to avoid the commission of that offence'.

The first task is for the employer to determine whether or not a substance is hazardous and then to assess the risk created by the manner in which the substance is used at work. A substance hazardous to health is defined as a substance for which a maximum exposure limit is specified in Schedule 1 of the Regulations or one which has an occupational exposure standard approved by the HSC. Substances covered by the Classification, Packaging and Labelling of Dangerous Substances Regulations 1984 are also included, as are significant amounts of dust, micro-organisms and any other substance which creates a hazard to the health of any person which is comparable with the hazards created by the previously mentioned substances.[54] The Approved Code of Practice states that a substance should be regarded as hazardous to health if it is hazardous in the form in which it occurs at work, whether or not the way it causes injury is known and whether or not the active constituent(s) have been identified. In many cases suppliers' information sheets prepared for users under section 6 HASAWA 1974 will be the most readily available source of information on hazardous substances.

The fundamental requirement of the Regulations is set out in Regulation 6(1):

an employer shall not carry on any work which is liable to

expose any employees to any substance hazardous to health unless he has made a suitable and sufficient assessment of the risks created by that work to the health of those employees and of the steps that need to be taken to meet the requirements of these Regulations.

Employers are required to review and, where necessary, change assessments where there is reason to suspect that they are no longer valid or there has been a significant change in the work to which they relate. Clearly, people appointed to carry out assessments must have the skills and training to do so[55] and, in all but the simplest cases, assessments should be recorded.[56]

Regulation 7 obliges employers to ensure that the exposure of employees to substances hazardous to health is either prevented or, where this is not reasonably practicable, adequately controlled. In determining whether controls are 'adequate' for these purposes only 'the nature of the substance and the nature and degree of exposure to substances hazardous to health' can be considered. It is important to note that, so far as is reasonably practicable, the prevention or control of exposure to such substances has to be secured by measures other than the provision of personal protective equipment.[57]

Control measures provided for the purposes of Regulation 7 must be maintained in good repair and in an efficient state and working order. Where engineering controls are provided the employer must ensure that thorough examinations and tests are carried out at suitable intervals. In addition, employers must keep a suitable record of examinations and tests in relation to engineering controls and respiratory protective equipment and of any consequential repairs. Such records should be kept available for at least five years from the date on which they were made.[58] Employers must also take all reasonable steps to ensure that 'any control measure, personal protective equipment or other thing or facility' provided in pursuance of the Regulations are properly used or applied. For their part, employees are required to make 'full and proper use' of any control measure, etc. and to report any defects.[59]

According to Regulation 10, employers must ensure that employees' exposure to hazardous substances is monitored in accordance with a suitable procedure where this is necessary to maintain adequate control over exposure or protect the health of employees. Paragraph 66 of the Approved Code of Practice defines 'monitoring' as 'the use of valid and suitable occupational hygiene techniques to derive a quantitative estimate of the exposure of employees to substances hazardous to health'. Where monitoring is considered necessary following the Regulation 6 assessment the ACOP suggests that it should be carried out at least once every 12 months. However, in the case of a small number of substances and processes detailed guidance is provided by schedule 4. Suitable records of any monitoring conducted for the purpose of this Regulation must be kept for at least five years, or at least 30 years where they refer to the exposures of identifiable employees, and should be made available to employees or their representatives, inspectors and employment medical advisers.[60]

Where it is appropriate for the protection of employees who are liable to be exposed to a hazardous substance, the employer must provide suitable health surveillance. Surveillance is treated as appropriate where exposure is such that an identifiable disease or adverse health effect may be related to it, there is a reasonable likelihood that the disease or effect may occur and there are valid techniques for detecting indications of the disease or effect. It will also be appropriate if an employee is exposed to one of the substances and is engaged in the process specified in Schedule 5, unless that exposure is not significant. Surveillance records should be kept in a form compatible with records containing exposure data 'so that, where appropriate, the nature and degree of exposure can be compared with the effects on health'. Employees who are subjected to surveillance in accordance with these Regulations must, when required by the employer and at the employer's expense, present themselves during working hours for the necessary surveillance procedures. Health records relating to such employees have to be kept in a suitable form for at least 30 years from the date on which the last entry was made. On giving reasonable notice employees are entitled to access to their own health records and employment medical advisers and appointed doctors are entitled to inspect any workplace or record kept for the purpose of the Regulations.[61]

Finally, employees who may be exposed to hazardous substances must be provided with such information, instruction and training as is 'suitable and sufficient' for them to know the risks to health created by that exposure and the precautions which should be taken. This information includes the results of exposure monitoring conducted under Regulation 10 and the collective results of any surveillance undertaken in accordance with Regulation 11 (in a form which prevents those relating to an individual being identified). The ACOP states that information should also be made available to safety representatives and that instruction should be aimed ensuring that people working on the employer's premises do not put themselves or others in danger through exposure to substances hazardous to health.[62]

The notification of accidents, etc.

The Reporting of Injuries, Diseases and Dangerous Occurrences Regulations 1985[63] impose three basic requirements:

(i)   major accidents (*i.e.* those causing death or defined injuries) and dangerous occurrences[64] must be notified by telephone and written reports on a standard form and must be sent within seven days

(ii) industrially linked diseases must also be reported on the standard form[65]

(iii) minor accidents leading to incapacity for work for more than three consecutive days must be reported on the standard form within seven days.

However, under Regulation 11 employers have a defence if they can prove that they were unaware of the event requiring them to notify or report and that they had taken all reasonable steps to have all such events brought to their notice. Records must be kept of all notified or reported matters and the Health and Safety Executive may seek further information from an employer who has reported one of the above. Finally, it should be noted that certain other pieces of legislation demand separate notification in specified circumstances.[66]

The 1992 Regulations

Apart from the MHSW Regulations, five other sets of regulations were introduced in 1992 in order to implement various EC Directives. The Workplace (Health, Safety and Welfare) Regulations 1992[67] provide that certain requirements must be met in relation to ventilation, temperature, lighting, work-station design, rest facilities, etc. Under the Provision and Use of Work Equipment Regulations 1992[68] employers have a specific obligation to ensure that all work equipment is suitable and well maintained. Workers must be supplied with information and training on the use of equipment. More specific requirements must be met in relation to a range of issues, for example dangerous parts of machinery and maintenance operations. The Personal Protective Equipment Regulations 1992[69] require employers to provide protective equipment where necessary. In addition they must ensure that it is suitable and well maintained and that workers are given information and training on its use.

According to the Manual Handling Operations Regulations 1992,[70] employees should not be obliged to undertake manual handling operations which involve a risk of injury where it is reasonably practicable to avoid this. If it is not, the employer must make a 'suitable and sufficient' assessment of the risk and take appropriate steps to reduce it as far as is reasonably practicable. Employees must also receive certain information on the loads they are required to handle. Finally, the Health and Safety (Display Screen Equipment) Regulations 1992[71] make it the employer's duty to assess work stations and take steps to reduce any risks that are identified. Work and display screen equipment must be planned to allow breaks, and users must be provided with free eye tests and information and training on the use of their work stations. However, it should be noted that these regulations only protect a person 'who habitually uses display screen equipment as a significant part of his normal work'.

Offences

Apart from the Crown, which for these purposes excludes National Health Service premises, any person or body corporate can be prosecuted for an offence under HASAWA 1974. However, if an offence is proved to have been committed with the consent or connivance of, or to have been attributable to neglect on the part of, any director, manager, secretary or other similar officer, then that person as well as the body corporate may be found guilty of an offence.[72] Thus in *Armour v Skeen*[73] a local authority Director of Roads was prosecuted for failing to prepare and carry out a sound safety policy. His neglect led to breaches of safety provisions which resulted in the death of a council employee. Where the commission of an offence by any person is due to the act of default of some other person, that other person may be charged whether or not proceedings are taken against the first-mentioned person.[74] Hence, Crown servants may be prosecuted despite the immunity of the Crown itself. Proceedings under this Act can be brought only by an inspector or with the consent of the Director of Public Prosecutions.

The normal maximum penalty for a person found guilty of an offence on summary conviction (*i.e.* in a magistrates' court) is a fine not exceeding level 5 on the standard scale (£5,000 in 1993). However, where there is a breach of sections 2–6 of HASAWA 1974 or of an improvement or prohibition notice a fine of up to £20,000 can be imposed. If there is a breach of a notice or a court order under section 42 HASAWA 1974 (*see* below) an offender may receive a sentence of up to six months' imprisonment. When proceedings are brought on indictment (in a Crown court) there is the possibility of an unlimited fine and, in specified circumstances, up to two years' imprisonment.[75] Finally, where people are convicted of offences in respect of any matters which appear to the court to be within their power to remedy, the court may, in addition to or instead of imposing any punishment, order them to take such steps as may be specified to remedy those matters.[76]

Enforcing the Act

The HASAWA 1974 established two new bodies, the HSC and the HSE. The HSC is appointed by the Secretary of State for Employment and consists of a chairperson together with three members appointed following consultations with employers' organizations, three members appointed after consultation with trade unions and three others appointed after local authorities and other appropriate organizations have been consulted. Apart from its general duty to 'do such things and make such arrangements as it considers appropriate' the HSC is required to:

(i)   assist and encourage persons concerned with matters relevant to any of the general purposes of the Act to further those purposes
(ii) make arrangements for carrying out research, provide information and training, and encourage others to perform these functions
(iii) make arrangements for providing an information and advisory service
(iv) submit proposed regulations.[77]

Except for the enforcement responsibilities of local authorities[78] HASAWA 1974 is enforced by the HSE, whose director is appointed by the HSC with the approval of the Secretary of State. Although the HSE is to give effect to any directions issued by the HSC the former cannot be directed to enforce a statutory provision in a particular case.

The enforcing authorities appoint inspectors who may exercise the following powers:[79]

(i)   at any reasonable time (or, if there is a dangerous situation, at any time) to enter premises
(ii)   to take with them a constable if they have reasonable cause to apprehend any serious obstruction in the execution of their duty
(iii) to take with them any other authorized person and any equipment or materials required
(iv)   to make such examination and investigation as may be necessary
(v)   to direct that the premises be left undisturbed for so long as is reasonably necessary for the purpose of examination or investigation
(vi)   to take such measurements, photographs and readings as they consider necessary
(vii) to take samples of any articles or substances found in any premises and of the atmosphere in, or in the vicinity of, any such premises[80]

(viii) in the case of an article or substance which appears to have caused or to be likely to cause danger, to dismantle it or subject it to any process or test. The article or substance may be damaged or destroyed if it is thought necessary in the circumstances. However, if they are so requested by a person who is present and has responsibilities in relation to those premises, this power must be exercised in that person's presence unless the inspector considers that to do so would be prejudicial to the safety of the State

(ix) in the case of an article or substance which appears to have caused or to be likely to cause danger, to take possession of it and detain it for so long as is necessary in order to examine it, to ensure that it is not tampered with before the examination is completed, and to ensure that it is available for use as evidence in any proceedings for an offence or any proceedings relating to a notice under section 21 or 22 HASAWA 1974 (*see* below). An inspector must leave a notice giving particulars of the article or substance stating that she or he has taken possession of it and, if it is practicable, she or he should give a sample of it to a responsible person at the premises.[81]

(x) if carrying out examinations or investigations under (iv), to require persons whom they have reasonable cause to believe to be able to give any information to answer such questions as the inspector thinks fit to ask and to sign a declaration of the truth of their answers

(xi) to require the production of, inspect and take copies of an entry in, any books of documents which are required to be kept and any other books or documents which it is necessary for them to see for the purpose of any examination or investigation under (iv) above

(xii) to require any persons to afford them such facilities and assistance with respect to any matters within that person's control or responsibilities as are necessary for the inspectors to exercise their powers

(xiii) any other power which is necessary for the purpose of carrying into effect the statutory provisions.

Where an inspector is of the opinion that a person is contravening or has contravened a relevant statutory provision in circumstances that make it likely that the contravention will continue or be repeated, he or she may serve an 'improvement notice' stating that opinion. The notice must specify the provision, give particulars of the reasons why he or she is of that opinion and will require that person to remedy the contravention within such period as may be specified in the notice.[82] This period must not be less than the time allowed for appealing against the notice, *i.e.* 21 days.[83] In respect of an activity covered by a relevant statutory provision, if any inspector believes that activities are being carried on or are about to be carried on which will involve a risk of serious personal injury, the inspector may serve a 'prohibition notice'. Such a notice will state the inspector's opinion, specify the matters which give rise to the risk, and direct that the activities to which the notice relates shall not be carried on by or under the control of the person on whom the notice is served (unless the matters specified in the notice have been remedied). A prohibition notice may take effect immediately, although ordinarily such a notice will take effect at the end of the period specified in the notice. Both types of notice may (but need not) include directions as to the measures to be taken to remedy the contravention or the matter to which the notice relates. Where a notice which is not to take immediate effect has been served, that notice may be withdrawn by the inspector within 21 days. Similarly the period specified for rectification may be extended by an inspector at any time when an appeal against the notice is not pending (*see* below). It is important to emphasize that such notices can be issued against individuals and on occasions employees who have refused to wear protective clothing have been prevented from working by the use of these administrative sanctions.

A person on whom a notice is served may appeal to an industrial tribunal which has the power to cancel or affirm the notice, or affirm it in a modified form.[84] For the purpose of hearing such appeals the tribunal may include specially appointed assessors. Bringing an appeal against an improvement notice has the effect of suspending the operation of that notice until the appeal is disposed of, but lodging an appeal against a prohibition notice only suspends it if the tribunal so directs and then only from the time when the direction is given.[85] Failure to comply with a notice is an offence.[86]

Since it is not possible to bring a prosecution against the

Crown,[87] it is equally impossible to enforce improvement and prohibition notices against Crown bodies. However, the HSE has been prepared to issue 'Crown notices' where in its opinion an improvement or prohibition notice would have been appropriate. Such notices have no legal effect but may be of some value in so far as they put moral pressure on the employing body. Of course, trade union representatives who receive copies of these notices may be in a position to apply industrial pressure.

Finally, it is worth noting that the Environment and Safety Information Act 1988 requires enforcement authorities to keep public registers giving details of notices issued under HASAWA 1974 and other safety legislation. However, this statute does not apply to notices which 'impose requirements or prohibitions solely for the protection of persons at work'.[88]

Notes

1 Sections 15 and 16 HASAWA 1974. See, for example, Regulation 27 of the Provision and Use of Work Equipment Regulations 1992 SI No 2932.
2 SI No 2051.
3 Except in so far as the regulations provide otherwise. See section 47(2) HASAWA 1974 and Regulation 15 MHSW Regulations 1992.
4 Section 17 HASAWA 1974.
5 See Regulation 3 and ACOP paragraphs 3–27.
6 See Regulation 6(5) and ACOP paragraphs 34–40.
7 See Regulation 7(2) and ACOP paragraphs 41–52.
8 Section 2(2) HASAWA 1974.
9 Defined in section 53 HASAWA 1974 as including any machinery, equipment or appliance.
10 On the general duty to reduce the risk of hearing damage to the lowest level reasonably practicable see Regulation 6 of the Noise at Work Regulation 1989.
11 Defined in section 54 HASAWA 1974 as 'any natural or artificial substance, whether in solid or liquid form or in the form of a gas or vapour'. See pages 107–11 on substances at work.
12 On hearing risks see Regulation 11 Noise at Work Regulations 1989.
13 See *West Bromwich Building Society v Townsend* [1983] IRLR 147.
14 Section 40 HASAWA 1974.
15 See *Martin v Boulton & Paul Ltd* [1982] ICR 366.
16 *Bolton Council v Malrod Insulation Ltd* [1993] IRLR 274.
17 1989 SI No 682.
18 For exceptions see Regulation 7(2) SRSC Regulations.

19 Section 28(8)(9) HASAWA 1974.
20 See definition in Regulation 2(1) SRSC Regulations.
21 An 'undertaking' is not defined for these purposes. See *Osborne v Taylor Ltd* [1982] IRLR 17.
22 Section 2(3) HASAWA 1974.
23 See *Writing a Safety Policy Statement: Advice to Employers*, HSC6 (revised).
24 In this context 'recognition' means recognition for the purposes of collective bargaining. See Regulation 2 SRSC Regulations and *Cleveland County Council v Springett* [1985] IRLR 131.
25 Section 2(6) HASAWA 1974.
26 Regulation 4A SRSC Regulations.
27 Regulation 3(4) SRSC Regulations.
28 Defined by Regulation 2(1) SRSC Regulations.
29 See Guidance Notes 8 and 9.
30 See the schedule to the SRSC Regulations.
31 *Time off for the Training of Safety Representatives*, HMSO, 1978.
32 [1980] IRLR 176.
33 Regulation 11 SRSC Regulations.
34 For definitions see Regulations 6(3) SRSC Regulations. See page 111 on the notification of accidents, etc.
35 Regulation 9 SRSC Regulations. See also the Guidance Notes on safety committees.
36 See *R v Trustees of the Science Museum* [1993] 3 AER 853.
37 *R v Mara* [1987] 1 WLR 87.
38 See *Inspector of Factories v Austin Rover* [1989] IRLR 404.
39 See the Health and Safety (Emissions into the atmosphere) Regulations 1983 (as amended 1989).
40 On the meaning of 'at work' see section 52(1) HASAWA 1974.
41 On the duty to use ear protectors see Regulations 8 of the Noise at Work Regulations 1989.
42 Regulation 12 MHSW Regulations 1992.
43 Section 9 HASAWA 1974.
44 Defined by section 53 HASAWA 1974 as any plant designed for use or operation (whether exclusively or not) by persons at work, and any article designed for use as a component in any such plant.
45 Section 6(6) HASAWA 1974.
46 Section 6(2) HASAWA 1974 but see also section 6(6) HASAWA 1974 (above).
47 See also Health and Safety (Leasing Arrangements) Regulations 1980 SI 1980.
48 See Regulation 9 Noise at Work Regulations 1989.
49 Defined in section 53 HASAWA 1974 as any substance intended for use (whether exclusively or not) by persons at work. See *Substances for Use at Work: the Provision of Information*, HS(G)27, HMSO 1989.
50 Section 6(4) as amended.

51 Section 6(5) HASAWA 1974 but subject to section 6(6) HASAWA 1974.
52 Section 6(7) HASAWA 1974.
53 SI No 1657. It should be noted that lead, asbestos and materials producing ionizing radiation are covered by their own legislation.
54 Regulation 2.
55 See Regulation 12(3) and ACOP paragraph 97.
56 See ACOP paragraphs 11–24 and *COSHH Assessments: a Step-by-step Guide* (HSE).
57 See Regulation 7(2) and ACOP paragraphs 25–44.
58 See Regulation 9 and ACOP paragraphs 25–44.
59 See Regulation 8 and ACOP paragraphs 45–46.
60 See ACOP paragraphs 66–76.
61 See Regulation 11 and ACOP paragraphs 77–92.
62 See Regulation 12 and ACOP paragraphs 93–7.
63 SI No 2023.
64 See Regulation 3 and Schedule 1.
65 See Regulation 5 and Schedule 2.
66 See Regulation 10 and Schedule 6.
67 SI 3004.
68 SI 2932.
69 SI 3139.
70 SI 2793.
71 SI 2792.
72 Section 37 HASAWA 1974. Directors who are convicted of an offence can be disqualified from office under the Directors Disqualification Act 1986.
73 [1977] IRLR 310. See also *R v Boal* [1992] IRLR 420.
74 Section 36 HASAWA 1974.
75 Section 33(2) (5) HASAWA 1974 (as amended).
76 Section 42(1) HASAWA 1974.
77 Section 11(1)(2) and section 50(3).
78 See Health and Safety (Enforcing Authority) Regulations 1989 SI No 1903.
79 Section 20 HASAWA 1974.
80 See *Laws v Keane* [1982] IRLR 500.
81 See also section 25 HASAWA 1974 on the power to deal with an imminent cause of danger.
82 See *West Bromwich Building Society v Townsend* (note 13).
83 Rule 2 Schedule 4 Industrial Tribunal (Constitution and Rules of Procedure) Regulations 1993 SI No. 2687.
84 Section 24(2) HASAWA 1974. Section 82(1)c defines 'modifications' as including additions, omissions and amendments. See *British Airways v Henderson* [1979] ICR 77.
85 Section 24(3) HASAWA 1974.
86 See section 33(1)g HASAWA 1974 and *Deary v Mansion Hide Upholstery Ltd* [1983] IRLR 195.

87   Section 48 HASAWA 1974.
88   Section 2(3).

8 Statutory sick pay and suspension on medical grounds

Statutory sick pay

The Social Security Contributions and Benefits Act 1992 (SSCBA 1992) makes employers responsible for paying statutory sick pay (SSP) to such of their employees as work within the EU.[1] SSP will be paid for up to 28 weeks of absence due to sickness or injury[2] in any single 'period of entitlement' (*see* below).[3] As well as those who pay full Class 1 National Insurance contributions married women and widows paying reduced contributions will be eligible for SSP. Part-timers who earn more than the current earnings limit (£56 per week in the tax year 1993–4), are to be treated in the same way as full-time employees and there is no minimum service qualification. Indeed, an employee may be entitled to SSP under more than one contract or with more than one employer if the relevant conditions are satisfied. Those who are ineligible for SSP can claim State sickness benefit while those who have exhausted their entitlement to SSP can claim invalidity benefit.

The qualifying conditions and limitations on entitlement

SSP is available for a 'day of incapacity for work' (not part of a day) which falls within 'a period of entitlement'.[4] In addition, a payment will only be made for the fourth and subsequent 'qualifying days' within that period of entitlement and employees must comply with provisions requiring them to notify the employer of incapacity to work.[5] According to section 151(4) SSCBA 1992 a day of incapacity for work is a day on which the employee is (or is deemed to be) 'incapable by reason of some specific disease or bodily or mental disablement of doing work of a kind which he might reasonably be expected to do' under his or her contract of employment.[6] When an employee has four or more consecutive 'days of incapacity for work' a 'period of incapacity for work' is formed. These successive days include non-working days, *e.g.* Sundays or bank holidays. Periods of 'incapacity for work' which are separated by eight weeks or less are treated as one for these purposes (the 'linking mechanism') so employees are not obliged to wait another three days to qualify for SSP.[7] However, a single period of incapacity cannot extend beyond three years.[8]

A 'period of entitlement' commences with the first 'day of incapacity for work' and ends when whichever of the following first occurs:[9]

(i) the period of incapacity for work ends
(ii) SSP entitlement is exhausted
(iii) a pregnant employee reaches the 'disqualifying period' *i.e.* the period of 18 weeks beginning with the eleventh week before the expected week of confinement
(iv) the employee is detained in legal custody or sentenced to a term of imprisonment[10]
(v) the employee's contract of service terminates. Regulation 4 of the SSP Regs 1982 deals with the situation where an employee is dismissed solely or mainly for the purpose of avoiding SSP liability. If on the day the contract is brought to an end the employee has a period of entitlement the employer must pay SSP until the period of entitlement would have ended under (i)-(iv) above or, if earlier, the date on which the contract would have expired
(vi) a period of three years has elapsed since entitlement commenced. At this point the employee will be transferred to State sickness benefit.

However, a 'period of entitlement' will not arise in the following circumstances:[11]

(i) if at the 'relevant date' (*see* page 123) the employee is over state pension age
(ii) if the employee was engaged for a specified period of three months or less and that period is not exceeded. Where an individual has been employed by the same employer within the previous eight weeks regard is to be had to the aggregate period of employment
(iii) if at the 'relevant date' the employee's normal gross weekly

earnings (*i.e.* average earnings including overtime and bonuses) are less than the current earnings limit for social security purposes[12]

(iv)   if the employee's first 'day of incapacity for work' is within 57 days of entitlement to an invalidity pension, a severe disablement allowance, sickness benefit or maternity allowance. In the case of sickness benefit it is sufficient that the employee would have been entitled if the contribution conditions had been satisfied

(v)   if the employee has done no work for the employer under the contract of service. Where the employee has been employed by the same employer within the previous eight weeks then the two contracts are to be treated as one[13]

(vi)   if on the 'relevant date' there is a stoppage of work due to a trade dispute at the employee's place of employment unless the employee can prove that he or she did not have a direct interest in the dispute[14]

(vii)   if before the 'relevant date' the employee has exhausted his or her SSP entitlement from the employer

(viii)   if the employee is pregnant and the 'relevant date' falls within the 'disqualifying period' (*see* above)

(ix)   if on the first day of the period of incapacity for work the employee is in legal custody or serving a prison sentence[15]

In this context the 'relevant date' is the date on which a period of entitlement would have begun if schedule 11 did not prevent it arising.[16]

If a period of incapacity for work has been formed but the employee is excluded from SSP, the employer must complete an 'exclusion form' and give or send it to the employee within seven days. Similarly, employers must issue a transfer form (SSP1(T)) to employees off sick at the start of the twenty-third week of SSP entitlement.[17] When completed, these forms will reveal why the employer is not paying SSP and will enable the employee to claim State sickness or invalidity benefits. Employers must also provide 'leaver's statements' to those who are leaving employment and had a period of incapacity for work not more than eight weeks before the contract ended.[18] Employers will generally be required to issue a statement (SSP1L) to the employee not later than the seventh day after the date the contract terminated which contains the following information:

(i)   the first day of sickness in the period of incapacity for work (including linked periods)
(ii) the number of weeks of SSP paid or due to be paid (to the nearest whole week)
(iii) the last day for which SSP was paid.

If the employee falls ill within eight weeks of the last date on which SSP was paid, a new employer who has received a statement must take the weeks of SSP shown on it into account in calculating his or her own 28 weeks' liability. However, the new employer need only consider a leaver's statement if it is received or posted on or before the seventh calendar day after the first qualifying day in a period of incapacity or such later date as the employer may require. Employers can accept the late receipt of a leaver's statement if they are satisfied that there was good cause for delay, but there is an absolute limit of 91 days after which the statement must be ignored. Employers should retain copies of any leaver's statements they issue and have received for a period of three years after the tax year to which the statement relates. Although employees are not obliged to give leaver's statements to their new employer it is clearly in the employer's interest to ask recruits whether they have been given such a form.

There must be at least one 'qualifying day' in each week.[19] Although such days may be agreed between the employer and the employee they are prevented from arranging that the qualifying days are those on which the employee was incapable of work. According to Regulation 5(2) of the SSP Regs 1982 where the employer and employee have not reached agreement the qualifying day or days will be:

(i)   the day or days on which the parties agreed that the employee was required to work;[20] or
(ii) on Wednesday, if it is agreed that there is no day on which work would be done.

Notification of sickness absence and proof of incapacity

Notification of absence is distinct from evidence of sickness. Notice of any day of incapacity for work must be given to the employer by (or on behalf of) an employee:[21]

(i)   where the employer has a fixed time limit and has taken reasonable steps to make it known to the employee, within that time limit. However, an employee cannot be required to notify 'earlier than the first qualifying day ... or by a specified time during that qualifying day'

(ii)   in any other case before the end of the seventh day after that day of incapacity.

Notice of a day of incapacity can be given later than as mentioned in (i) or (ii) if there is a 'good cause' for doing so, but in any event it must be submitted before the end of the ninety-first day after the day of incapacity. Where the employer has taken reasonable steps to make the desired manner of notification known to the employee that manner must be followed. However, the employer cannot insist on notice being given:

(i)   personally, or
(ii)   in the form of medical evidence, or
(iii) more than once in every seven days during a period of entitlement, or
(iv)   on a document supplied by him or her, or
(v)   on a printed form.

Employees can notify in any way they wish, provided they do so in writing (unless otherwise agreed). Where the employee fails to comply with the notification procedure the employer may withhold SSP for the unnotified days, although the employee's maximum entitlement will be unaffected.[22]

Section 17(2) of the Social Security and Housing Benefits Act 1982 (SSHBA 1982) stipulates that an employee must provide such information as may reasonably be required to enable the employer to determine whether there is a period of entitlement and, if so, its duration. Evidence of sickness must be supplied by means of a doctor's statement in a prescribed form.[23] On it the medical practitioner must specify that the employee has been advised that he or she should refrain from work for a period (usually up to six months) specified in the statement. It should be noted that medical information cannot be required in respect of the first seven days of absence in any period of incapacity for work.

The amounts payable and recoverable by employers

Employees receive different amounts of SSP according to their normal gross weekly earnings. The amounts fixed from April 1994 are £47.80 per week for those earning between £56 and £195 per week and £52.50 if normal weekly earnings exceed £195.[24] The daily rate of SSP will be the appropriate weekly rate divided by the number of 'qualifying days' in the week (starting with Sunday). Employers must pay the stipulated amount of SSP for each day that an employee is eligible but any other sums paid in respect of the same day can count towards the SSP entitlement *e.g.* normal wages.[25] Any agreement which purports to exclude, limit or modify an employee's right to SSP or which requires an employee to contribute (directly or indirectly) towards any cost incurred by the employer will be void.[26] For many employees SSP will be worth less than State sickness benefit because the former is subject to tax and national insurance contributions and will be paid at a flat rate without additions for dependants. It is therefore hardly surprising that trade unions endeavour to negotiate sick pay schemes which ensure that their members do not suffer any detriment as a result of this legislation.

Employers are entitled to deduct 80 per cent of SSP paid out from their monthly payments of national insurance contributions and, if SSP exceeds the value of these contributions, deductions can also be made from the tax element of the monthly remittance.[27] From April 1994 there will be no reimbursement of SSP except for small employers.

Enforcing the right to SSP

Section 17(3) SSHBA 1982 gives employees the right to ask their employer for a written statement, in relation to a period before the request is made, of one or more of the following matters:

(i)   the days for which the employer regards himself or herself as liable to pay SSP

(ii) the reasons why the employer does not consider himself or herself liable to pay for other days

(iii) the amount of SSP to which the employer believes the employee is entitled

and, to the extent to which the request is reasonable, the employer must comply with it within a reasonable time.

Unless it is reserved for the determination of the Secretary of State, any question as to entitlement to sick pay can be referred to an adjudication officer who, so far as it is practicable, must dispose of it within 14 days or refer it to a social security appeal tribunal. Appeals against an adjudication officer's decision go to the Social Security Appeal Tribunal and must normally be lodged within 28 days.[28] Further appeals (with leave) go to the Social Security Commissioners and then the Court of Appeal. Any party to proceedings who is notified by the Secretary of State that information is required from him or her for the determination of any question arising in connection with those proceedings must provide the information sought within ten days of receiving the notification.[29]

According to Regulation 9 of the SSP Regs 1982, SSP must be paid not later than the first pay day after:

(i)   where an appeal has been brought, the day on which the employer receives notification that it has been finally disposed of

(ii) where leave to appeal has been refused and there is no further opportunity to apply for leave, the day on which the employer receives notification of the refusal

(iii) in any other case, the day on which the time for lodging an appeal expires.

Where as a result of the employer's methods of accounting for and paying remuneration it is impracticable to comply with the above requirement it must be met not later than the next following pay day. Once entitlement to SSP is established any outstanding sums can be recovered through the county courts if necessary, although to the extent that SSP has not been paid by the employer liability passes to the Secretary of State.[30]

The duty to keep records

Employers are obliged to keep records showing:

(i)   the amount of SSP paid to each employee on each pay day
(ii) the amount of SSP paid to each employee during each tax
      year
(iii) the total amount of SSP paid to all employees during the
      tax year.

Additionally, Regulation 13 of the SSP Regs 1982 stipulates that
for three years after the end of each tax year employers must keep
a record in relation to each employee of the following matters:

(i)   any day in that tax year which was one of four or more
      consecutive days of incapacity for work, whether or not
      the employee would normally have been expected to work
      on that day
(ii) any day recorded under (i) for which the employer did not
      pay SSP
(iii) the reason why the employer did not pay SSP
(iv) the qualifying days in each period of entitlement which fell
      wholly or partly in that tax year.

Penalties

An employer who knowingly produces false information in order
to recover a sum allegedly paid out as SSP commits an offence.
The maximum penalty for knowingly making a false claim is a
fine not exceeding level 5 on the standard scale or three months'
imprisonment, or both. A reckless claim may lead to a fine not
exceeding level 4 on the standard scale. Any person who without
reasonable excuse fails to:

(i)   comply with the time limit for paying SSP, or
(ii) maintain the records required, or
(iii) provide the information sought by the Secretary of State in
      connection with proceedings, or
(iv) provide information to employees in accordance with
      Regulation 15 of the SSP Regs 1982

may receive a fine not exceeding level 3 on the standard scale. If the contravention continues after conviction a daily fine may be imposed.[31] Where an offence is proved to have been committed with the consent or connivance of, or to have been attributable to neglect on the part of, any director, manager, secretary or other similar officer then that person as well as the company may be found guilty of an offence.

Suspension on medical grounds

Employees with at least a month's continuous service who are suspended from work in consequence of a requirement imposed by specified health and safety provisions or a recommendation contained in a code of practice issued or approved under section 16 HASAWA 1974 are entitled to a week's pay (*see* chapter 15) for each week of suspension up to a maximum of 26 weeks.[32] The relevant health and safety provisions are listed in Schedule 1 of EPCA 1978 (as amended) and cover certain hazardous substances and processes, *e.g.* lead and ionizing radiation. It should be observed that this statutory right can be invoked only where the specified safety legislation has affected the employer's undertaking and not the employee's health. Therefore, employees are not entitled to remuneration under this provision for any period during which they are incapable of work by reason of illness or injury. Additionally, if employees unreasonably refuse to perform suitable alternative work (whether or not it is within the scope of their contract), or if they do not comply with reasonable require-ments imposed by their employer with a view to ensuring that their services are available, no payment is owed.[33]

It is important to note that these sections do not grant employers the right to suspend, they merely give rights to employees who are lawfully suspended. If there is no contractual right to suspend employees will be entitled to sue for their full wages anyway, although the set-off formula will apply here.[34] Where the employer fails to pay remuneration which is owed to the employee by virtue of the statute the latter can apply to an industrial tribunal within three months.[35] Section 22(3)EPCA 1978 provides that if the tri-bunal finds a complaint to be well founded the employer must be ordered to pay the amount due to the employee. As long as any replacement for a suspended employee is informed in writing by the employer that the employment will be terminated at the end of the suspension, dismissal of the replacement in order to allow the original employee to resume work will be deemed to have been for a 'substantial reason of a kind such as to justify the dismissal of an employee holding the position which that employee held'.[36] However, an industrial tribunal must be still satisfied that it was reasonable in all the circumstances to dismiss (*see* chapter 12).

Notes

1 On the definition of 'employee' see Regulation 16 of SSP (General) Regulations 1982, Regulations 5–8 of SSP (Mariners, Airmen and Persons Abroad) Regulations 1982 and SSP (Compensation of Employers) and Miscellaneous Provisions Regulations 1983 and SI No 376 (the Compensation Regulations 1983)

2 Injury benefit was abolished by section 39 SSHBA 1982.

3 Section 155 SSCBA 1992 sets the entitlement limit at '28 times the appropriate weekly rate' and Regulation 6 of SSP (General) Regulations 1982 explains how this limit should be calculated.

4 Sections 152–3 SSCBA 1992.

5 Sections 154 and 156 SSCBA 1992.

6 Regulation 2 of SSP (General) Regulations 1982 describes the circumstances in which a person may be deemed incapable of work.

7 Section 152 SSCBA 1992.

8 See Regulation 3 SSP (General) Amendment Regulations 1986.

9 Section 153(2) SSCBA 1992.

10 Regulation 3(1) of SSP (General) Regulations 1982.

11 See Schedule 11 paragraph 2 SSCBA 1992.

12 The meaning of 'earnings' and 'normal weekly earnings' is dealt with in Regulations 17 and 19 of SSP (General) Regulations 1982 (as amended).

13 See Regulation 20 SSP (General) Regulations 1982 (as amended).

14 See also Schedule 11 paragraph 7 SSCBA 1992.

15 Regulation 3(2) of SSP (General) Regulations 1982.

16 See Schedule 11 paragraph 3 SSCBA 1992.

17 See Regulation 15 of SSP (General) Regulations 1982.

18 See Regulation 15A SSP (General) Regulations 1982 (as amended).

19 Section 154 SSCBA 1992.

20 See Regulation (SSP) 1/85.

21 See Regulation 7 of SSP (General) Regulations 1982 (as amended).

22 See Section 156(2)(3) SSCBA 1992.

23 See SSP (Medical Evidence) Regulations 1985 (as amended).

24 See section 157 SSCBA 1992. From April 1995 the lower rate will be abolished.
25 See Schedule 12 paragraph 2 SSCBA 1992.
26 Section 151(2) SSCBA 1992.
27 See section 158 SSCBA, SSP (Compensation of Employers) Regulations 1983 (as amended) and SSP (Small Employers Relief) Regulations 1991.
28 See Social Security (Adjudication) Regulations 1986 SI 2218.
29 See Regulation 14 of SSP (General) Regulations 1982.
30 See Regulation 9A SSP (General) Regulations 1982 (as amended).
31 See Regulation 22 of SSP (General) Regulations 1982 (as amended).
32 Section 19 EPCA 1978 (as amended).
33 Section 20 EPCA 1978.
34 See section 21(2)(3) EPCA 1978 and chapter 6 note 3.
35 Unless the 'time limit escape clause' applies (*see* chapter 3 note 14); section 22 EPCA 1978.
36 See section 61(2) EPCA 1978.

9 Time off work owing to lay-off, short time or public duties

The implications of lay-off and short-time working

At common law entitlement to payment during a period of lay-off or short-time working depends on whether there is an express or implied term in the contract of employment dealing with the situation. In the absence of contractual authority to lay off or introduce short time, which may be secured in advance or may result from an agreement at the relevant time, an employee can treat the suspension of payment as repudiatory conduct (*i.e.* a breach of a fundamental term) by the employer and hence as dismissal. If the dismissal is found to be on grounds of redundancy, a redundancy payment can be claimed by those who are qualified to do so (*see* chapter 13). In *Macrae & Co v Dawson*[1] the EAT held that where employers have a contractual right to lay off their employees indefinitely, normally they are not to be regarded as in breach of their obligation to supply work simply by virtue of the passage of time. If employees think that too long a time has elapsed, their remedy is to follow the statutory redundancy procedure (see page 134).

Guarantee payments

Employees with one month's continuous service qualify for a guarantee payment if they are not provided with work throughout a day in which they would normally be required to work in accordance with their contract of employment because of:

(i) a diminution in the requirements of the employer's business for work of the kind which the employee is employed to do, or

(ii) any other occurrence affecting the normal working of the employer's business in relation to work of that kind.[2]

However, if a contract of employment is not expected to last more than three months there is no right to a guarantee payment unless a person is in fact employed for more than three months.[3] The words 'normally required to work' are significant for two reasons. First, an employee who is not obliged to work when requested may be regarded as not being subject to a contract of employment.[4] Secondly, if contracts of employment are varied to provide for a reduced number of working days, for example four instead of five, employees will be unable to claim a payment for the fifth day because they are no longer 'required to work' on that day. 'Any other occurrence . . .' would seem to contemplate something like a power failure or natural disaster rather than works holidays.

No guarantee payment is available if the workless day is a consequence of a strike, lock-out or other industrial action involving any employee of the employer or any associated employer.[5] The entitlement to a guarantee payment may be lost in two other circumstances:

(i) where the employer has offered to provide alternative work which is suitable in the circumstances (irrespective of whether it falls inside or outside the scope of the employee's contract) but this has been unreasonably refused

(ii) the employee does not comply with reasonable requirements imposed by the employer with a view to ensuring that his or her services are available.[6] This is to enable the employer to keep the workforce together, perhaps in the hope that the supplies which have been lacking will be delivered.

A guarantee payment is calculated by multiplying the number of normal working hours (*see* chapter 15) on the day of lay-off by the guaranteed hourly rate.[7] Accordingly, where there are no normal working hours on the day in question no guarantee payment can be claimed. The guaranteed hourly rate is one week's pay divided by the number of normal hours in a week and, where the number of normal hours varies, the average number of such hours over a 12 week period will be used.[8] In 1993 the statutory maximum in respect of any day was £14.10 and payment cannot be claimed for more than five days in any period of three months.[9] It should be noted that contractual payments in respect of workless days not only discharge an employer's liability to make guarantee payments for those days[10] but are also to be taken into account when calculating the maximum number of days for which employees are entitled to statutory payments.[11] Where guaranteed weekly remuneration has been agreed, this sum is to be 'apportioned rateably between the workless days'.[12] If an employer fails to pay the whole or part of a guarantee payment an employee can complain to an industrial tribunal within three months of the last workless day.[13] Where a tribunal finds a complaint to be well founded, it must order the employer to pay the amount which it finds owing to the employee.[14]

If guaranteed remuneration is the subject of a collective agreement currently in force all the parties may choose to apply for an exemption order. So long as the Secretary of State is satisfied that the statutory provisions should not apply the relevant employees will be excluded form the operation of section 12 EPCA 1978. However, the Secretary of State cannot make an order unless a collective agreement permits employees to take a dispute about guaranteed remuneration to arbitration, an independent adjudicating body or an industrial tribunal.[15]

Finally, it should be noted that under the Social Security (Unemployment, Sickness and Invalidity Benefit) Regulations 1983[16] an employee is disqualified from receiving unemployment benefit on any day in respect of which a guarantee payment is payable.

Redundancy payments

Sections 87–9 EPCA 1978 enable employees to claim redundancy payments on the grounds that they have been laid off or kept on short time for four or more consecutive weeks or for a series of six or more weeks within a 13 week period.[17] It is immaterial that during these periods the employee was partly laid off and partly on short time, although no account can be taken of any week in which the lay-off or short time is wholly or mainly attributable to a strike or lock-out (whether or not it is in the trade or industry in which the person is employed and whether it is in Great Britain or elsewhere).[18] For these purposes employees are deemed to be laid off if they are not provided with work for a week and are thereby not entitled to any remuneration under their contracts. Short time is where, by reason of diminution of the work, the employee's remuneration for any week is less than half a week's pay.[19] However, employees are not on short time if they refuse work that has been offered.[20]

Employees seeking payments in these circumstances must give written notice of their intention to claim within four weeks of the lay-off or short time finishing, and must give notice to terminate their contracts within three weeks of the seven days allowed to the employer to issue a 'counter notice'.[21] This 'counter notice' must be in writing and indicate that the employer will contest any liability to make a redundancy payment.[22] In *Fabar Construction v Race*[23] the EAT did not accept that an offer of employment in itself indicated that a redundancy claim would be contested. Employees are not entitled to a redundancy payment in pursuance of a notice of intention to claim if, at the date that notice was received, it was reasonable to expect that they would, not later than four weeks after that date, enter upon a period of not less than 13 weeks' employment during which they would not be laid off or kept on short time. If no 'counter notice' is given, or the employee is laid off or kept on short time during each of the four weeks following the date the notice of intention to claim was received, a redundancy payment is owed.[24] Where the employer gives 'counter notice' within the time allowed and does not subsequently withdraw it, employees are not entitled to a payment except in accordance with a tribunal decision.[25]

Time off for public duties

Section 29 EPCA 1978 (as amended) permits employees who are:

(i)   justices of the peace
(ii) members of a local authority
(iii) members of any statutory tribunal
(iv) members of a health authority, NHS trust or a Family Practitioner Committee
(v)   members of the governing body of an educational establishment maintained by a local authority or a grant-maintained school

(vi)   members of the National Rivers Authority
(vii) prison visitors

to take time off during working hours for the purpose of performing any of the duties of their office or as members. Employees are
eligible for time off irrespective of their length of service, but
are not entitled to a payment from their employer by virtue of
this section.

The duties referred to are attendance at meetings of the body
(or its committees or sub-committees) and 'the doing of any other
thing approved by the body' for the purpose of discharging its
functions. The amount of time off which is to be allowed and the
occasions on which and conditions subject to which it may be
taken are those that are reasonable in the circumstances. No code
of practice exists for these purposes but regard must be had to
the following matters:[26]

(i)   how much time off is required for the performance of the
       public duty as a whole and how much is required for
       the particular duty
(ii)   how much time off has already been permitted for trade
       union duties and activities (*see* chapter 18)
(iii) the circumstances of the employer's business and the effect
       of the employee's absence on the running of it.

The EAT has commented that an employee who undertakes a
variety of public and other duties may have some responsibility
to plan the absences from work, and to scale down the level of
commitment which such public duties involve, so as to produce a
pattern which can be regarded as reasonable in the circumstances.[27]

A complaint that an employer has failed to permit time off in
accordance with the above provisions must be lodged in the same
way as a claim that the employer has not complied with sections
27 or 28 EPCA 1978 and the remedies available are identical (*see*
chapter 18). However, two observations may be helpful at this
stage. First, rearranging employees' hours of work but requiring
them to perform the same duties does not constitute giving time
off. Second, it is not the function of industrial tribunals to stipulate
what amounts of, or conditions for, time off would be appropriate
in the future.[28]

Notes

1   [1984] IRLR 5.
2   Section 12(1) EPCA 1978.
3   Section 13(2) EPCA 1978 (as amended).
4   See *Mailway (Southern) Ltd v Willsher* [1978] IRLR 322.
5   Section 13(1) EPCA 1978. 'Associated employer' is defined by section 153(4) EPCA 1978 (*see* chapter 15).
6   Section 13(2) EPCA 1978.
7   Section 14(1) EPCA 1978.
8   Section 14(2) EPCA 1978.
9   Section 15 EPCA 1978 (as amended).
10   Section 16(2) EPCA 1978 (*see* chapter 6, note 3).
11   See *Cartwright v Clancey Ltd* [1983] IRLR 355.
12   Section 16(3) EPCA 1978.
13   Unless the 'time limit escape clause' applies (*see* chapter 3, note 14). Section 17(2) EPCA 1978.
14   Section 17(3) EPCA 1978.
15   Section 18 EPCA 1978.
16   SI No 1598 Regulation 7(1)(k)(i).
17   On general exclusions from and qualifications for a redundancy payment see pages 150–1.
18   Section 89(2)(3) EPCA 1978.
19   Section 87(1)(2) EPCA 1978.
20   See *Spinpress Ltd v Turner* [1986] ICR 433.
21   See *Walmsley v Ferguson Ltd* [1989] IRLR 112.
22   Section 88(4) EPCA 1978.
23   [1979] IRLR 232.
24   Section 89(1) EPCA 1978.
25   Section 89(4) EPCA 1978.
26   Section 29(4) EPCA 1978. On local authority employees requiring time off to perform duties as a council member see section 10 Local Government and Housing Act 1989.
27   *Borders Regional Council v Maule* [1993] IRLR 199.
28   See *Corner v Buckinghamshire County Council* [1978] IRLR 320.

10 Variation, breach and termination of the contract of employment at common law

Variation

Theoretically neither employer nor employee can unilaterally alter the terms and conditions of employment, for these can only be varied by mutual agreement. It follows that an employer cannot lawfully vary a contract simply by giving 'notice to vary'. Such a notice will have legal effect only if it terminates the existing contract and offers a new contract on revised terms.[1] Consent to change may be obtained through individual or collective negotiation or may be implied from the conduct of the parties. Thus, if employees remain at work for a considerable period of time after revised terms have been imposed they may be deemed to have accepted the changes. Where the individual continues in employment but works 'under protest' it is a question of fact whether or not the variation has been accepted. In *WPM Retail v Lang*[2] it was held that the employer's obligation to pay a bonus in accordance with the terms when the employee was promoted in September 1974 remained in force until the employment was terminated in August 1977, notwithstanding that the bonus had been paid only in the first month after promotion and the employee had carried on working thereafter. As a general rule, courts and tribunals will be reluctant to find that there has been a consensual variation 'where the employee has been faced with the alternative of dismissal and where the variation has been adverse to his interest.'[3]

A unilateral variation which is not accepted will constitute a breach and could amount to a repudiation of the contract. However, there is no law that any breach which an employee is entitled to treat as repudiatory brings the contract to an end automatically.[4] Where there is repudiatory conduct by the employer, the employee has the choice of affirming the contract (by continuing in employment) or accepting the repudiation as bringing the contract to an end. If the latter option is exercised and the employee resigns within a short period, there will be a constructive dismissal for statutory purposes (*see* chapter 11). In practice, developments in the law of unfair dismissal make it very difficult for an employee to resist a unilateral variation. This is dealt with more fully in chapter 12. Suffice it to say at this stage that employers can offer, as a fair reason for dismissal, the fact that there was a sound business reason for insisting on changes being put into effect. So long as a minimum amount of consultation has taken place, it is relatively easy to satisfy a tribunal, particularly where the majority of employees has been prepared to go along with the employer's proposals, that an employer has acted reasonably in treating a refusal to accept a variation as a sufficient reason for dismissing.[5]

Breach of contract

The options open to an innocent party will depend on whether the breach is of a minor or serious nature. An innocent party may choose to continue with the contract as if nothing had happened (*i.e.* waive the breach), may sue for damages, or, in the case of a serious or fundamental breach, regard the contract as at an end (*i.e.* accept the other party's repudiation of it). Although the employer could sue or possibly dismiss for breach of contract, there are a number of reasons why disciplinary rather than legal action is preferred. First, the potential defendant may be unable to pay any damages awarded. Secondly, the amount likely to be obtained may not be worth the time and effort involved. Thirdly, taking legal action against individual employees is not conducive to harmonious industrial relations.

What options are open to employers when employees refuse to carry out all or part of their contractual obligations? Apart from the measures outlined in the previous paragraph, the employer may withhold pay on the grounds that employees who are not ready and willing to render the services required by their contracts are not entitled to be paid.[6] In *Wiluszynski v London Borough of Tower Hamlets*[7] the employee refused to perform the full range of his duties and had been told by the employer that until he did he would not be required for work or be paid. Although he went to work and performed a substantial part of his duties the Court of Appeal held that the local authority was entitled to withhold the whole of his remuneration. Clearly employees are not entitled to pick and choose what work they will do under their contracts but if employers are prepared to accept part performance they will be required to pay for such work as is agreed.

The principal remedies for breach of contract are an injunction (an order restraining a particular type of action), a declaration of the rights of the parties, and damages. Traditionally, great emphasis was placed on the personal nature of the contract of employment and courts were extremely reluctant to order a party to continue to perform the contract. However, in recent years the courts have been more willing to grant injunctions against employers who act in breach of contract. Nevertheless, they need to be satisfied not only that it would be just to make such an order but also that it would be workable.[8] The mere fact that the employer and employee are in dispute does not mean that mutual confidence has evaporated.[9] The position remains that an employee cannot be compelled to return to work,[10] although a tribunal has the power to order the re-employment of someone who has been unfairly dismissed and seeks this remedy (see pages 211–14). Those who seek damages can be compensated for the direct and likely consequences of the breach, although nothing can be recovered for the mental stress, frustration or annoyance caused.[11]

At the time of writing industrial tribunals have no jurisdiction to hear ordinary breach of contract cases. The Courts and Legal Services Act 1990 establishes criteria for deciding where certain actions will normally be started, heard and enforced. For example, proceedings will normally be heard in the County Court if the value of the action is less than £25,000 and in the High Court if the value of the action is £50,000 or more. However, the appropriate Minister is empowered to make an order allowing claims to be brought before an industrial tribunal in respect of the following matters:

(i)   damages for breach of a contract of employment
(ii) a claim for a sum owed under such a contract
(iii) a claim for recovery of a sum in pursuance of any enactment relating to the terms or performance of such a contract

The Minister can also extend the types of claim that may be

brought to a tribunal or provide for exceptions to the tribunal's contractual jurisdiction. Similarly an order may specify the maximum amount of compensation that may be awarded by a tribunal in relation to a claim.[12]

Automatic termination: frustration

A contract is said to have been frustrated where events make it physically impossible or unlawful for the contract to be performed, or where there has been a change such as to radically alter the purpose of the contract. A contract which is still capable of being performed but becomes subject to an unforeseen risk is not frustrated.[13] As long as the frustrating event is not self-induced there is an automatic termination of the contract, *i.e.* there is no dismissal.[14] This being so it was not uncommon for an employer to resist a claim for unfair dismissal by alleging that the contract had been frustrated, *e.g.* on grounds of sickness. Although the EAT thought that the concept of frustration should normally only come into play where the contract is for a long term which cannot be determined by notice, the Court of Appeal has allowed this doctrine to be applied to a contract of employment determinable by short notice.[15]

The following principles are relevant to the application of the doctrine of frustration in the event of illness.[16] First, the courts must guard against too easy an application of the doctrine. Second, an attempt to decide the date that frustration occurred may help to decide whether it is a true frustration situation. Third, the factors below may help to decide the issue:

(i)   length of previous employment
(ii) how long the employment was expected to continue
(iii) the nature of the job
(iv) the nature, length and effect of the illness or disabling event
(v)   the employer's need for the work to be done and the need for a replacement employee
(vi) whether wages have continued to be paid
(vii) the acts and statements of the employer in relation to the employment. In *Hart v Marshall & Sons*[17] the EAT held

that the employer's acceptance of sick notes did not
prevent a tribunal finding that the contract had been
frustrated

(viii) whether in all the circumstances a reasonable employer
could have been expected to wait any longer

(ix) the terms of the contract as to sick pay, if any

(x) a consideration of the prospects of recovery.

A prison sentence is a potentially frustrating event but the
circumstances of each case have to be examined to discover
whether such a sentence has in fact operated to frustrate the
contract or whether its termination was due to some other cause.[18]

Termination without notice: summary dismissal

A summary dismissal occurs where the employer terminates the
contract of employment without notice. It must be distinguished
from an instant dismissal, which has no legal meaning but normally
refers to a dismissal without investigation or inquiry. Whereas an
instant dismissal is likely to be procedurally defective in unfair
dismissal terms (*see* chapter 12) a summary dismissal may be
lawful under both common law and statute.

In order to justify summary dismissal the employee must be in
breach of an important express or implied term of the contract,
i.e. be guilty of gross misconduct. Although certain terms are
always regarded as important, for example the duty not to steal
or damage the employer's property, the duty to obey lawful orders
and not to engage in industrial action, the significance of other
terms will depend on the nature of the employer's business and
the employee's position in it. Thus smoking may not normally be
viewed as an act of gross misconduct, but if it occurs at a gas-
bottling plant it is likely to be so regarded! If an employer feels
that a particular act or omission would warrant summary dismissal,
this fact should be communicated clearly to all employees.[19]

One consequence of the contractual approach is that everything
hinges upon the facts in the particular case and previous decisions
usually have little bearing. Nevertheless, a number of general
principles can be discerned. First, single acts of misconduct are
less likely to give rise to a right of summary dismissal than a

persistent pattern. Secondly, it is the nature of the act rather than its consequences which is relevant. Thirdly, an employer is more likely to be entitled to dismiss summarily for misconduct within the workplace than outside it. Fourthly, a refusal to obey instructions can still amount to repudiation even though the employee has mistakenly proceeded in the *bona fide* belief that the work which he or she had been instructed to do fell outside the scope of the contract.[20]

If employers do not invoke the right to end the contract within a reasonable period they will be taken to have waived their rights and can only seek damages. What is a reasonable period will depend on the facts of the particular case. In *Allders International v Parkins*[21] it was held that nine days was too long a period to be allowed to pass in relation to an allegation of stealing before deciding what to do about the alleged repudiatory conduct.

Prior to 1980 the balance of opinion seemed to be that a summary dismissal must be accepted even if it is unlawful, *i.e.* wrongful. However, in *Gunton v London Borough of Richmond*[22] the Court of Appeal decided that the general doctrine that repudiation by one party does not terminate a contract applies to employment law. Thus, it would now appear that an unlawful summary dismissal does not terminate a contract of employment until the employee has accepted the employer's repudiation and certain contractual rights and obligations will survive until that time, *e.g.* in relation to a disciplinary procedure. (*see* chapter 11 on the effective date of termination for *statutory* purposes). Nevertheless, in the absence of special circumstances a court will easily infer that the repudiation has been accepted. Finally, at common law an employer is not required to supply a reason for dismissal. However, this position has been modified by the operation of the unfair dismissal provisions and the statutory right of a pregnant employee or a worker with more than two years' continuous service to receive a written statement giving particulars of the reasons for dismissal (*see* chapter 12).[23]

Termination with notice

Usually either party is entitled to terminate a contract of employment by giving notice and once notice has been given it cannot be unilaterally withdrawn.[24] (Of course, an employer who makes a mistake could offer to re-employ.) The courts have consistently ruled that for notice to be effective it must be possible to ascertain the date of termination and not infrequently employees have confused an advanced warning of closure with notice of dismissal.[25] The length of the notice will be determined by the express or implied terms of the contract and, if no term can be identified, both parties are required to give a reasonable period of notice. What is reasonable will depend on the circumstances of the relationship, *e.g.* the employee's position and length of service. Thus in *Hill v C. A. Parsons & Co. Ltd*[26] a 63 year old engineer with 35 years' service was held to be entitled to at least six months' notice.

Apart from the situation where individuals are disentitled to notice by reason of their conduct,[27] section 49(1) EPCA 1978 provides that certain minimum periods of notice must be given. After a month's service an employee is entitled to a week's notice and this applies until the employment has lasted for two years. At this point two weeks' notice is owed and from then on the employee must receive an extra week's notice for each year of service up to a maximum of 12 weeks. According to section 49(2) EPCA 1978 an employee with a month's service or more need only give one week's notice to terminate, but there is nothing to prevent the parties agreeing that both should receive more than the statutory minimum.

Although the statute does not prevent an employee accepting a payment in lieu of notice, strictly speaking an employer must have contractual authority for insisting on such a payment. Without such authority a payment in lieu of notice will be construed as damages for the failure to provide proper notice. Thus a payment in lieu can properly terminate a contract of employment if the contract provides for such a payment or the parties agree that the employee will accept a payment in lieu, provided the payment relates to a period no shorter than that of the notice to which the employee would by entitled either under the contract of employment or section 49(1) EPCA 1978.[28] The date of termination at common law is the day notice expires or the day wages in lieu are accepted.

Except where the notice to be given by the employer is at

least one week more than the statutory minimum, an employee is entitled to be paid during the period of notice even if:

(i) no work is provided by the employer
(ii) the employee is incapable of work because of sickness or injury
(iii) the employee is absent from work wholly or partly because of pregnancy or childbirth
(iv) the employee is absent in accordance with the terms of his or her employment relating to holidays.[29]

Any payments by the employer by way of sick pay, maternity pay, holiday pay or otherwise go towards meeting this liability.[30] If employees take part in a strike after they have been given notice, payment is due for the period when they were not on strike. However, where employees give notice and then go on strike they do not qualify for any payment under the schedule.[31]

Remedies for wrongful dismissal

Basically a wrongful dismissal is a dismissal without notice or with inadequate notice in circumstances where proper notice should have been given. The expression also covers dismissals which are in breach of agreed procedures. Thus where there is a contractual disciplinary procedure, an employee may be able to obtain an injunction or declaration from the courts so as to prevent a dismissal, or declare a dismissal void if the procedure has not been followed.[32] However, an injunction will only be granted if the court is convinced that the employer's repudiation has not been accepted, that the employer has sufficient trust and confidence in the employee and that damages would not be an adequate remedy.[33]

Judicial review is available where an issue of public law is involved, although employment by a public authority does not by itself inject any element of public law.[34] Indeed, where an alternative remedy is available judicial review will only be exercised in exceptional circumstances. Factors to be taken into account in considering whether the circumstances are exceptional include: the speed of the alternative procedure, whether it was as convenient and whether the matter depended on some particular knowledge available to the appellate body.[35]

For the reason mentioned earlier the courts are reluctant to enforce a contract of employment, so in the vast majority of cases the employee's remedy will lie in damages for breach of contract. A person who suffers a wrongful dismissal is entitled to be compensated for such loss as arises naturally from the breach and for any loss which was reasonably foreseeable by the parties as being likely to arise from it. Hence an employee will normally recover only the amount of wages lost between the date of the wrongful dismissal and the date when the contract could lawfully have been terminated.[36] However, an employee may be compensated for loss suffered as a result of being deprived of a right to exercise options under a share option scheme.[37] Damages are not available for hurt feelings or the manner in which the dismissal took place even though the manner might have made it more difficult to obtain other employment.

Employees have a duty to mitigate their loss, which means in effect that they are obliged to look for another job. Any wages earned elsewhere during the notice period will be deducted from the amount the employer has to pay,[38] and where there is a failure to mitigate the court will deduct a sum which it feels the employee might reasonably have been expected to earn. As regards State benefits, it would appear that any benefit received by the dismissed employee should only be deducted where not to do so would result in a net gain to the employee.[39] Finally, the first £30,000 of damages is to be awarded net of tax but any amount above this figure will be awarded gross since it is taxable in the hands of the recipient.

Notes

1   *Alexander v STC Ltd* [1991] IRLR 286.
2   [1978] IRLR 343.
3   See *Sheet Metal Components Ltd v Plumridge* [1974] IRLR 86.
4   See *Rigby v Ferodo Ltd* [1987] IRLR 516.
5   See *Hollister v National Farmers' Union* [1979] IRLR 238.
6   See *Ticehurst v British Telecom* [1992] IRLR 219.
7   [1989] IRLR 279.
8   See *Robb v London Borough of Hammersmith* [1991] IRLR 72.

9 See *Hughes v London Borough of Southwark* [1988] IRLR 55.
10 Section 236 TULRCA 1992.
11 See *Bliss v South East Thames Regional Health Authority* [1985] IRLR 308.
12 Section 131 EPCA 1978 (as amended by TURERA 1993).
13 See *Converfoam Ltd v Bell* [1981] IRLR 195.
14 Where the employer dies or the business is destroyed a dismissal is deemed to occur for the purpose of safeguarding an employee's right to a redundancy payment: section 93(1) EPCA 1978.
15 See *Notcutt v Universal Equipment Ltd* [1986] 1 WLR 641.
16 See *Williams v Watson's Ltd* [1990] IRLR 164.
17 [1977] IRLR 61.
18 See *F. Shepherd Ltd v Jerrom* [1986] IRLR 358.
19 See ACAS *Code of Practice on Disciplinary Practice and Procedures in Employment* paragraph 8.
20 See *Blyth v Scottish Liberal Club* [1983] IRLR 245.
21 [1981] IRLR 68.
22 [1980] IRLR 321.
23 Section 53 EPCA 1978 (as amended).
24 See *Harris & Russell Ltd v Slingsby* [1973] IRLR 221.
25 See *ICL v Kennedy* [1981] IRLR 28.
26 [1971] 3 WLR 995.
27 See section 49(5) EPCA 1978.
28 *Ginsberg Ltd v Parker* [1988] IRLR 483.
29 Schedule 3 paragraph 2(1) EPCA 1978 (as amended).
30 Schedule 3 paragraph 2(2) EPCA 1978 (as amended).
31 Schedule 3 paragraph 6 EPCA 1978.
32 See *Jones v Gwent County Council* [1992] IRLR 521.
33 See *Dietman v London Borough of Brent* [1988] IRLR 299 and *Wall v STC Ltd* [1990] IRLR 55.
34 See *R v East Berkshire Health Authority ex parte Walsh* [1984] IRLR 278 and *McLaren v Home Office* [1990] IRLR 338.
35 See *R v Chief Constable of Merseyside Police ex parte Calveley* [1986] 2 WLR 144.
36 See *Marsh v National Autistic Society* [1993] ICR 453.
37 See *Chapman v Aberdeen Construction Group* [1991] IRLR 505 and *Micklefield v SAC Ltd* [1990] IRLR 218.
38 On the effect of payments received under an occupational pension scheme see *Hopkins v Norcross PLC* [1994] IRLR 18.
39 See *Westwood v Secretary of State* [1984] IRLR 209.

11 Unfair dismissal and redundancy rights (1)

Exclusions and qualifications

Unfair dismissal

Every employee has the right not to be unfairly dismissed[1] although there are a number of general exclusions and qualifications. Certain share fishers cannot lodge a complaint, but Crown employees are covered.[2] The right does not apply 'where under his contract of employment the employee ordinarily works outside Great Britain', but employees who work on oil rigs or off-shore installations in British territorial waters or areas designated under the Continental Shelf Act 1964 are not excluded.[3] In *Wilson v Maynard Shipbuilding*[4] the Court of Appeal rejected the notion that for these purposes an employee could work both ordinarily inside and outside Great Britain. They held that the issue could not be decided by looking at what actually happens alone. Tribunals must look at the terms of the contract and in the absence of special factors it is the country where the employee's base is that is likely to be the place where he or she is ordinarily working. Attention is focused on the contract subsisting at the time of the relevant dismissal. If under that contract the employee ordinarily worked in Great Britain he or she is not excluded even if under a preceding contract he or she ordinarily worked outside Great Britain within the period of two years prior to dismissal (*see* page 149 on the qualifying period).[5]

No claim can be made if on or before the effective date of termination (*see* pages 157–8) the individual had attained the normal retiring age for an employee in his or her position or was 65 years old.[6] However, there is no age limit if the reason or principal reason for dismissal is inadmissible (*see* pages 163–5).[7] In *Nothman v London Borough of Barnet*[8] the House of Lords ruled that there was one upper age limit per person and that the 65 years restriction only applied when there is no normal retiring age fixed by the contract of employment. 'Normal retirement age' is the age at which employees in a group[9] can reasonably expect to be compelled to retire unless there is some special reason in a particular case for a different age to apply. The contractual retirement age does not conclusively fix the normal retirement age. Where there is a contractual retirement age there is a presumption that that age is the normal retirement age, but this presumption can be rebutted by evidence that there is in practice some higher age at which employees are regularly retired and which they have reasonably come to regard as their normal retirement age. If the contractual retirement age is regularly departed from it is irrelevant that employment beyond that age was at management's discretion or that continued employment was subject to regular review.[10] Where there is evidence that employees retire at a variety of ages then there will be no normal retirement age and the statutory alternative applies. If there is no contractual retirement age, the correct approach is to consider whether there is evidence of a practice which establishes a normal retirement age.[11]

According to the Court of Appeal, in determining normal retirement age it is necessary to establish what, at the effective date of the termination of the employee's employment (*see* pages 157–8), and on the basis of the facts then known, was the age at which employees of all ages in the employee's position could reasonably regard as the normal retirement age applicable to the group.[12] Thus the expectation is that of the group as a whole and need not be the universal expectation of each and every member of it.[13] Finally, it should be noted that the normal retirement age must be a definite age rather than an age band.[14]

In order to complain of unfair dismissal two years' continuous service is required. Again, this qualification does not apply if the reason or principal reason for dismissal was inadmissible.[15] Two other exceptions should be noted. If an employee is dismissed rather than suspended on medical grounds (*see* chapter 8) only a month's service is required,[16] and where sex or race discrimination is being alleged no minimum period of service is needed because the case will be brought under the SDA 1975 or RRA 1976 rather than EPCA 1978. Continuity is to be calculated up to the effective date of termination in accordance with Schedule 13 EPCA 1978 (*see* chapter 15). However, employees who are wrongfully deprived of their statutory minimum entitlement to notice or receive a payment in lieu can add on that period of notice in ascertaining their length of service.[17] Longer contractual notice cannot be added and it should be remembered that employees who are guilty of gross misconduct forfeit their entitlement to notice.[18]

It is only possible to contract out of the unfair dismissal provisions in three ways. First, an employee will be excluded if a dismissal procedures agreement has been designated by the Secretary of State as exempting those covered by it. An application must be made jointly by all the parties to the agreement and the Secretary of State must be satisfied about the matters listed in section 65(2) EPCA 1978. Secondly, an agreement to refrain from presenting a complaint will be binding if it has been reached after the involvement of a conciliation officer or satisfies the conditions regulating 'compromise agreements' (*see* page 210).[19] Finally, section 54 EPCA 1978 does not apply to a dismissal under a fixed term contract for a year or more, where the dismissal consists only of the expiry of that term without it being renewed, if before the term expires the employee has agreed in writing to waive his or her right to claim.[20] Normally attention will focus solely on the period of the final contract. However, if this would produce an unreasonable result the Northern Ireland Court of Appeal has suggested that it would be permissible to enquire whether the employee's contract had been extended or renewed or whether there was a re-engagement under a new contract. Thus in *Mulrine v University of Ulster*[21] it was held that the waiver clause could be relied upon when the employee's appointment was extended for a period of four months beyond the original two-year term.

Redundancy payments

Employees who, at the relevant date, have two years' continuous service over the age of 18 qualify for a payment. Again, employees who were not given their statutory minimum entitlement to notice of dismissal are to be treated as if they had received it.[22] Certain categories are specifically excluded, for example public office holders, civil servants and certain National Health Service employees.[23] Also ineligible are employees who have reached the age of 65 (or a normal retirement age of less than 65) and those who ordinarily work outside Great Britain, unless on the 'relevant date' (*see* pages 157–8) the employee is in Great Britain in accordance with instructions given by the employer.[24] Additionally, if at, or within 90 weeks of the date of leaving employment an individual is entitled to pension rights which represent the equivalent of one third or more of leaving salary, the right to a redundancy is excluded.[25]

People employed under fixed term contracts for two years or more cannot claim if before the term expires they have agreed in writing to waive the right to do so.[26] Finally, an employer or employer organization and one or more trade unions may apply to the Secretary of State for exemption from the operation of the redundancy provisions so long as the conditions laid down in section 96 EPCA 1978 are fulfilled.

The meaning of dismissal

Unfair dismissal and redundancy payments

Apart from the lay-off and short-time provisions (*see* chapter 9) an employee is to be treated as dismissed if:[27]

(i)   the contract under which he or she is employed is terminated by the employer with or without notice, or
(ii) a fixed term contract expires without being renewed under the same contract, or
(iii) the employee terminates the contract with or without notice in circumstances such that he or she is entitled to terminate it without notice by reason of the employer's conduct.

For redundancy purposes section 93 EPCA 1978 provides that a contract is terminated by the employer's death unless the business is carried on by the personal representatives of the deceased.[28] Similarly, if the employee dies after being given notice of dismissal she or he is to be treated as dismissed.[29] Finally, a court order for the compulsory winding up of a company, the appointment of a receiver by a court and a major split in a partnership can all constitute a termination by the employer.

Where the contract is terminated by the employer with or without notice

It is vitally important not to confuse a warning of impending dismissal, for example through the announcement of a plant closure, with an individual notice to terminate.[30] For the giving of notice to constitute a dismissal at law the actual date of termination must be ascertainable. Where an employer has given notice to terminate, an employee who gives counter-notice indicating that he or she wishes to leave before the employer's notice has expired is still to be regarded as dismissed.[31] However, in the case of redundancy this counter-notice must be given within the 'obligatory period' of the employer's notice. This 'obligatory period' is the minimum period which the employer is required to give by virtue of section 49(1) EPCA 1978 (*see* chapter 10) or the contract of employment.[32] Before the counter-notice is due to expire the employer can write to the employee and ask for it to be withdrawn, stating that unless this is done liability to make a redundancy payment will be contested.[33] If employees do not accede to such a request a tribunal is empowered to determine whether they should receive the whole or part of the payment to which they would have been entitled. Tribunals decide what is just and equitable 'having regard to the reason for which the employee seeks to leave the employment and those for which the employer requires him to continue in it'.[34] Another possibility is that an employee leaves before the expiry of the employer's notice of termination for reasons of redundancy by mutual consent. This will not affect entitlement to a redundancy payment.[35]

A mutually agreed termination does not amount to a dismissal at law, although as a matter of policy tribunals will not find an agreement to terminate unless it is proved that the employee really did agree with full knowledge of the implications. Thus in *Hellyer Bros v Atkinson*[36] it was held that the employee was merely accepting the fact of his dismissal rather than agreeing to terminate his employment. Whether a mutual agreement is void because of duress is a matter for the industrial tribunal.[37] Moreover, where a provision for automatic termination is introduced by way of a variation to a subsisting contract it may be declared void if its effect is to exclude or limit the operation of EPCA 1978.[38] It is possible to have a mutual determination of a contract in a redundancy situation and in *Birch and Humber v University of Liver-*

pool[39] the Court of Appeal held that there was no dismissal when the employer accepted the employees' applications for premature retirement. However, where an employer seeks volunteers for redundancy those who are dismissed will be eligible for a payment despite their willingness to leave.[40]

Obviously if people resign of their own volition there is no dismissal at law, yet if pressure has been applied the situation will be different, *e.g.* where the employee is given the choice of resigning or being dismissed. However, an invitation to resign must not be too imprecise and in *Haseltine Lake & Co. v Dowler*[41] it was held that there was no dismissal when the employee was told that if he did not find a job elsewhere his employment would eventually be terminated. It would also appear that there is no dismissal when an employee resigns on terms offered by an employer's disciplinary sub-committee. In *Staffordshire County Council v Donovan*[42] the EAT stated:

> It seems to us that it would be most unfortunate if, in a situation where the parties are seeking to negotiate in the course of disciplinary proceedings and an agreed form of resignation is worked out by the parties, one of the parties should be able to say subsequently that the fact that the agreement was reached in the course of disciplinary proceedings entitles the employee thereafter to say that there was a dismissal.

Problems can arise in determining whether the words used by an employee can properly be regarded as amounting to a resignation. Normally where the words are unequivocal and are understood by the employer as a resignation it cannot be said that there was no resignation because a reasonable employer would not have so understood the words. However, exceptions will be made in the case of immature employees, decisions taken in the heat of the moment or under pressure exerted by an employer.[43] An objective test of whether the employee intended to resign applies only where the language used is ambiguous or where it is not plain how the employer understood the words. In *Southern v Franks Charlesly*[44] the Court of Appeal decided that the words 'I am resigning' were unambiguous and indicated a present intention of resigning. Equally doubts can arise in relation to expressions used by an employer and in *Tanner v Kean*[45] it was decided that the words 'You're finished with me' were merely spoken in annoyance and amounted to a reprimand rather than a dismissal. The EAT has advised tribunals that in deciding whether the employer's words constituted a dismissal in law they should consider all the circumstances of the case to determine whether the words were intended to bring the contract to an end.

Where a fixed term contract expires without being renewed under the same contract

Here 'fixed term' refers to a contract which has a defined beginning and a defined end. It is to be distinguished from a contract to complete a particular task which is discharged by performance when it is fulfilled[46] or a contract which ends on the occurrence of a specified event.[47] Nevertheless, if the duration of the task can be established with reasonable precision a court may hold that the contract was for a fixed term.[48] So long as it is for a specified period a fixed term contract exists even though it is terminable by notice within that period.[49]

The employee terminates the contract with or without notice in circumstances such that he or she is entitled to terminate it without notice by reason of the employer's conduct

This is commonly referred to as a 'constructive' dismissal, for in these circumstances the employer's behaviour constitutes a repudiation of the contract and the employee accepts that repudiation by resigning. Employees are only entitled to treat themselves as constructively dismissed if the employer is guilty of conduct which is a significant breach going to the root of the contract or which shows that the employer no longer intends to be bound by one or more of its essential terms. Whether the repudiatory conduct of a supervisor binds the employer depends on whether the acts were done in the course of the supervisor's employment.[50]

If employees continue for any length of time without leaving they will be regarded as having elected to affirm the contract and will lose the right to treat themselves as discharged.[51] However, provided that employees make clear their objection to what is being done they are not to be taken to have affirmed the contract by continuing to work and draw pay for a limited period of time, even if their purpose is merely to find another job.[52] Where the employer has allowed the employee time to make up his or her mind there is no need to expressly reserve the right to accept repudiation.[53] Even though a repudiatory breach of an express term has been waived it could still form part of a series of acts which cumulatively amounted to a breach of the employer's implied duty to show trust and confidence.[54] If there is merely a threat to repudiate, the employee is not to be treated as constructively dismissed unless there has been unequivocal acceptance of the repudiation before the threat is withdrawn.[55]

It is not necessary to show that the employer intended to repudiate the contract. The tribunal's function is to look at the employer's conduct as a whole and determine whether it is such that its cumulative effect judged reasonably and sensibly is such that the employee cannot reasonably be expected to tolerate it. The mere fact that a party to a contract takes a view of its construction which is ultimately shown to be wrong does not of itself constitute repudiatory conduct. It has to be shown that he or she did not intend to be bound by the contract as properly construed.[56] According to the Court of Appeal whether or not there is a fundamental breach of contract is a question of fact, so the EAT cannot substitute its decision for that of an industrial tribunal unless the latter misdirected itself in law or the decision was one which no reasonable tribunal could reach.[57]

A physical assault, demotion, or significant change in job duties or place of work can obviously amount to a constructive dismissal. In relation to the place of work, it is now established that even an express right to transfer may be subject to an implied right to reasonable notice, since employers must not exercise their discretion in such a way as to prevent employees from being able to carry out their part of the contract.[58] However, this does not mean that an employer repudiates a contract simply by introducing a general rule with which a particular employee is unable to comply, for example, a no-smoking policy.[59]

In *Millbrook Furnishing Ltd v McIntosh*[60] the EAT accepted that 'if an employer, under the stresses of the requirements of his business, directs an employee to transfer to other suitable work on a purely temporary basis and at no diminution in wages that may, in the ordinary case, not constitute a breach of contract'. Nevertheless, the EAT have also held that for a breach to go to the root of the contract it need not involve a substantial alteration to terms and conditions on a permanent basis. A substantial alteration is sufficient by itself.[61] As regards demotion, even where this is provided for within a disciplinary procedure it may amount to repudiation if it can be said that the punishment was grossly out of proportion to the offence.[62]

It is clear that an employer is not entitled to alter the formula whereby wages are calculated, but whether a unilateral reduction in additional pay or fringe benefits is of sufficient materiality as to entitle the employee to resign is a matter of degree.[63] Indeed, depending on the circumstances, a failure to pay the employee's salary on the due date might constitute a fundamental breach.[64] In *Gardner Ltd v Beresford*,[65] where the employee resigned because she had not received a pay increase for two years while others had, the EAT accepted that in most circumstances it would be reasonable to infer a term that the employer will not treat employees arbitrarily, capriciously or inequitably in the matter of remuneration. However, if a contract makes no reference at all to pay increases, it is impossible to say that there is an implied term that there will always be a pay rise.[66]

Many cases have been decided on the basis that the employer failed to display sufficient trust and confidence in the employee (*see* chapter 3). Thus unjustified accusations of theft, foul language or a refusal to act reasonably in dealing with matters of safety or incidents of harassment could all give rise to a claim of constructive dismissal. According to the EAT, whatever the respective actions of employer and employee at the time of termination, the relevant question is: who really terminated the contract? So when an employer falsely inveigled an employee to resign and take another job with the express purpose of avoiding liability for redundancy it was held that there was a dismissal at law.[67]

Finally, given the consequences of being found to have dismissed at law, it was to be expected that employers would seek to establish the notion of 'constructive resignation.' However, the Court of Appeal has refused to accept such a concept. Thus, if an employee acts in a manner which demonstrates that he or she no longer intends to be bound by the contract of employment, for example through lengthy unauthorized absence, the contract will only be regarded as terminated if the employer has expressly or impliedly accepted the repudiation.[68]

The effective and relevant date of termination

Whether a person is qualified to complain of unfair dismissal or has presented a claim within the prescribed time period (*see* chapter 14) must be answered by reference to the effective date of termination. Similarly, entitlement to a redundancy payment and the computation of it, together with the time limit for submitting a claim, all depend on ascertaining the 'relevant date' of dismissal. Thus, as a matter of policy, employers should ensure that there is no doubt as to what constitutes the effective or relevant date. Sections 55(4) and 90(1) EPCA 1978 provide that:

(i)   where the contract is terminated by notice the effective or relevant date is the date on which the notice expires even though the employee does not work out that notice.[69] Where the employee gives counter-notice, the effective date is when the employee ceased working in accordance with that notice.[70] If the employee has given counter-notice in accordance with section 85(2) EPCA 1978 the 'relevant date' is the date the counter-notice expires. However, once an employee has been given notice of redundancy, to take effect on a specified date, there is nothing to prevent the employer and employee altering that date by mutual agreement.[71] In *West v Kneels Ltd*[72] the EAT concluded that oral notice starts to run the day after it is given. Logically, the same should be true of notice in writing

(ii) where the contract is determined without notice the effective or relevant date is the date on which the termination takes effect.[73] Hence the date of termination of people dismissed with payments in lieu of notice is the date on which they are told they are dismissed.[74] According to the Court of Appeal, where an employee is summarily dismissed during the course of a working day, and no question arises as to whether that dismissal constitutes a repudiation which the employee has not accepted, both the contract of employment and the status of employee cease at the moment when the dismissal is communicated to the employee.[75] Where employees are given notice of dismissal and told to work it but the employer subsequently requires

them to leave immediately the effective or relevant date
is the date when they stop working[76]

(iii) where a fixed term contract expires without being renewed
under the same contract the effective or relevant date is
the date on which the term expires

(iv) where under the redundancy provisions a statutory trial
period has been served (*see* page 194), for the purpose of
submitting a claim in time the relevant date is the day that
the new or renewed contract terminated. This is to be
assessed in accordance with (i)-(iii) above.

It is worth noting that the form P45 has nothing to do with the
date on which employment terminates.[77]

Whether in a particular case the words of dismissal evince an
intention to terminate the contract at once or an intention only
to terminate it at a future date depends on the construction of
those words. Such construction should not be technical but reflect
what an ordinary reasonable employee would understand by the
language used. Moreover, words should be construed in the light
of the facts known to the employee at the time of notification.[78]
If the language used is ambiguous it is likely that tribunals will
apply the principle that words should be interpreted most strongly
against the person who uses them.[79] It should also be observed that
where a dismissal has been communicated by letter, the contract of
employment does not terminate until the employee has actually
read the letter or had a reasonable opportunity of reading it.[80]
What is the effective (or relevant) date where there is an appeal
against dismissal? According to the House of Lords, unless there
is a contractual provision to the contrary, the date of termination is to be ascertained in accordance with the above formula
and is not the date on which the employee was informed that his
or her appeal had failed.[81]

Notes

1   Section 54 EPCA 1978; see chapter 4 on who is an employee.
2   See sections 144(2) and 138 EPCA 1978 respectively. On the dismissal
    of local authority staff see model standing orders issued under section
    8 of the Local Government Housing Act 1989.

3   See section 141(2) EPCA 1978 and the Employment Protection
     (Offshore Employment) Order 1976.
4   [1977] IRLR 491. See also *Sonali Bank v Rahman* [1989] ICR 314.
5   See Schedule 13 paragraph 1(2) EPCA 1978 and *Weston v Vega Co-
     op Ltd* [1989] IRLR 429.
6   Section 64(1)b EPCA 1978. 'Position' is defined in section 153 EPCA
     1978 as meaning the following matters taken as a whole: status, the
     nature of the work and the terms and conditions of employment.
     See *Brooks v British Telecom* [1992] IRLR 67.
7   See section 64(3) EPCA 1978 and section 154 TULRCA 1992.
8   [1979] IRLR 35.
9   See *Barber v Thames TV* [1992] IRLR 410.
10   See *Whittle v MSC* [1987] IRLR 441.
11   See *Waite v GCHQ* [1983] IRLR 341.
12   See *Brooks v British Telecom* [1992] IRLR 67. On identifying the
     relevant group see *Barber v Thames TV* [1992] IRLR 410.
13   See *Barclays Bank PLC v O'Brien* [1993] ICR 347.
14   See *Swaine v HSE* [1986] IRLR 205.
15   See note 7 above.
16   Section 64(2) EPCA 1978.
17   Section 55(5–7) and paragraph 11(1) Schedule 13 EPCA 1978. See
     Staffordshire CC v Secretary of State [1989] IRLR 117.
18   See *Lanton Leisure Ltd v White* [1987] IRLR 119.
19   Section 140(2)d and 86 EPCA 1978 (as amended).
20   Section 142(1) EPCA 1978 (as amended).
21   [1993] IRLR 545.
22   Section 90(3) EPCA 1978.
23   See sections 99(1), 111, 138 EPCA 1978.
24   See sections 82(1) (as amended) and 141(3) EPCA 1978.
25   See section 98 EPCA 1978, Redundancy Payments Pensions Regu-
     lations 1965 SI No 1932 and *Royal Ordnance PLC v Pilkington* [1989]
     IRLR 489.
26   Section 142(2) EPCA 1978.
27   Sections 55(2) and 83(2) EPCA 1978. See *Mulrine v University of
     Ulster* (note 21 above).
28   See Schedule 12 Part 3 EPCA 1978.
29   See Schedule 12 Part 3 EPCA 1978.
30   See *Doble v Firestone Tyre* [1981] IRLR 300.
31   Section 55(3) EPCA 1978 and *Ready Case Ltd v Jackson* [1981]
     IRLR 312.
32   Section 85(1) (2) (5) EPCA 1978.
33   Section 85(3) EPCA 1978.
34   Section 85(4) EPCA 1978.
35   See *CPS Recruitment Ltd v Bowen* [1982] IRLR 54.
36   [1994] IRLR 88.
37   See *Logan Salton v Durham CC* [1989] IRLR 99.
38   See *Igbo v Johnson Matthey* [1986] IRLR 215 and ACAS Advisory
     Handbook *Discipline at Work*, page 44.

39 [1985] IRLR 165. See also *Scott v Coalite* [1988] IRLR 131.
40 *Burton v Peck* [1975] IRLR 87.
41 [1981] IRLR 25.
42 [1981] IRLR 108. See also *Logan Salton v Durham CC* (note 37 above).
43 See *Kwik-fit v Lineham* [1992] IRLR 156.
44 [1981] IRLR 278.
45 [1978] IRLR 110.
46 See *Ironmonger v Movefield* [1988] IRLR 461.
47 See *Brown v Knowsley BC* [1986] IRLR 102.
48 See *Wiltshire County Council v NATFHE and Guy* [1980] IRLR 198.
49 See *Dixon v BBC* [1979] IRLR 114.
50 See *Hilton Hotels v Protopapa* [1990] IRLR 316.
51 See *Wilton v Cornwall Health Authority* [1993] IRLR 482.
52 See *Cox Toner Ltd v Crook* [1981] IRLR 443.
53 See *Bliss v South East Thames Regional Health Authority* [1985] IRLR 308.
54 See *Lewis v Motorworld Garages* [1985] IRLR 465.
55 See *Harrison v Norwest Holst* [1985] IRLR 240.
56 See *Brown v JBD Engineering Ltd* [1993] IRLR 568.
57 See *Martin v MBS Fastenings* [1983] IRLR 198.
58 See *White v Reflecting Roadstuds* [1991] IRLR 332.
59 See *Dryden v Greater Glasgow Health Board* [1992] IRLR 469.
60 [1981] IRLR 309.
61 See *McNeil v Crimin Ltd* [1984] IRLR 179.
62 See *Cawley v South Wales Electricity Board* [1985] IRLR 89.
63 See *Gillies v R. Daniels & Co.* [1979] IRLR 457.
64 See *Adams v C. Zub Ltd* [1978] IRLR 551.
65 [1978] IRLR 63.
66 See *Murco Petroleum v Forge* [1987] IRLR 50.
67 See *Caledonian Mining Ltd v Bassett* [1987] IRLR 165.
68 *London Transport Executive v Clarke* [1981] IRLR 166.
69 See *TBA Industrial Products Ltd v Morland* [1982] IRLR 331.
70 See *Thompson v GEC Avionics* [1991] IRLR 448.
71 see *Mowlem Ltd v Watson* [1990] IRLR 500.
72 [1986] IRLR 430.
73 This principle was applied to a constructive dismissal in *BMK Ltd v Logue* [1993] ICR 601.
74 See *R. Cort & Son Ltd v Charman* [1981] IRLR 437.
75 See *Octavius Atkinson Ltd v Morris* [1989] IRLR 158.
76 See *Stapp v Shaftesbury Society* [1982] IRLR 326.
77 See *Leech v Preston BC* [1985] IRLR 337.
78 See *London Borough of Newham v Ward* [1985] IRLR 509.
79 See *Chapman v Letheby & Christopher Ltd* [1981] IRLR 440.
80 See *Brown v Southall & Knight* [1980] IRLR 130.
81 See *West Midlands Co-op Ltd v Tipton* [1986] IRLR 112.

12 Unfair dismissal and redundancy rights (2)

Giving a reason for dismissal

Once employees have proved that they were dismissed, the burden shifts to the employer to show the reason, or, if there was more than one, the principal reason, for the dismissal and that it falls within one of the following categories:[1]

(i)   it related to the capacity or qualifications of the employee for performing work of the kind which he or she was employed to do

(ii) it related to the conduct of the employee

(iii) the employee was redundant

(iv) the employee could not continue to work in the position held without contravention, either on the employee's part or that of the employer, of a duty or restriction imposed by or under a statute

(v)   there was some other substantial reason of such a kind as to justify the dismissal of an employee holding the position which the employee held.[2]

Several points need to be made at this stage. First, where no reason is given by the employer a dismissal will be unfair simply because the statutory burden has not been discharged. Equally, if a reason is engineered in order to effect dismissal because the real reason would not be acceptable, the employer will fail because the underlying principal reason is not within section 57(1) or (2).[3] Secondly, the fact that an employer has used a wrong label is not necessarily fatal, for it is the tribunal's task to discover what reason actually motivated the employer at the time of dismissal. That the correct approach is the subjective one has been confirmed by the Court of Appeal: 'A reason for the dismissal of an employee is a set of facts known to the employer, or it may be of beliefs

161

held by him which causes him to dismiss the employee'.[4] Subsequently the Court of Appeal has been prepared to attribute a reason for dismissal even where the employers had argued throughout the case that they had not dismissed but the employee had resigned.[5] Thirdly, the reason for dismissal must have existed and been known to the employer at the time of dismissal, which makes it impossible, for example, to rely on subsequently discovered misconduct.[6] Equally, an employer cannot justify a dismissal by a reason that was not the reason for the original dismissal but was the reason for which it was confirmed by an internal appeal.[7] Fourthly, section 63 EPCA 1978 provides that in determining the reason for dismissal, or whether it was sufficient to dismiss, a tribunal cannot take account of any pressure, in the form of industrial action or a threat of it, which was exercised on the employer to secure the employee's dismissal. It is not necessary that those exerting the pressure explicitly sought the dismissal of the employee, the test is whether it could be foreseen that the pressure would be likely to result in dismissal.[8]

According to section 53 EPCA 1978 (as amended) a person who has been continuously employed for two years[9] and has been dismissed or is under notice of dismissal has the right to be supplied with a written statement giving particulars of the reasons for dismissal. The employer must provide the statement within 14 days of a specific request being made. In *Gilham v Kent County Council*[10] the Court of Appeal held that the council had responded adequately by referring the employee's legal representative to two previous letters in which the reasons for dismissal were fully set out, enclosing copies of those letters and stating that their contents contained the reasons for dismissal. A claim may be presented to an industrial tribunal on the ground that the employer unreasonably failed to provide such a statement or that the particulars given were inadequate or untrue. However, section 53 merely obliges employers to indicate truthfully the reasons they were relying on when they dismissed. Only if an unfair dismissal claim is brought will a tribunal have to examine whether the reasons given justify dismissal.[11] The same time limit applies as for unfair dismissal claims (*see* chapter 14).

The test for determining the reasonableness of an employer's failure is objective. Thus, where the employer maintains that there was no dismissal in law but the tribunal finds that there was, it must then decide whether there was an unreasonable failure to supply a statement.[13] If the complaint is well founded a tribunal may make a declaration as to what it finds the employer's reasons were for dismissing and must order that the employee receive two weeks' pay from the employer. Perhaps the most important aspect of this section is that such a statement is admissible in evidence in any proceedings. This means that an employee who detects any inconsistency between the particulars given and the reasons offered as a defence to an unfair dismissal claim, *e.g.* on the employer's 'notice of appearance', can exploit the situation to the full.

Automatically unfair dismissal

In certain circumstances a dismissal will be unfair because the reason for it was 'inadmissible'. Thus a dismissal will be automatically unfair if the reason for it related to any of the following:

(i)   the assertion of a statutory right (*see* below)
(ii) trade union membership or activities, or non-union membership (*see* chapter 18).
(iii) pregnancy or maternity (*see* page 85), or
(iv) certain health and safety grounds (*see* below).

Additionally, if an inadmissible reason was used to select a person for redundancy, or if a person was selected in contravention of a customary arrangement or agreed procedure and there were no special reasons justifying a departure from that arrangement or procedure, then dismissal will also be unfair (*see* pages 176–7).[14]

As regards the assertion of statutory rights, employees are protected if they have brought proceedings against the employer to enforce a 'relevant' statutory right or have alleged that the employer has infringed such a right. The 'relevant' statutory rights are:

(i)   any right conferred by EPCA 1978 or the Wages Act 1986 which may be the subject of a complaint to an industrial tribunal
(ii) minimum notice rights under section 49 EPCA 1978
(iii) certain rights relating to the unlawful deduction of union

contributions from pay, action short of dismissal on union membership grounds, and time off for union duties and activities.

It should be noted that employees are protected irrespective of whether they qualify for the right that has been asserted or whether the right was actually infringed. All that has to be demonstrated is that the employee's claim was made in good faith.[15]

In relation to health and safety, section 57A EPCA 1978 provides that a dismissal is unfair if the reason for it was that the employee:

(i)   carried out, or proposed to carry out, activities designated by the employer in connection with preventing or reducing risks to the health and safety of employees

(ii)   performed, or proposed to perform, any of his or her functions as a safety representative or a member of a safety committee

(iii) brought to the employer's attention, by reasonable means, circumstances connected with his or her work which he or she reasonably believed were harmful or potentially harmful to health and safety

(iv)   left or proposed to leave, or refused to return to (while the danger persisted), his or her place of work or any dangerous part of the workplace, in circumstances of danger which he or she reasonably believed to be serious and imminent

(v)   took, or proposed to take, appropriate steps to protect himself or herself or other persons, in circumstances of danger which he or she reasonably believed to be serious and imminent. Whether those steps were 'appropriate' must be judged by reference to all the circumstances, including the employee's knowledge and the facilities and advice available at the time. A dismissal will not be regarded as unfair if the employer can show that it was, or would have been, so negligent for the employee to take the steps which he or she took, or proposed to take, that a reasonable employer might have dismissed on these grounds.

According to Regulation 8 (1) and (2) of the Transfer Regulations where there is a relevant transfer (*see* pages 201–2) if the transfer 'or a reason connected with it' is the reason or principal reason for dismissal then the dismissal is to be treated as unfair, unless there is an 'economic, technical or organizational reason entailing changes in the workforce'. In this context an 'economic' reason must be one which relates to the conduct of the business.[16] Thus the desire to obtain an enhanced price or achieve a sale are not in themselves acceptable reasons for dismissal. As regards the phrase 'entailing changes in the workforce' it is worth referring to the case of *Berriman v Delabole Slate*.[17] Here the employee resigned following the acquisition of the company in which he was employed because the new owners sought to reduce his guaranteed wage so that he would be engaged on the same basis as their existing staff. The Court of Appeal held that it must be an objective of the employer's plan to achieve changes in the workforce not just a possible consequence of it.[18] Changes in the identity of the individuals who make up the workforce do not constitute changes in the workforce itself so long as the overall number and functions of the employees looked at as a whole remain unchanged. Thus there may be a change in the workforce if the same people are kept on but they are given entirely different jobs to do.[19] Even if the dismissal is for an 'economic, etc. . . . reason entailing changes in the workforce' it must still pass the test of reasonableness under section 57(3) EPCA 1978.[20]

Both the SDA 1975 and the RRA 1976 stipulate that it is unlawful to discriminate on the prohibited grounds by way of dismissal (*see* chapter 5). In addition, the Rehabilitation of Offenders Act 1974 states that 'a conviction which has become spent . . . shall not be a proper ground for dismissing'.[21] Finally, section 9(5) of the Disabled Persons (Employment) Act 1944 provides that an employer must not discontinue the employment of a registered disabled person unless there is 'reasonable cause for doing so' if as a result the number of registered disabled persons would fall below the statutory quota (*see* page 53).

Industrial action and lack of jurisdiction

Official action

Where at the date of dismissal the employee was locked out or taking part in a strike or other industrial action, a tribunal cannot determine whether the dismissal was fair or unfair unless it is shown that one or more 'relevant employees' of the same employer have not been dismissed or that, within three months of the complainant's dismissal, any such employee has been offered re-engagement and the complainant has not. For the purposes of determining whether 'relevant employees' have not been dismissed, the word 'employees' must be interpreted as excluding persons who at the relevant date have retired or resigned voluntarily.[22] The phrase 'unless it is shown' requires a complainant to demonstrate that at least one employee of the same employer has not been dismissed by the time the tribunal hearing is concluded.[23] Thus dismissals during the course of a hearing could deprive the tribunal of jurisdiction! According to the EAT there is no selectivity where an employee is offered re-engagement within three months of the date of dismissal, even if other employees are re-engaged at an earlier date.[24] If no re-engagement was offered the employer has to show the reason or principal reason for not re-engaging rather than for dismissal.[25]

According to the EAT, for there to be an offer of re-engagement the employer must have actual knowledge of the first job and the reason for dismissal, or the means of obtaining knowledge of the fact that what is being offered is re-engagement within the meaning of section 238 TULRCA 1992. Thus in *Bigham v GKN Ltd*[26] an industrial tribunal erred in finding that the re-engagement of an employee dismissed when taking part in a strike at a different site was not an effective re-engagement for these purposes because it came about by mistake. Nevertheless, if a job application involved fraud any offer of re-engagement (or contract of employment) would be rendered void. Finally, it is worth noting that a general advertising campaign offering employment to those who apply does not in itself constitute an offer of employment to a particular individual.[27]

'Relevant employees' means, in relation to a lock-out, 'employees who were directly interested in the dispute in contemplation of furtherance of which the lock-out occurred' and, in relation to a strike or other industrial action, 'those employees at the establishment who were taking part in the action at the complainant's date of dismissal'. It is clear from the language of the statute that the test of who were 'relevant employees' is a retrospective one.[28] In this context 'establishment' refers to the 'establishment of the employer at or from which the complainant works', and the 'date of dismissal' means either the date on which the employer's notice was given or, if the contract was not terminated by notice, the effective date of termination.[29]

Thus employers can retain the services of employees who have returned to work while dismissing those who are still on strike. Only those employees who were still on strike when the complainant was dismissed form the constituency amongst whom there must be no selectivity, and three months after the date of dismissal an employer can re-engage former employees who were dismissed for industrial action without facing a claim from anyone who was not re-engaged. In *Hindle Gears Ltd v McGinty*[30] the EAT decided that two employees who had returned to work while dismissal letters were in the post and who were unaware of their existence had not been dismissed in law. Thus their acceptance back for duty by the employer did not operate as a re-engagement conferring jurisdiction on the tribunal. If an industrial tribunal does have jurisdiction to hear a complaint employers will have to give a reason for their selection. For example, it might be argued that as a result of the industrial action fewer jobs were available and the complainant had a comparatively poor work record.

The phrase 'strike or other industrial action' is not defined for these purposes, although the threat of taking industrial action does not of itself amount to industrial action.[31] The meaning of 'other industrial action' is not restricted to action in breach of contract and these words will cover a refusal to do something used as a bargaining weapon. However, if there is no contractual obligation to perform, for example overtime, a refusal will not constitute industrial action if it is because of a private commitment or personal preference.[32] Whether employees are taking part in industrial action must be determined as an objective fact and not by reference to what the employer knew or whether the employer acted properly in trying to collect information on the subject.[33] The fact that employees are in breach of their duty to attend work is relevant to the question of whether they are taking part in a strike but it is not an essential ingredient. Thus employees who are off sick or on holiday could be held to be taking part in a strike if they associated themselves with it, for example by attending a picket line.[34] By way of contrast, if sick employees merely wish their colleagues well, this may be regarded as supportive but would not amount to 'taking part' in industrial action.[35]

Although there is no statutory definition of a lock-out, dictionary definitions suggest that it means an employer's refusal to provide employees with work, except on conditions which have to be accepted by the workforce collectively.[36] According to the EAT, if an employer does no more than insist that his employees should abide by their existing terms and conditions of employment if they are to return to work, that does not constitute a lock-out.[37]

An offer of re-engagement refers to an offer (made either by the employer, a successor or an associated employer) to re-engage either 'in the job which he held immediately before the date of dismissal, or in a different job which would be reasonably suitable in his case'.[38] In *Williams v National Theatre*[39] it was decided that treating employees who had been on strike as having received a second warning nevertheless constituted an offer to re-engage in the same job. However a job may have conditions attached to it which are so disadvantageous compared to the position before the dismissal that it cannot realistically be suggested that the employee is being offered re-employment.

Unofficial action

By virtue of section 237 TULRCA 1992 employees cannot complain of unfair dismissal if at the time of dismissal they were taking part in an unofficial strike or other unofficial industrial action. For these purposes, a strike or other industrial action will be treated as unofficial unless the employee:

(i)   is a union member and the action is authorized or endorsed by that union, or

(ii) is not a union member but there are among those taking part in the industrial action members of a union by which the action has been authorized or endorsed within the meaning of section 20(2) TULRCA 1992 (*see* page 300)

A strike or other industrial action will not be regarded as unofficial if none of those taking part in it is a union member. However, employees who were union members when they began to take industrial action will continue to be treated as such even if they have subsequently ceased to be union members.[40]

Section 237(4) provides that the issue of whether or not the action is unofficial is to be determined by reference to the facts at the time of the dismissal. Nevertheless, where the action is repudiated in accordance with section 21 TULRCA 1992 (*see* page 301), the industrial action is not to be treated as unofficial before the end of the next working day after the repudiation has taken place. On the absence of statutory immunity for acts in support of those dismissed for taking unofficial action *see* page 297.

Potentially fair reasons for dismissal

Capability or qualifications

According to section 57(4) EPCA 1978 'capability' is to be assessed by reference to 'skill, aptitude, health or any other physical or mental quality', and it has been held that an employee's inflexibility or lack of adaptability came within his or her aptitude and mental qualities.[41] 'Qualifications' means 'any degree, diploma, or other academic, technical or professional qualification relevant to the position which the employee held'. In *Blue Star Ltd v Williams*,[42] it was held that a mere licence, permit or authorization is not such a qualification unless it is substantially concerned with the aptitude or ability of the person to do the job. For our purposes it is convenient to consider capability in terms of competence and ill health.

Competence
The ACAS Advisory Handbook *Discipline at Work* recommends that the following principles should be observed when employment commences:[43]

(i)   the standard of work required should be explained and employees left in no doubt about what is expected of them. Special attention should be paid to ensuring that standards are understood by employees whose English is limited and by young persons with little experience of working life

(ii)   where job descriptions are prepared they should accurately convey the main purpose and scope of each job and the tasks involved

(iii) employees should be made aware of the conditions which attach to any probation period

(iv) the consequences of any failure to meet the required standards should be explained

(v)   where an employee is promoted, the consequences of failing to 'make the grade' in the new job should be explained.

It almost goes without saying that proper training and supervision are essential to the achievement of satisfactory performance and that performance should be discussed regularly with employees.[44] Measures should be taken to ensure that inadequate performance is identified as soon as possible so that remedial action can be taken. In all cases, the cause of poor performance should be investigated and ACAS suggest the following guidelines to ensure that appropriate action is taken:[45]

(i)   the employee should be asked for an explanation and the explanation checked

(ii)   where the reason is a lack of the required skills, the employee should, wherever practicable, be assisted through training and given reasonable time to reach the required standard of performance

(iii) where despite encouragement and assistance the employee is unable to reach the required standard of performance, consideration should be given to finding suitable alternative work

(iv) where alternative work is not available, the position should be explained to the employee before dismissal action is taken

(v)   an employee should not normally be dismissed because of poor performance unless warnings and a chance to improve have been given

(vi) if the main cause of poor performance is the changing nature of the job, employers should consider whether the situation may properly be treated as a redundancy matter rather than a capability or conduct issue.

Finally, it is important to distinguish cases of sheer incapability owing to an inherent incapacity to function from those where there is a failure to exercise to the full such talent as is possessed. According to the EAT, cases where people have not come up to standard through their own carelessness, negligence or idleness are much more appropriately dealt with as cases of misconduct than of incapability.[46]

Ill health
It must be emphasized at the outset that the decision to dismiss is not a medical one but a matter to be determined by the employer in the light of the medical evidence available. The basic question is whether in all the circumstances the employer could have been expected to wait any longer for the employee to recover, and the factors taken into account in deciding whether a contract has been frustrated will be relevant here (*see* pages 141–2).

Where an employee is absent owing to long term illness the ACAS Advisory Handbook recommends that the following procedure be invoked:[47]

(i)   the employee should be contacted periodically and in turn should maintain regular contact with the employer[48]
(ii)   the employee should be kept fully informed if employment is at risk
(iii) the employee's GP should be asked when a return to work is expected and what type of work the employee will be capable of
(iv)   on the basis of the GP's report the employer should consider whether alternative work is available
(v)   the employer is not expected to create a special job for the employee concerned, nor to be a medical expert, but to take action on the basis of the medical evidence
(vi)   where there is reasonable doubt about the nature of the illness or injury, the employee should be asked if he or she would agree to be examined by a doctor to be appointed by the company
(vii) where an employee refuses to co-operate in providing medical evidence or to undergo an independent medical examination, the employee should be told in writing that

a decision will be taken on the basis of the information
available and that it could result in dismissal

(viii)   where the employee is allergic to a product used in the
workplace, the employer should consider remedial action or
a transfer to alternative work

(ix)   where the employee's job can no longer be kept open and
no suitable alternative work is available, the employee
should be informed of the likelihood of dismissal

(x)   where dismissal action is taken, the employee should be
given the period of notice to which he or she is entitled
and informed of any right of appeal.

In cases of intermittent absences owing to ill health, there is no
obligation on an employer to call medical evidence. According to
the EAT, an employer has to have regard to the whole history of
employment and to take into account a range of factors including:
the nature of the illness and the likelihood of its recurrence; the
lengths of absences compared with the intervals of good health;
the employer's need for that particular employee; the impact
of the absences on the rest of the workforce and the extent to
which the employee was made aware of his or her position. There
is no principle that the mere fact that the employee is fit at the
time of dismissal makes that dismissal unfair.[49]

In deciding whether an employer acted fairly in dismissing,
tribunals must determine as a matter of fact what consultation, if
any, was necessary or desirable in the known circumstances; what
consultation took place; and whether that consultation process
was adequate in the circumstances.[50] Thus, in *Elipse Blinds v
Wright*[51] the Court of Appeal ruled that it was not unfair to dismiss
without consultation where the employer was genuinely concerned
about giving the employee information about her health of which
she seemed unaware.

Three further points need to be made. First, an employee's
incapability need only 'relate to' the performance of contractual
duties; there is no requirement to show that the performance of
all those duties has been affected.[52] Second, although employees
who are sick will hope to remain employed at least until their
contractual sick pay entitlement (if any) is exhausted, this does
not mean that a person cannot be dismissed before the period of
sick pay has elapsed (*see* pages 122–3 on avoiding liability for

SSP). Equally, it will be unfair to dismiss simply because the sick pay period has expired. Finally, people who are registered as disabled are entitled to special consideration.[53]

Conduct

It is the function of tribunals to decide not whether misconduct is gross or criminal but whether the employer has, in the circumstances of the case, acted reasonably in dismissing. There is no necessary inference that, because an employee is guilty of gross misconduct in relation to his or her actual employment, they must necessarily be considered unsuitable for any employment whatsoever.[54] Clearly there will be cases where the misconduct is sufficiently serious that an employee can be dismissed without warning, and paragraph 8 of the ACAS *Code of Practice on Disciplinary Practice and Procedures in Employment* (1977) advocates that employees should be given 'a clear indication of the type of conduct which may warrant summary dismissal'. According to the EAT, disciplinary rules which contain a catalogue of offences that carry the potential sanction of dismissal may be useful in assessing the quality of the offence, but it does not follow that misconduct which does not fall within it can never merit dismissal. However, if employees are required to report the misdemeanours of colleagues it has been suggested that such a rule should be clearly spelt out.[55]

Fighting is an example of an area where it is not necessary to state that such behaviour will be regarded very gravely, since the courts have decided that whether or not to dismiss for this reason is essentially a matter for the employer. The test is what would be the reaction of a reasonable employer in the circumstances. Thus, if without proper inquiry an employer implements a policy of dismissing any employee who struck another there could be a finding of unfairness.[56] Similarly, false clocking or claims in respect of hours done are serious offences which can justify dismissal without a warning if the employer has had due regard to all the circumstances.[57]

As a general rule, if an order is lawful a refusal to obey it will be a breach of contract and amount to misconduct even though similar refusals have been condoned in the past. Nevertheless, in disobedience cases the primary factor to be considered is whether the employee is acting reasonably in refusing to carry out an instruction.[58] Acknowledging that employers are obliged to issue instructions in order to ensure compliance with health and safety legislation, tribunals have readily accepted that non-compliance with safety rules or procedures constitute sufficient grounds for dismissal. The intention to set up in competition with the employer is not in itself a breach of the implied duty of loyalty. Unless the employer has reasonable grounds for believing that the employee has done or is about to do some wrongful act, dismissal will not be justified.[59] Thus in *Marshall v Industrial Systems Ltd*[60] the EAT held that it was reasonable to dismiss a managing director after discovering that, with another manager, he was planning to set up in competition and take away the business of their best client, and that he tried to induce another key employee to join them in that venture.

Theft of an employer's property will amount to a fair reason for dismissal; far more difficult to handle are cases of *suspected* dishonesty. The Court of Appeal has approved of the approach taken to this delicate matter in *British Home Stores v Burchell*,[61] where it was stated that tribunals had to decide whether the employer entertained a reasonable suspicion amounting to a belief in the guilt of the employee at that time. There are three elements to this:

(i)   the employer must establish the fact of that belief
(ii) the employer must show that there were reasonable grounds upon which to sustain that belief
(iii) at the stage at which the belief was formed the employer must have carried out as much investigation into the matter as was reasonable in the circumstances.

Thus the question to be determined is not whether, by an objective standard, the employer's belief that the employee was guilty of the misconduct was well founded but whether the employer believed that the employee was guilty and was entitled so to believe having regard to the investigation conducted.[62] If these requirements are met it is irrelevant that the employee is acquitted of criminal charges or that they are dropped.

Where there is a reasonable suspicion that one or more employees within a group have acted dishonestly, it is not necessary for the employer to identify which of them acted dishonestly.[63]

Thus provided certain conditions are satisfied, an employer who cannot identify which member of a group was responsible for an act can fairly dismiss the whole group, even where it is probable that not all were guilty of the act. These conditions are:

(i) the act must be such that, if committed by an identified individual it would justify dismissal

(ii) the employer had made a sufficiently thorough investigation with appropriate procedures

(iii) as a result of that investigation the employer reasonably believed that more than one person could have committed the act

(iv) the employer had acted reasonably in identifying the group of employees who could have committed the act and each member of the group was individually capable of doing so

(v) as between the members of the group the employer could not reasonably identify the individual perpetrator.

The fact that one or more of the group is not dismissed does not necessarily render the dismissal of the remainder unfair, provided the employer is able to show solid and sensible grounds for differentiating between members of the group.[64]

In certain cases it will be reasonable to rely on the results of extensive police investigation rather than carry out independent inquiries.[65] Similarly where an employee admits dishonesty, there is little scope for the kind of investigation referred to in *Burchell's* case. Where the probability of guilt is less apparent the safer course may be to suspend pending the outcome of any criminal proceedings. Whether a conviction forms an adequate basis for dismissal will depend to some extent on the nature of the crime. Clearly there may be cases where the offence is trivial and dismissal would be unreasonable.[66]

The fact that employees have been charged with a criminal offence does not prevent the employer communicating with them or their representatives to discuss the matter. What needs to be discussed is not so much the alleged offence as the action which the employer is proposing to take. If the employee chooses not to give a statement to the employer, the latter is entitled to consider whether the evidence available is strong enough to justify dismissal.[67] However, it will not always be wrong to dismiss before a belief in guilt has been established, because involvement in an alleged criminal offence often involves a serious breach of duty or discipline, quite apart from the guilt. For example, a cashier charged with a till offence may well have ignored the proper till procedure.

In the context of unfair dismissal, conduct means actions of such a nature, whether done in the course of employment or outside, that reflect in some way on the employer/employee relationship.[68] Thus it may cover the wilful concealment of convictions which are not 'spent', criminal offences outside employment, such as stealing or gross indecency, or even 'moonlighting'. Finally, in an appropriate case it may be unfair to dismiss without first considering whether the employee could be offered some other job.[69]

Redundancy

It is possible for a dismissed employee to claim both a redundancy payment and unfair dismissal, although double compensation cannot be obtained.[70] For unfair dismissal purposes the statutory presumption of redundancy does not apply, so it is up to the employer to establish this as the reason, or principal reason, for dismissal. However, tribunals will not investigate the background which led to the redundancy or require the employer to justify redundancies in economic terms. According to the Court of Appeal the correct test for redundancy is whether there has been a diminution in the employer's need for the kind of work which the employee was employed to do, under his or her contract, rather than in the need for the kind of work the employee was actually doing at the time of dismissal.[71] Thus employers are obliged to look for vacancies within the scope of the contract before dismissing an employee on grounds of redundancy.

As mentioned earlier, a dismissal on grounds of redundancy will be unfair if it is shown that 'the circumstances constituting the redundancy applied equally to one or more other employees in the same undertaking who held positions similar' and either the reason, or principal reason, for which the employee was selected was inadmissible (*see* page 163), or the employee was selected for dismissal in contravention of a customary arrangement or agreed procedure, and there were no special reasons justifying a departure in the particular case.[72] To fall within section 59 a customary arrangement must relate directly to the actual selection of an employee for redundancy. A more structured scheme than a mere call for volunteers is required.[73] In addition, a customary arrangement must be sufficiently certain, *i.e.* it must be possible to deduce from the evidence a comprehensible definition of what is ordinarily done when selections are made.[74]

Agreed procedures can be express or implied[75] and may provide for selection on a variety of grounds including, for example, disciplinary record or seniority. As regards seniority, 'last in, first out' (LIFO) is frequently adopted, but it is assumed to be based on periods of continuous rather than cumulative service.[76] Arguably this form of selection indirectly discriminates against women and needs to be justified (*see* page 57).[77] A procedure which required part-timers to be dismissed first has already been the subject of a successful action under the SDA 1975 (*see* chapter 5).[78] Where it is argued that there were special reasons justifying a departure from the agreed procedure the employer will have to prove what those reasons were. In *Cross International v Reid*[79] the Court of Appeal held that a serious downturn in trade caused by the loss of a valuable contract did not justify a departure from a LIFO procedure. However, in *Robinson v Ulster Carpet Mills*[80] the Northern Ireland Court of Appeal were satisfied that the employer's desire to avoid religious discrimination constituted a special reason justifying departure from an agreed service-based procedure.

Since section 59 EPCA 1978 is concerned purely with selection on impermissible grounds, a failure to comply with a procedural requirement to consult trade unions and to consider volunteers will not be automatically unfair.[81] Nevertheless section 57(3) EPCA 1978 can still have a considerable impact on dismissals for redundancy, a point which has been emphasized by the decision in *Williams v Compair Maxam*.[82] In this case it was held that it is not enough to show that it was reasonable to dismiss *an* employee, a tribunal must be satisfied that the employer acted reasonably in treating redundancy as 'sufficient reason for dismissing *the* employee'.

According to the EAT, where employees are represented by a recognized independent trade union reasonable employers will seek to act in accordance with the following principles:

(i) The employer will seek to give as much warning as possible of impending redundancies so as to enable the union and employees who may be affected to take early steps to inform themselves of the relevant facts, consider possible alternative solutions, and, if necessary, find alternative employment in the undertaking or elsewhere.

(ii) The employer will consult the union as to the best means by which the desired management result can be achieved fairly and with as little hardship to the employees as possible.[83] In particular, the employer will seek to agree with the union the criteria to be applied in selecting the employees to be made redundant.[84] When a selection has been made the employer will consider with the union whether the selection has been made in accordance with those criteria.

(iii) Whether or not an agreement as to the criteria to be adopted has been agreed with the union, the employer will seek to establish criteria for selection which so far as possible do not depend solely upon the opinion of the person making the selection but can be objectively checked against such things as attendance record, efficiency at the job or length of service.

(iv) The employer will seek to ensure that the selection is made fairly in accordance with these criteria and will consider any representations the union may make as to such selection

(v) The employer will seek to see whether instead of dismissing an employee could be offered alternative employment. (*See* chapter 13 on the statutory procedure for handling redundancies.)

It is now well established that employers have a duty to consider the alternatives to compulsory redundancy. Indeed, paragraph 45 of the Industrial Relations Code of Practice 1972 (now revoked) suggested the following methods of avoiding such redundancies:

(i) restrictions on recruitment
(ii) retirement of employees who are beyond normal retiring age and seeking applicants for early retirement or voluntary redundancy
(iii) reductions in overtime
(iv) short-time working

(v)   retraining and redeployment to other parts of the organization.

Of course, if the size of reduction in the workforce that needs to be achieved is sufficiently large an employer may be able to persuade a tribunal that none of these alternatives, together with voluntary redundancies, could have produced a solution which would have affected the employee's position. If compulsory redundancies cannot be avoided, in the absence of an agreed procedure or customary practice, the personal circumstances of employees must be taken into account. In addition, the Court of Appeal has accepted that selection of the longest serving employee can be challenged under section 57(3) EPCA 1978 on the grounds that it was not 'in accordance with equity and the substantial merits of the case'.[85]

The importance of length of service was highlighted in the case of *Watling Ltd v Richardson*.[86] Here the custom and practice in the electrical contracting industry of dealing with contracts entirely separately was declared unreasonable since its effect had been that an employee with a little over a week's service was retained in preference to one who had been employed for a substantial period. As a matter of policy, therefore, if employers adopt criteria for selection other than 'last in, first out' they must be able to demonstrate both that the criteria adopted are reasonable and that they have been applied rationally and objectively. Indeed, in *Rolls Royce v Price*[87] the EAT accepted that a reasonable employer would have seen each employee affected by the application of the criteria and disclosed their assessments to them so that they could then have brought forward any relevant matters. In practice many employers have established redundancy appeal procedures to deal with complaints from employees who feel that selection criteria have been unfairly applied.

Consultation has been described as one of the foundation stones of modern industrial relations practice and an employer will be expected to show an exceptional reason for not consulting.[88] Although proper consultation may be regarded as a procedural matter it might have a direct bearing on the substantive decision to select a particular employee, since a different employee might have been selected if, following proper consultation, different criteria had been adopted. It is not normally permissible for an employer to argue that a failure to consult or warn would have made no difference to the outcome in the particular case. It is what the employer did that is to be judged, not what might have been done. Nevertheless, if the employer could reasonably have concluded in the light of the circumstances known at the time of dismissal that consultation or warning would be 'utterly useless' he or she might well have acted reasonably.[89] It remains to be seen whether the test to be used is objective or whether the exception only applies where the employer himself or herself has considered whether consultation would be useful.[90] In *Ferguson v Prestwick Circuits*[91] the EAT held that the lack of consultation could not be excused on the basis that when there had been consultation in relation to previous redundancies some employees had indicated that they would not wish to go through that process again. While the size of an undertaking might affect the nature or formality of the consultation, it cannot excuse lack of any consultation at all.[92]

As regards alternative employment, 'the size and administrative resources' of the employer will be a relevant consideration here. (see also page 204 on time off to look for work, etc.) However, if a vacancy exists an employer would be advised to offer it rather than speculate about the likelihood of the employee accepting it. This is so even if the new job would entail demotion or other radical changes in the terms and conditions of employment. Nevertheless, only in very rare cases will a tribunal accept that a reasonable employer would have created a job by dismissing someone else. Finally, employers should consider establishing both redundancy counselling services, which would provide information on alternative employment, training, occupational and state benefits, and hardship committees, which would seek to alleviate 'undue hardship'.[93]

Statutory ban

Section 57(2)d EPCA provides that if it would be unlawful to continue to work in the position which the employee held there will be a valid reason for dismissing. In *Bouchaala v Trust House Forte*[94] the EAT held that the absence of the words 'related to' in this section were significant and that a genuine but erroneous belief is insufficient for these purposes. Again, a tribunal must be satisfied that the requirements of section 57(3) EPCA 1978 have been met. Thus the loss of a permit or licence may fall within section 57(2)d EPCA 1978 but, in deciding what is reasonable, attention will focus on whether the legal ban is permanent or temporary. If the former, an employer might be expected to consider the feasibility of redeployment, and if the latter, short-term alternative work might be offered. Whether such measures need to be taken will depend on the type of business and the employee's work record. Of course in some circumstances it may be possible for employees to continue in their normal job by making special arrangements, *e.g.* a sales representative who has been disqualified from driving may be prepared to hire a driver at his or her own expense in order to remain in employment.

Some other substantial reason

Section 57(1)b EPCA 1978 was included in the legislative scheme so as to give tribunals the discretion to accept as a fair reason for dismissal something that would not conveniently fit into any of the other categories. It covers such diverse matters as dismissal for being sentenced to imprisonment,[95] failing to obtain a fidelity bond,[96] refusing to sign an undertaking not to compete,[97] personality clashes between employees,[98] or because the employer's best customer was unwilling to accept the particular individual.[99] However, in *Wadley v Eager Electrical*[100] the EAT decided that an employee's dismissal on the grounds that there had been breaches of trust by his wife during her employment with the employer did not amount to a substantial reason. Whether the non-renewal of a fixed term contract amounts to some other substantial reason depends on whether the case is one where the employee has, to his or her own knowledge, been employed for a particular period or a particular job on a temporary basis. Tribunals have to draw a balance between the need to protect employers who have a genuine requirement for fixed term employment which can be seen from the outset not to be ongoing and the need to protect employees.[101]

According to the Court of Appeal, tribunals have to decide whether the reason established by the employer falls within the category of reasons which *could* justify the dismissal of an employee holding the position that the employee held.[102]

Employers cannot claim that a reason for dismissal is substantial if it is whimsical or capricious. Nevertheless, if they can show that they genuinely believed a reason to be fair and that they had it in mind at the time of dismissal,[103] this would bring the case within section 57(1)b EPCA 1978. It may be held that the reason was substantial even though more sophisticated opinion can be adduced to demonstrate that the belief had no scientific foundation.[104] The notion of genuine belief has also been invoked to assist employers who are unable to rely on any other reasons for dismissal owing to an error of fact. Thus this sub-section could be relied on where an employee was dismissed as a result of the employer's mistaken belief that a work permit was needed.[105]

'Some other substantial reason' has frequently provided a convenient peg where employees have been dismissed as a result of a reorganization of the business. The Court of Appeal has taken the view that it is not necessary for an employer to show that in the absence of a reorganization there would be a total business disaster. It is sufficient if there is a sound business reason, which means only that there is a reason which management thinks on reasonable grounds is sound.[106] If the employer can satisfy a tribunal that a certain policy has evolved which was thought to have discernible advantages then dismissal in accordance with that policy can be said to be for 'some other substantial reason'. Where an employee refuses to agree changes consequent upon a reorganization the test to be applied by tribunals is not simply whether the terms offered were those which a reasonable employer could offer. Looking at the employer's offer alone would exclude from scrutiny everything that happened between the time the offer was made and the dismissal. For example, a potentially significant factor is whether other employees accepted the offer.[107] Obviously the reasonable employer will explore all the alternatives to dismissal but, like consultation with trade unions and the individual concerned, such a consideration is only one of the factors which must be taken into account under section 57(3) EPCA 1978.

Reasonableness in the circumstances

Section 57(3) EPCA 1978 (as amended)

Where the employer has given a valid reason for dismissal the determination of the question whether the dismissal was fair or unfair depends on:

> whether in the circumstances (including the size and administrative resources of the employer's undertaking), the employer acted reasonably or unreasonably in treating it as a sufficient reason for dismissing the employee; and that question shall be determined in accordance with equity and the substantial merits of the case.

As a matter of law, a reason cannot be treated as a sufficient reason where it has not been established as true or that there were reasonable grounds on which the employer could have concluded that it was true.[108]

Under section 57(3) tribunals must take account of the wider circumstances. In addition to the employer's business needs attention must be paid to the personal attributes of the employee, for example seniority and previous work record. Thus when all the relevant facts are considered a dismissal may be deemed unfair notwithstanding the fact that the disciplinary rules specified that such behaviour would result in immediate dismissal.[109] Conversely, employers may act reasonably in dismissing even though they have breached an employee's contract.[110]

Employers will be expected to treat employees in similar circumstances in a similar way. The requirement that the employer must act consistently between all employees means that an employer should consider truly comparable cases which were known about or ought to have been known about. Nevertheless, the overriding principle seems to be that each case must be considered on its own facts and with the freedom to consider mitigating circumstances.[111] The words 'equity and the substantial merits' also allow tribunals to apply their knowledge of good industrial relations practice and to ensure that there has been procedural fairness (*see* below).[112]

However, it is not the function of tribunals to ask themselves whether they would have done what the employer did in the circumstances; it is merely to assess the employer's decision to dismiss to see if it falls within a range of responses which a reasonable employer could have taken.[113] Even so, the range of reasonable responses test does not mean that such a high degree of unreasonableness must be shown so that nothing short of a perverse decision to dismiss can be held unfair.[114] Finally, it would seem that in determining the reasonableness of a dismissal tribunals are not barred from taking into account events which occurred between the giving of notice and its expiry, for example, if alternative work becomes available after redundancy notices have been issued.[115]

The Code of Practice and procedural fairness

The ACAS *Code of Practice on Disciplinary Practice and Procedures in Employment* (1977) does not have the force of law, so failure to comply with it does not make a dismissal automatically unfair. Indeed, where there is a procedural defect the question to be answered is, did the employer's procedure constitute a fair process? A dismissal will be unfair either where there was a defect of such seriousness that the procedure itself was unfair or where the results of the defect taken overall were unfair. Thus in *Fuller v Lloyds Bank*[116] the failure to provide witness statements was a breach of company policy but the dismissal was fair because the employee knew exactly what was being alleged.

In certain circumstances there may be a good excuse for not following the Code, for example, if the inadequacy of the employee's performance is extreme or the actual or potential consequences of a mistake are grave, warnings may not be necessary.[117] Although it is management's responsibility to ensure that there are adequate disciplinary rules and procedures, the Code emphasizes the desirability of union involvement in agreeing procedural arrangements.[118] Naturally, tribunals tend to pay greater attention to agreed rather than unilaterally imposed procedures. The rules required will again depend on the nature of the employment but they should be reasonable in themselves, consistently enforced, and reviewed in the light of legal developments and organizational needs. Employees should know and understand the rules and be made aware of the likely consequences of breaking them.[119]

The essential features of a disciplinary procedure are outlined in paragraph 10 of the Code. They should:

(i)   be in writing
(ii)   specify to whom they apply
(iii)   provide for matters to be dealt with quickly[120]
(iv)   indicate the disciplinary actions which may be taken
(v)   specify the levels of management which have the authority to take the various forms of disciplinary action, ensuring that immediate superiors do not normally have the power to dismiss without reference to senior management
(vi)   provide for individuals to be informed of the complaints against them and to be given an opportunity to state their case before decisions are reached. (It is clear that allowing access to a grievance procedure does not constitute the giving of an opportunity to explain[121])
(vii)   give individuals the right to be accompanied by a trade union representative or by a fellow employee of their choice
(viii) ensure that any investigatory period of suspension is with pay (unless the contract of employment clearly provides otherwise) and specify how pay is to be calculated during such a period
(ix)   ensure that, except for gross misconduct, no employees are dismissed for a first breach of discipline
(x)   ensure that disciplinary action is not taken until the case has been carefully investigated
(xi)   ensure that individuals are given an explanation for any penalty imposed
(xii)   provide a right of appeal and specify the procedure to be followed.[122]

It is clear from the above that natural justice is an important element in such procedures. Fairness requires that accused persons should know the case to be met; should hear or be told the important points of the evidence in support of that case; should have an opportunity to criticize or dispute that evidence and to adduce their own evidence and argue their case.[123] However, natural justice in this context does not include the automatic right to be present throughout a disciplinary hearing if the employee's interests are safeguarded by a representative. Similarly, employers are not required to conduct a quasi-judicial investigation, with cross-examination and confrontation of witnesses.[124] However, if allegations are made by an informant a careful balance must be maintained between the desirability of protecting informants who are genuinely in fear and providing a fair hearing of the issues for employees who are accused.[125] In *Rowe v Radio Rentals*[126] the EAT decided that the employer's appeal procedure did not conflict with the rules of natural justice because the person hearing the appeal had been informed of the decision to dismiss before it took place and the person who took that decision was also present throughout the appeal hearing. It was recognized as inevitable that those involved in the original decision to dismiss will be in daily contact with their supervisors who will be responsible for deciding the appeal. However, if it is not necessary for the same person to act as both witness and judge in the procedure leading to dismissal, there may be a finding of unfairness.[127]

Warnings are particularly appropriate in cases of misconduct but may also be useful in dealing with other types of case. Basically there are two types of warnings which need to be distinguished: a 'resolutive' warning means that the employee will be dismissed unless an existing situation is rectified, whereas a 'suspensive' warning indicates that the employee will be dismissed if further unacceptable behaviour occurs. Suspensive warnings are dealt with in paragraph 12 of the Code of Practice, where it is recommended that written warnings should set out the nature of the offence and the likely consequences of it being repeated. According to the Court of Appeal, provided a formal disciplinary warning has been given on adequate evidence, and not for an oblique or improper motive, it is a relevant consideration to which an industrial tribunal should have regard in deciding whether the dismissal was unfair, even where the warning was under appeal and the appeal had not been determined at the time of the dismissal.[128] It follows that systematic records will have to be kept by employers, although it is suggested in paragraph 18 of the Code of Practice that 'except in agreed special circumstances, breaches of disciplinary rules should be disregarded after a specified period of satisfactory conduct'. The ACAS Advisory Handbook indicates that warnings for minor offences may be valid for up to six months whereas final warnings may remain in force for a year or longer.

As regards appeal procedures, the House of Lords has confirmed that a dismissal is unfair if the employer unreasonably treats the reason for dismissal as a sufficient one, either when the original decision to dismiss is made or when that decision is maintained at the conclusion of an internal appeal.[129] Indeed, a dismissal may also be unfair if the employer refuses to entertain an appeal or to comply with the full requirements of the appeal procedure.[130] Where two employees are dismissed for the same incident and one is successful on appeal and the other is not, in determining the fairness of the latter's dismissal the question is whether the appeal panel's decision was so irrational that no employer could reasonably have accepted it.[131] Whether procedural defects can be rectified on appeal will depend on the degree of unfairness at the original hearing. If there is to be a correction by the appeal, then that appeal must be of a comprehensive nature, in essence a rehearing and not merely a review.[132]

Finally paragraph 15 of the Code of Practice urges that special consideration be given to the way in which disciplinary procedures operate in particular cases. Three examples are given:

(i) employees to whom the full procedure is not immediately available, such as those who work on shifts or in isolated locations

(ii) trade union officials: 'Although normal disciplinary standards should apply to their conduct as employees, no disciplinary action beyond an oral warning should be taken until the circumstances of the case have been discussed with a senior trade union representative or full time official'

(iii) criminal offences outside employment.

Notes

1   Section 57(1)(2) EPCA 1978.
2   On the meaning of 'position' *see* chapter 11, note 6.
3   See *Maund v Penwith District Council* [1984] IRLR 24.
4   See *Abernethy v Mott, Hay and Anderson* [1984] IRLR 213.
5   See *Ely v YKK Ltd* [1993] IRLR 500.
6   See *Devis & Sons Ltd v Atkins* [1977] IRLR 314.
7   See *Monie v Coral Racing Ltd* [1980] IRLR 464.

8   See *Ford Motor Co. Ltd v Hudson* [1978] IRLR 66. On pressure to dismiss on union grounds *see* chapter 18.
9   No service qualification applies if the dismissal is on the grounds of pregnancy or maternity (*see* page 85).
10 [1985] IRLR 16
11 See *Harvard Securities PLC v Younghusband* [1990] IRLR 17.
12 Section 53(4) EPCA 1978.
13 See *Broomsgrove v Eagle Alexander* [1981] IRLR 127.
14 The Deregulation and Contracting Out Bill 1994 will affect this provision.
15 Section 60A EPCA 1978.
16 See *Wheeler v Patel* [1987] IRLR 211.
17 [1985] IRLR 305.
18   See also *Porter v Queen's Medical Centre* [1993] IRLR 486.
19 See *Crawford v Swinton Insurance* [1990] IRLR 42.
20 See *McGrath v Rank Leisure Ltd* [1985] IRLR 323.
21 Section 4(3)b Rehabilitation of Offenders Act 1974.
22 *Manifold Industries Ltd v Sims* [1991] IRLR 242.
23 See *P&O v Byrne* [1989] IRLR 254.
24 See *Highland Fabricators v McLaughlin* [1984] IRLR 482.
25 Section 239(3) TULRCA 1992.
26 [1992] IRLR 4.
27 *Crosville Ltd v Tracey* [1993] IRLR 60.
28 See *Campey Ltd v Bellwood* [1987] ICR 311.
29 Section 238(3)(5) TULRCA 1992.
30 [1984] IRLR 477.
31 See *Midland Plastics Ltd v Till* [1983] IRLR 9 but note *Lewis v Mason & Sons* [1994] IRLR 4.
32 See *Faust v Power Packing Ltd* [1983] IRLR 117.
33 See *Manifold Industries Ltd v Sims* [1993] EAT 223/91.
34 See *Bolton Roadways Ltd v Edwards* [1987] IRLR 392.
35 See *Rogers v Chloride Systems* [1992] ICR 198.
36 See *Express & Star Ltd v Bunday* [1987] IRLR 422.
37 See *Manifold Industries Ltd v Sims* [1993] EAT 223/91.
38 Section 238(4) TULRCA 1992.
39 [1982] IRLR 377.
40 Section 237(6) TULRCA 1992.
41 See *Abernethy v Mott, Hay and Anderson* (*see* note 4).
42 [1979] IRLR 16.
43 See Advisory Handbook, page 47.
44 On appraisal see ACAS Advisory Booklet No 11.
45 See Advisory Handbook, pages 48–9.
46 See *Sutton & Gates Ltd v Boxall* [1978] IRLR 486.
47 See Advisory Handbook, pages 42–3.
48 See *Mitchell v Arkwood Plastics* [1993] ICR 471.
49 See *Cereal Packaging Ltd v Lynock* [1988] IRLR 510 and Advisory Handbook, page 41.
50 See *A. Links Ltd v Rose* [1991] IRLR 353.

51 [1992] IRLR 133.
52 See *Shook v London Borough of Ealing* [1986] IRLR 46.
53 See *Hobson v GEC* [1985] ICR 377.
54 See *Hamilton v Argyll and Clyde Health Board* [1993] IRLR 99.
55 See *Distillers Co. v Gardner* [1982] IRLR 47.
56 See *Taylor v Parson's Peebles Ltd* [1981] IRLR 199 where the employee concerned had a good conduct record extending over 20 years.
57 See also *United Distillers v Conlin* [1992] IRLR 503.
58 See *UCATT v Brain* [1981] IRLR 224.
59 See *Laughton v Bapp Industrial Ltd* [1986] IRLR 245.
60 [1992] IRLR 294.
61 [1978] IRLR 379.
62 *Scottish Midland Co-op v Cullion* [1991] IRLR 261.
63 See *Parr v Whitbread PLC* [1990] IRLR 39.
64 *Frames Snooker v Boyce* [1992] IRLR 472.
65 See *Parker v Dunn Ltd* [1979] IRLR 56.
66 See *Secretary of State v Campbell* [1992] IRLR 263.
67 See *Harris v Courage Ltd* [1982] IRLR 509.
68 See *Thomson v Alloa Motor Co.* [1983] IRLR 403.
69 See *P v Nottingham County Council* [1992] IRLR 363.
70 Section 73(9) EPCA 1978.
71 See *Pink v White* [1985] IRLR 489.
72 Section 59 EPCA (as amended); 'undertaking' is not defined in this context. 'Position' is defined in note 6 to chapter 11. On 'positions similar' see *Powers and Villiers v A. Clarke & Co.* [1981] IRLR 483. Note the effect of the Deregulation and Contracting Out Bill 1994.
73 See *Rogers v Vosper Thornycroft* [1989] IRLR 82.
74 See *Suflex Ltd v Thomas* [1987] IRLR 435.
75 See *Henry v Ellerman Liners* [1984] IRLR 409.
76 See *International Paint Co. v Cameron* [1979] IRLR 62.
77 See *Brook v London Borough of Haringey* [1992] IRLR 478.
78 See *Clarke and Powell v Eley (IMI) Kynoch Ltd* [1982] IRLR 482.
79 [1985] IRLR 387.
80 [1991] IRLR 348.
81 See *McDowell v Eastern BRS Ltd* [1981] IRLR 482.
82 [1982] IRLR 83.
83 See *Hough v Leyland DAF* [1991] IRLR 194.
84 See *Rolls Royce Ltd v Price* [1993] IRLR 203.
85 See *Bessenden Properties v Corness* [1974] IRLR 338.
86 [1978] IRLR 255.
87 See note 84.
88 See *Heron v Citylink-Nottingham* [1993] IRLR 368.
89 See *Polkey v Dayton Ltd* [1987] IRLR 503.
90 Compare *Duffy v Yeoman & Partners* [1993] IRLR 368 with *Robertson v Magnet Ltd* [1993] IRLR 512.
91 [1992] IRLR 266.
92 See *De Grasse v Stockwell Tools* [1992] IRLR 269.

93   See generally ACAS Advisory Booklet No 12, *Redundancy Handling*.
94   [1980] IRLR 382.
95   See *Kingston v British Rail* [1984] IRLR 146.
96   See *Moody v Telefusion Ltd* [1978] IRLR 311.
97   See *RS Components v Irwin* [1973] IRLR 239.
98   See *Turner v Vestric Ltd* [1981] IRLR 23.
99   See *Scottpacking Ltd v Paterson* [1978] IRLR 166.
100 [1986] IRLR 93.
101 See *North Yorkshire County Council v Fay* [1985] IRLR 247.
102 *Dobie v Burns International* [1984] IRLR 329.
103 See *Ely v YKK Ltd* (note 5).
104 See *Saunders v Scottish National Camps Association* [1981] IRLR 277.
105 See *Bouchaala v Trusthouse Forte* (note 94).
106 See *Hollister v National Farmers' Union* [1979] IRLR 238.
107 See *St John of God Ltd v Brooks* [1992] IRLR 546.
108 See *Smith v City of Glasgow DC* [1987] IRLR 326.
109 See *Ladbroke Racing v Arnott* [1983] IRLR 154.
110 See *Brandon v Murphy Bros* [1983] IRLR 54.
111 See *Proctor v British Gypsum Ltd* [1992] IRLR 7.
112 See *Williams v Compair Maxam Ltd* (note 82).
113 See *British Leyland (UK) Ltd v Swift* [1981] IRLR 91.
114 See *Rentokil Ltd v Mackin* [1989] IRLR 286.
115 See *Stacey v Babcock Power Ltd* [1986] IRLR 3.
116 [1991] IRLR 336.
117 See *Alidair Ltd v Taylor* [1978] IRLR 82.
118 See Code of Practice paragraph 5.
119 See Code of Practice paragraphs 7 and 8.
120 See *RSPCA v Cruden* [1986] IRLR 83.
121 See *Clarke v Trimoco Ltd* [1993] IRLR 148.
122 See *Vauxhall Motors Ltd v Ghafoor* [1993] ICR 376.
123 See *Spink v Express Foods* [1990] IRLR 320.
124 See *Ulsterbus Ltd v Henderson* [1989] IRLR 251.
125 See *Linfood Cash & Carry v Thomson* [1989] IRLR 235.
126 [1982] IRLR 177.
127 See *Byrne v Boc Ltd* [1992] IRLR 505.
128 See *Tower Hamlets Health Authority v Anthony* [1989] IRLR 394.
129 See *West Midlands Co-op Ltd v Tipton* [1986] IRLR 112.
130 See *Stoker v Lancashire County Council* [1992] IRLR 75.
131 See *Securicor Ltd v Smith* [1989] IRLR 356.
132 See *Clark v CAA* [1991] IRLR 412 on what is required at such hearings.

13 Unfair dismissal and redundancy rights (3)

The definition of redundancy
(*see also* page 134–5 on lay-off and short time)

According to Section 81(2) EPCA 1978 employees are to be regarded as being redundant if their dismissals are attributable wholly or mainly to:

(i)   the fact that the employer has ceased, or intends to cease, to carry on the business[1] for the purposes for which the employees were employed, or

(ii) the fact that the employer has ceased, or intends to cease, to carry on that business in the place where the employees were so employed, or

(iii) the fact that the requirement of that business for employees to carry out work of a particular kind, or for employees to carry out work of a particular kind in the place where they were so employed, have ceased or diminished or are expected to cease or diminish.

In this context 'cease' or 'diminish' mean either permanently or temporarily and from whatever cause.[2] The scope and extent of the business is a question of fact for the tribunal.[3]

As regards the place where workers are employed, it is crucial to establish where employees are contractually obliged to work rather than where they have in fact been working.[4] Thus, where contracts expressly provide that employees may be required to work anywhere, a refusal to move could lead to a dismissal for misconduct but not redundancy. However, the EAT has suggested that where employers are intending to rely on a mobility clause in a situation of job or location change, rather than dismiss for redundancy and offer alternative employment, they must make the position clear.[5] If there is no express term relating to mobility a tribunal will have to examine all the evidence to see if a term should be implied.[6] However, even though an employee may be contractually justified in declining to move, a request to do so may have to be considered as an offer of suitable alternative employment (*see* below).

One of the most onerous tasks of tribunals is to determine what constitutes 'work of a particular kind'. It is clear that a change in the time when the work is to be performed will not give rise to a redundancy payment[7] nor will a reduction of overtime if the work to be done remains the same. Thus in *Lesney Products Ltd v Nolan*[8] the Court of Appeal held that the company's reorganization, whereby one long day shift plus overtime was changed into two day shifts, was done in the interests of efficiency and was not a result of any diminution in the employer's requirements for employees to carry out work of a particular kind. However, a dismissal caused by a reorganization can give rise to a redundancy payment if the tribunal decide that the reallocation of functions amongst the staff was such as to change the particular kind of work which a particular employee was required to carry out.[9]

Three further points need to be made. First, employees will be entitled to a payment notwithstanding that it could be seen from the commencement of the contract that they would be dismissed for redundancy. The fact that the contract was temporary and short-term makes no difference in this respect.[10] Second, the statutory definition of redundancy focuses on the employer's requirements rather than needs. Thus even where there is still a need for the work to be done if, owing to lack of funds, the requirement for the employee's service has ceased, the employee is redundant.[11] Finally, section 91(2) EPCA 1978 states that an employee who is dismissed is presumed to have been dismissed by reason of redundancy unless the contrary is proved.[12]

Offers of alternative employment

If, before the ending of a person's employment, the employer or an associated employer makes an offer, in writing or not, to renew the contract or to re-engage under a new contract which is to take effect either on the ending of the old one or within four weeks thereafter, then section 82(5) EPCA 1978 has the following effect:

(i)   if the provisions of the new or renewed contract as to the capacity and place in which the person would be employed, together with the other terms and conditions, would not differ from the corresponding terms of the previous contract, or

(ii)   the terms and conditions would differ, wholly or in part, but the offer constitutes an offer of suitable employment, and

(iii) in either case the employee unreasonably refuses that offer, then he or she will not be entitled to a redundancy payment.

The burden is on an employer to prove both the suitability of the offer and the unreasonableness of the employee's refusal.[13] Offers do not have to be formal nor do they have to contain all the conditions which are ultimately agreed.[14] However, supplying details of vacancies is not the same as an offer of employment.[15] Clearly, sufficient information must be provided to enable the employee to take a realistic decision.[16]

The suitability of the alternative work must be assessed objectively by comparing the terms on offer with those previously enjoyed. A convenient test has been whether the proposed employment will be 'substantially equivalent' to that which has ceased.[17] Merely offering the same salary will not be sufficient[18] but short-term employment could be suitable if it is full-time.[19] The fact that the employment will be at a different location does not necessarily mean that it will be regarded as unsuitable.

By way of contrast, in adjudicating upon the reasonableness of an employee's refusal, subjective considerations can be taken into account *e.g.* domestic responsibilities. In *Spencer v Gloucestershire County Council*[20] the employees had refused offers of suitable employment on the grounds that they would not be able to do their work to a satisfactory standard in the reduced hours and with reduced staffing levels. The Court of Appeal held that it was for employers to set the standard of work they wanted carried out but it was a different question whether it was reasonable for a particular employee, in all the circumstances, to refuse to work to the standard which the employer set. This is a question of fact for the tribunal. Similarly, it might be reasonable for an employee to refuse an offer of employment which, although suitable, involved loss of status.[21] Although in theory the questions of suitability and the reasonableness of refusal are distinct they are often run together in practice.

To allow an employee to make a rational decision about any alternative employment offered, section 84(3) EPCA 1978 provides that if the terms and conditions would differ, wholly or in part, from those of the previous contract a trial period may be invoked. Such a period commences when the employee starts work under the new or renewed contract and ends four calendar weeks later[22] unless a longer period has been agreed for the purpose of retraining. Any such agreement must be made before the employee starts work under the new or renewed contract, it must be in writing, and specify the date the trial period ends, and the terms and conditions which will apply afterwards.[23] In order to have an agreement an employee must do something to indicate acceptance. However it is not necessary for the employer to provide all the information required by section 1 EPCA 1978 (*see* chapter 2); the agreement need only embody important matters such as remuneration, status and job description.[24] If, during the trial period, the employee for any reason terminates or gives notice to terminate the contract, or the employer terminates or gives notice to terminate it for any reason connected with or arising out of the change, the employee shall be treated, for redundancy payment purposes, as having been dismissed on the date the previous contract ended. Of course, the employee's contract may be renewed again or he or she may be re-engaged under a new contract in circumstances which give rise to another trial period.[25] Indeed, the termination of a trial period could lead to a finding of unfair dismissal.[26]

The statutory trial period applies to those who have been dismissed by their employer and have unconditionally accepted a new or renewed contract. However, at common law if the employer is guilty of repudiating the contract employees are allowed a reasonable period within which to decide whether or not to regard themselves as constructively dismissed (*see* chapter 11) or to carry on with the contract. In these circumstances the statutory trial period will not commence until after the expiry of the common law period, so the employee gets the benefit of both.[27] Among the circumstances to be considered in determining the length of the common law period are the steps taken by the employer to enquire what the employee is going to do. If the employer makes no such enquiries the period continues until either the employee has announced a decision or a period expires which is long enough for it to be said that it would be unreasonable to consider the trial as subsisting.[28]

Dismissal for misconduct or striking during the notice period

If an employee who is working out notice of dismissal for redundancy commits an act of misconduct which justifies summary dismissal and is dismissed for that reason, a tribunal is empowered to determine whether it is just and equitable for him or her to receive the whole or part of the redundancy payment.[29] The burden is on the employer to show that the employee's conduct was such as to entitle the employer to terminate the contract without notice[30] and the tribunal's discretion only applies if the misconduct occurred during the 'obligatory period' of the employer's notice or after the employee has given notice of an intention to claim a payment in respect of lay-off or short time[31] (*see* page 152 for the definition of 'obligatory period'). Where the misconduct takes place at any other time the employee is not entitled to a payment.[32] Equally, section 92(1) EPCA 1978 prevents employees who have been given notice of dismissal on the ground of redundancy from being denied a payment if they take part in a strike during the 'obligatory period'[33] If the employee is sacked before redundancy notices have been issued no payment is owed,[34] but the fact that redundancy is the result of industrial action will not bar an employee from obtaining a payment.[35]

The procedure for handling redundancies

Consultation

Employers proposing to dismiss as redundant employees of a description in respect of which an independent trade union is recognized must consult representatives of that union about the dismissal 'at the earliest opportunity'. For these purposes only, redundancy is defined as 'dismissal for a reason not related to the individual concerned or for a number of reasons all of which are not so related'[36]. This might include, for example, dismissals resulting from a refusal to accept a change in terms and conditions of employment. In this context also it will be presumed that a dismissal is by reason of redundancy unless the contrary is proved.

Employers are to be identified by the contracts of employment they issue and the EAT has been unwilling to lift the corporate veil.[37] It is important to note that the employees covered need not be union members or be employed for any minimum number of hours per week. However, those who work under a contract for a fixed term of three months or less will be excluded unless the employment lasted for more than three months.[38] Section 196 TULRCA 1992 defines a trade union representative as an official or other person authorized to carry on collective bargaining with the employer.

Without prejudice to the basic obligation section 188(2) TULRCA 1992 sets out the following minimum periods which must be allowed for consultation before a dismissal takes effect:

(i) where the employer is proposing to dismiss 100 or more at one establishment within a period of 90 days or less, 90 days, and

(ii) where the employer is proposing to dismiss 10 or more at one establishment within a period of 30 days or less, 30 days.

'Establishment' is not defined by the statute and the EAT has ruled that this is a question for the tribunal acting as an industrial jury using its common sense on the particular facts of the case. In *Bakers' Union v Clark's of Hove Ltd*[39] it was accepted that separate premises could be regarded as one establishment if there was common management and accounting.

The consultation required must include consultation about ways of:

(i) avoiding the dismissals
(ii) reducing the numbers to be dismissed, and
(iii) mitigating the consequences of the dismissal.

Section 188(6) TULRCA 1992 also specifies that this consultation must be undertaken 'with a view to reaching agreement with trade union representatives'.[39A] According to the EAT, employers are required to begin consultation before they give notice of dismissal[40] but notices can be issued during the consultation period so long as the dismissals do not take effect until after the period has elapsed. Of course, if an employer gives notice of dismissal immediately after consultation has begun it could be argued that no meaningful consultation took place.[41]

A fundamental question in relation to these provisions is: how concrete does the intention to make employees redundant have to be before the duty applies? In *Hough v Leyland DAF*[42] the EAT suggested that the duty to consult arose when matters had reached a stage where a specific proposal had been formulated. This is a later stage than the diagnosis of a problem and the appreciation that one answer would be redundancies. Hence an employer must have formed some view as to how many employees are to be dismissed, when this is to take place and how it is to be arranged. It is important to note that Article 2 of EC Directive 75/129 requires consultation where an employer is 'contemplating' collective redundancies.

The employer must disclose in writing the following matters at the beginning of the consultation period:[43]

(i)   the reason for the proposals
(ii) the number and description of employees whom it is proposed to dismiss
(iii) the total number of employees of any such description employed by the employer at that establishment
(iv) the proposed method of selecting the employees who may be dismissed
(v)   the proposed method of carrying out the dismissals, with due regard to any agreed procedure, including the period over which the dismissals are to take effect
(vi) the proposed method of calculating the redundancy payment if this differs from the statutory sum.

This information must be delivered to the trade union representatives, or sent by post to an address notified by them or to the union head office. In *E. Green Ltd v ASTMS and AUEW*[44] it was held that items (iv) and (v) had not been complied with when the method of selecting employees who might be dismissed was given as 'to be in consultation with union representatives'.

If there are 'special circumstances' which render it not reasonably practicable for the employer to comply with the above-mentioned provisions an employer must take 'all such steps towards compliance' as are reasonably practicable in the circumstances. 'Special circumstances' mean circumstances which are uncommon or out of the ordinary, so insolvency by itself will not provide an excuse as it may well be foreseeable.[45] However, that the employer has continued trading in the face of adverse economic pointers in the genuine and reasonable expectation that redundancies would be avoided can justify non-compliance.[46] Additionally, a pending application for government financial aid, the withdrawal of a prospective purchaser from negotiations combined with a bank's immediate appointment of a receiver, and the need for confidentiality in negotiating a sale, have all constituted 'special circumstances'. By way of contrast, the following have not been accepted as being 'special':

(i)   the alarm and chaos caused by the disclosure of information about the proposed redundancies
(ii) a genuine belief that the union had not been recognized. In *Wilson & Bros v USDAW*[47] it was held that such a belief must be reasonable
(iii) the fact that the employer had been informed by the Department of Employment that there was no duty to consult in the particular case.[48]

Section 188(7) TULRCA 1992 also provides that where the decision leading to the proposed dismissals is that of a person controlling the employer, a failure on the part of that person to provide information to the employer will not constitute 'special circumstances'.

Where the employer has failed to comply with any of the requirements of section 188 TULRCA 1992 the recognized union can complain to an industrial tribunal before the proposed dismissal takes effect or within three months of it doing so unless the 'time limit escape clause' applies.[49] Employers wishing to argue that there were 'special circumstances' justifying non-compliance must prove that these circumstances existed and that they took all such steps towards compliance as were reasonably practicable.[50] If a complaint is well founded the tribunal must make a declaration to that effect and may also make a protective award. A protective award refers to the wages payable for a protected period to employees who have been dismissed or whom it is proposed to dismiss. The protected period begins with the date on which the first of the dismissals to which the complaint relates takes effect (*i.e.* the proposed date of dismissal)[51] or the date of the award (whichever is the earlier) and will be of such length as the tribunal determines 'to be just and equitable in all the circumstances having regard to the seriousness of the employer's default'. However, the protected period is to be limited in the following ways:

(i) where it was proposed to make 100 or more employees redundant within 90 days, the period cannot exceed 90 days

(ii) where it was proposed to make 10 or more redundant within 30 days the period cannot exceed 30 days

(iii) in any other case, the period must not exceed 28 days.[52]

Two types of decision emerged at tribunal level in relation to the protective award. Whereas some tribunals linked the award to the period over which consultations could have been expected to have taken place, others based the size of the award on the merits of the employer's excuse. The prevailing view would seem to be that the object of an award is to compensate employees for their employer's failure to consult with the union even where compliance with the statute would have made no difference.[53] One consequence of focusing on the loss of days of consultation rather than the loss or potential loss of remuneration during the relevant period is that it becomes possible to make a protective award in favour of employees who have suffered no pecuniary damage, for example, where alternative employment was immediately secured.[54] The rate of remuneration payable under a protective award is a week's pay for each week of the protected period, with proportionate reductions being made in respect of periods less than a week.[55]

If during the protected period employees are fairly dismissed for a reason other than redundancy, or if they unreasonably resign, then their entitlement to remuneration under the protective award ceases on the day the contract is terminated. Similarly, employees who unreasonably refuse an offer of employment on the previous terms and conditions or an offer of suitable alternative employment will not be entitled to any remuneration under a protective award in respect of any period during which, but for that refusal, they would have been employed.[56] Employees who are of a description to which a protective award relates may complain to a tribunal, within three months unless the 'time limit escape clause' applies, that their employer has failed, wholly or in part, to pay the remuneration under that award. If the complaint is well founded the employer will be ordered to pay the amount due to the complainant.[57]

Finally, it may be of interest to note that section 198 TULRCA 1992 enables the parties to a collective agreement to apply to the Secretary of State for an exemption order in respect of the consultation provisions.

Notification

An employer proposing to dismiss as redundant 100 or more employees at one establishment within a period of 90 days, or more than 10 employees within 30 days, must notify the Secretary of State in writing of the proposal within 90 or 30 days respectively.[58] Hence there is no obligation to notify if less than 10 employees are to be dismissed. In addition, the employer must give a copy of the notice to the representatives of any independent trade union which is recognized in relation to the employees affected. The written notice must be in such form and contain such particulars as the Secretary of State may direct but it is expressly provided that where consultation with union representatives is required by section 188 TULRCA 1992 the employer must identify the union concerned and state when consultation began.[59] At any time after receiving a notice under this section the Secretary of State may require the employer to give further information.[60]

If there are special circumstances rendering it not reasonably practicable for the employer to comply with the requirements of section 193 TULRCA 1992 an employer must take all such steps as are reasonably practicable in the circumstances. Again, where the decision leading to the proposed dismissals is that of a person controlling the employer, a failure on the part of that person to provide information to the employer will not constitute 'special circumstances.'[61] Employers who fail to give notice in accordance with this section may be prosecuted and suffer a fine not exceeding level 5 on the standard scale.[62]

The procedure for handling transfers of undertakings

The types of transfer covered

The Transfer Regulations 1981 were introduced in order to comply with EC Directive 77/187 and cover the transfer of any undertaking which was situated wholly or partly in the United Kingdom prior to the transfer.[63] For these purposes an undertaking includes any trade or business and it would seem that there could be a temporary closure of the undertaking and an absence of staff at the time of the transfer.[64] Regulation 3(2) provides that the transfer may be 'effected by sale or some other disposition or by operation of law'.

European Court of Justice decisions suggest that the Transfer Regulations should apply wherever there is a change in the legal or natural person responsible for carrying on the business and who incurs the obligations of an employer towards the employees of the undertaking.[65] The decisive question for establishing whether there has been a transfer is whether the unit in question retains its identity. It is also necessary to consider the type of undertaking concerned, whether tangible assets are transferred, the value of intangible assets at the time of the transfer, whether the majority of employees are taken over by the new employer, whether customers are transferred, the degree of similarity between the activities carried on before and after the transfer, and the period, if any, for which these activities were suspended.[66] Thus, in principle, the Transfer Regulations can apply where part of a business is contracted out.

Regulation 3(4) states that 'a transfer of an undertaking or part of one may be effected by a series of two or more transactions between the same parties', and makes it clear that a transfer may take place whether or not any property is transferred to the transferee by the transferor. Regulation 4 is concerned with 'hiving down'. This is the process whereby a receiver or liquidator transfers a part of a business to a wholly owned subsidiary which, in turn, transfers the business to a third party as if the intermediate transfer had not occurred. It is provided that when an undertaking has been 'hived down' to a wholly owned subsidiary company the automatic transfer of contracts of employment (*see* chapter 2) is postponed until the subsidiary either transfers the undertaking to the final purchaser or is itself taken over by that purchaser. This means that the new owners are only obliged to engage those employees whose contracts are still in force immediately prior to the final transfer.

The duty to inform and consult the representatives of recognized trade unions

There are two parts to the duty created by Regulation 10 of the Transfer Regulations 1981. First both the transferor and the transferee employers must provide information to the union representatives of any employees 'who may be affected by the transfer or . . . measures taken in connection with it'.[67] Arguably, since any substantial transfer is likely to affect the profitability of a corporate group all employees of that group may be affected by the transfer. Secondly, where either the transferor or transferee employer envisages that they will 'be taking measures' in connection with the transfer which affect the employees concerned they are required to consult with the representatives of a recognised trade union 'with a view to reaching their agreement to measures to be taken'.[68] Regulation 10(2) states that 'long enough before a relevant transfer to enable consultations to take place' the employer must inform the trade union representatives of:

(i) the fact that the relevant transfer is to take place, when, approximately, it is to occur and the reasons for it

(ii) the legal, economic and social implications of the transfer for the affected employees

(iii) the measures which it is envisaged will, in connection with the transfer, be taken in relation to those employees or, if it is envisaged that no measures will be so taken, that fact

(iv) if the employer is the transferor, the measures which the transferor envisages will, in connection with the transfer, be taken in relation to such of those employees as become employees of the transferee after the transfer or, if it is envisaged that no measures will be so taken, that fact.[69]

A number of points need to be made at this stage. First, despite the words 'long enough before a relevant transfer to enable consultations to take place' the obligation to consult arises only in the circumstances described by Regulation 10(5) of the Transfer Regulations 1981. Secondly, it is interesting that the information to be given relates to the *fact* of a transfer rather than one that is proposed. Thirdly, Regulation 10(3) of the Transfer Regulations 1981 obliges the transferee to give the transferor employer 'such information at such time as will enable the transferor to perform the duty imposed' by (iv) above. Fourthly, the information to be given to trade union representatives under this Regulation must be delivered to them or posted to an address notified by them or to the union's head office.

Turning to consultation, it is important to note that the transferor employer has a duty to consult representatives of recognized trade unions about measures that he or she will be taking in connection with affected employees, *i.e.* those being transferred together with those being retained (if they are affected). Similarly, the transferee employer is obliged to consult recognized trade unions about the measures he or she will be taking in so far as they affect existing employees. However, neither employer is required to consult the union recognized in respect of the employees being transferred about the measures which the transferee proposes to take in relation to them. An employer must consider any representations made by the trade unions and reply to them. If the employer rejects any representations, reasons for doing so must be given. Again, if there are 'special circumstances' which render it not reasonably practicable for employers to perform a duty imposed on them by this Regulation, they must still take all such steps towards performing that duty as are reasonably practicable in the circumstances.[70]

The remedies available for a failure to inform or consult parallel those that can be awarded for non-compliance with section 188 TULRCA 1992. In addition, a transferee employer is potentially liable if the reason the transferor did not fulfil his or her duty was the result of the transferee failing to supply the requisite information.[71] The maximum compensation which can be awarded in respect of a failure to inform or consult under the Transfer Regulations 1981 is four weeks' pay for each employee affected.[72]

Time off to look for work

A person who has been continuously employed for two years or more and is under notice of dismissal by reason of redundancy is entitled to reasonable time off during working hours to look for new employment or make arrangements for training for future employment.[73] Such an employee should be paid at the appropriate hourly rate for the period of absence. This is one week's pay divided by the number of normal weekly hours or, where the number of normal working hours varies, the average of such hours[74] (*see* chapter 15 for the meaning of a week's pay and normal working hours).

A complaint that an employer has unreasonably refused time off or has failed to pay the whole or part of any amount to which the employee is entitled must be presented to an industrial tribunal within three months of the day on which it is alleged that the time off should have been allowed.[75] If the complaint is well founded the tribunal must make a declaration to that effect and order the employer to pay the amount which it finds due to the employee. Curiously, although the employee is entitled to be paid 'an amount equal to the remuneration to which he would have been entitled if he had been allowed the time off', the maximum that a tribunal can award is two fifths of a week's pay.[76] There are a few reported decisions in this area but in *Dutton v Hawker Siddeley Aviation Ltd*[77]the EAT rejected the argument that employees had to give details of any appointment or interviews for which they wished to take time off.

Notes

1   'Business' is defined in section 153(1) EPCA 1978.
2   Section 81(3) EPCA 1978.
3   See *Babar Restaurant v Rawat* [1985] IRLR 57 and section 81(2A) EPCA 1978.
4   See *Rank Xerox v Churchill* [1988] IRLR 280.
5   See *Curling v Securicor Ltd* [1992] IRLR 549.
6   See *O'Brien v Associated Fire Alarms Ltd* [1969] 1 AER 93.
7   See *Johnson v Nottingham Police Authority* [1974] ICR 170.
8   [1977] IRLR 77.
9   See *Murphy v Epsom College* [1984] IRLR 271.

10   See *Lee v Nottinghamshire County Council* [1980] IRLR 284.
11   See *AUT v Newcastle University* [1987] ICR 317.
12   See *Willcox v Hastings* [1987] IRLR 299.
13   See *Jones v Aston Cabinet Ltd* [1973] ICR 292.
14   See *Singer Co. v Ferrier* [1980] IRLR 300.
15   See *Curling v Securicor Ltd* (note 5).
16   See *Modern Injection Moulds Ltd v Price* [1976] IRLR 172.
17   See *Hindes v Supersine Ltd* [1979] IRLR 343.
18   See *Taylor v Kent County Council* [1969]2 QB 560.
19   See *Morganite Crucible v Street* [1972] ICR 110.
20   [1985] IRLR 393.
21   See *Cambridge and District Co-op v Ruse* [1993] IRLR 156.
22   See *Benton v Sanderson Kayser* [1989] IRLR 299.
23   Section 84(4) (5) EPCA 1978.
24   See *McKindley v W. Hill Ltd* [1985] IRLR 492.
25   Section 84(6) EPCA 1978.
26   See *Hempell v W. H. Smith & Sons Ltd* [1986] IRLR 95.
27   See *Turvey v Cheyney Ltd* [1979] IRLR 105.
28   See *Air Canada v Lee* [1978] IRLR 392.
29   Section 92(3) and 82(2)c EPCA 1978.
30   See *Bonner v H. Gilbert Ltd* [1989] IRLR 475.
31   Section 92(2) EPCA 1978.
32   Section 82(2) EPCA 1978.
33   On the possibility of extending the contract to make up for days lost see section 110 EPCA 1978.
34   See *Simmons v Hoover Ltd* [1976] IRLR 266.
35   See *Sanders v E. Neale Ltd* [1974] ICR 565.
36   Section 195(1) TULRCA 1992.
37   See *E. Green Ltd v ASTMS and AUEW* [1984] IRLR 135.
38   Section 282(1) TULRCA 1992.
39   [1978] IRLR 366.
39A On what is 'fair consultation' see *R v British Coal ex parte Price* [1994] IRLR 72.
40   See *NUT v Avon County Council* [1978] IRLR 55.
41   See *TGWU v Ledbury Preserves* [1985] IRLR 412 and *Sovereign Distribution v TGWU* [1989] IRLR 334.
42   *Hough v Leyland DAF* [1991] IRLR 194.
43   Section 188(4) TULRCA 1992 (as amended).
44   See note 37.
45   See *GMB v Rankin* [1992] IRLR 514.
46   See *APAC v Kirvin* [1978] IRLR 318.
47   [1978] IRLR 20.
48   See *UCATT v Rooke & Son Ltd* [1978] IRLR 204.
49   Section 189(1)(5) TULRCA 1992; see chapter 3, note 14, on 'time limit escape clause'.
50   Section 189(6) TULRCA 1992.
51   See *E. Green Ltd v ASTMS and AUEW* (note 37).
52   Section 189(3)(4) TULRCA 1992.

53   See *Sovereign Distribution v TGWU* (note 41).
54   See *Spillers-French Ltd v USDAW* [1979] IRLR 339.
55   Section 190(2) TULRCA 1992.
56   Section 191(1–3) TULRCA 1992.
57   Section 192 TULRCA 1992.
58   Section 193 TULRCA 1992.
59   Section 193(4)(6) TULRCA 1992.
60   Section 193(5) TULRCA 1992.
61   See section 193(7) TULRCA 1992.
62   Section 194 TULRCA 1992.
63   See Regulation 3(1)(3) Transfer Regulations 1981.
64   See *Landsorganisationen I Danmark v Ny Molle Kro* [1989] IRLR 37.
65   See *Stichting v Bartol* [1992] IRLR 366.
66   See *Kenny v South Manchester College* [1993] IRLR 265.
67   See Regulation 10(1) of Transfer Regulations 1981. The trade union must be independent and recognized in relation to the affected employees.
68   See Regulation 10(5) of Transfer Regulations 1981 (as amended).
69   On the meaning of 'measures', 'envisages' and 'in connection with the transfer' see *IPCS v Secretary of State* [1987] IRLR 373.
70   See Regulation 10(7) Transfer Regulations 1981.
71   See Regulation 11(3)(4) Transfer Regulations 1981.
72   See Regulation 11(11) Transfer Regulations 1981 (as amended).
73   Section 31(1)(2) EPCA 1978. Paragraph 64 of ACAS *Code of Practice on Disciplinary and other Procedures in Employment* suggests that 'where possible employers should extend such assistance to all employees who are affected by redundancy'.
74   Section 31(4) EPCA 1978.
75   Section 31(7) EPCA 1978. The 'time limit escape clause' applies here (see chapter 3, note 14).
76   Section 31(5)(8) EPCA 1978. The 'set-off formula' applies here (see chapter 6, note 3).
77   [1978] IRLR 390.

14 Unfair dismissal and redundancy rights (4)

Making a claim

Unfair dismissal

Unless the 'time limit escape clause' applies[1] complaints of unfair dismissal must normally arrive at an industrial tribunal within three months of the effective date of termination (*see* chapter 11). However, where employees dismissed for taking part in industrial action allege that they should have been offered re-engagement (*see* chapter 12) a complaint must be lodged within six months of the date of dismissal.[2] A time limit expires at midnight on the last day of the stipulated period even when that is a non-working day.[3] A complaint can also be presented before the effective date of termination provided it is lodged after notice has been given. This includes notice given by an employee who is alleging constructive dismissal.[4] What is or is not reasonably practicable is a question of fact and the onus is on the employee to prove that it was not reasonably practicable to claim in time. The meaning of reasonably practicable lies somewhere between reasonable and reasonably capable physically of being done.[5]

The Court of Appeal has dealt with this jurisdictional point on several occasions and has taken the view that since the unfair dismissal provisions have been in force for some time tribunals should be fairly strict in enforcing the time limit. The fact that an internal appeal or criminal action is pending does not by itself provide a sufficient excuse for delaying an application.[6] The correct procedure is for employees to submit their applications, known as originating applications, and request that they be held in abeyance. It is a general principle of English law that ignorance does not afford an excuse. Nevertheless in *Wall's Meat Co. Ltd v Khan*[7] it was decided that ignorance or mistaken belief can be grounds for holding that it was not reasonably practicable if it could be shown that the ignorance or mistaken belief was itself reasonable. Thus in *Churchill v Yeates Ltd*[8] the EAT held that it was not reasonably practicable for an employee to bring a complaint until he or she had knowledge of a fundamental fact which rendered the dismissal unfair. In this case, after the three-month period had elapsed an employee who had been dismissed on the grounds of redundancy discovered that he had been replaced. Ignorance or mistaken belief will not be reasonable if it arises from the fault of complainants in not making such inquiries as they reasonably should have in the circumstances. However, there is no general principle that a failure by an adviser, such as a trade union official, citizens' advice bureau worker or solicitor, to give correct advice about a time limit will prevent the employee from arguing that it was not reasonably practicable to claim in time.[9]

The correct way to calculate the period of three months beginning with the effective date of termination is to take the day before the effective date and go forward three months. If there is no corresponding date in that month, the last day of the month is taken.[10] Where an application is posted within three months but arrives after the period has expired, the question to be determined is whether the claimant could reasonably have expected the application to be delivered in time in the ordinary course of the post.[11] The unexplained failure of an application to reach the tribunal is insufficient to satisfy the statutory test unless all reasonable steps were taken to confirm that the application was duly received.[12]

Redundancy

Employees who have not received a redundancy payment will normally only be entitled to make a claim if within six months of the relevant date (*see* chapter 11) they have:

(i)   given written notice to the employer that they want a payment, or
(ii) referred a question as to their right to a payment, or its amount, to a tribunal, or
(iii) presented a complaint of unfair dismissal to a tribunal.[13]

The written notice to the employer does not have to be in a particular form. The test is whether it is of such a character that the recipient would reasonably understand in all the circumstances that it was the employee's intention to seek a payment.[14] In this context the words 'presented' and 'referred' seem to have the same meaning, *i.e.* an application must have been received by the industrial tribunal within the six-month period.[15] Nevertheless, if any of the above steps are taken outside this period but within 12 months of the relevant date, a tribunal has the discretion to award a payment if it thinks that it would be just and equitable to do so. In such a case a tribunal must have regard to the employee's reasons for failing to take any of the steps within the normal time limit.[16]

Conciliation and compromise agreements

Copies of unfair dismissal applications, but not redundancy claims, and subsequent correspondence are sent to an ACAS conciliation officer who has the duty to endeavour to promote a settlement of the complaint:

(i) if requested to do so by the complainant and the employer (known as the respondent), or

(ii) if, in the absence of any such request, the conciliation officer considers that he or she could act with a reasonable prospect of success.

In *Moore v Duport Furniture*[17] the House of Lords decided that the expression 'promote a settlement' should be given a liberal construction capable of covering whatever action by way of such promotion is appropriate in the circumstances. Where the complainant had ceased to be employed the conciliation officer must seek to promote that person's re-employment (*i.e.* reinstatement or re-engagement) on terms which appear to be equitable. If the complainant does not wish to be re-employed, or this is not practicable, the conciliation officer must seek to promote agreement on compensation.[18] In addition section 134(3) EPCA 1978 requires conciliation officers to make their services available before a complaint has been presented if requested to do so by either a potential applicant or respondent. However, conciliation officers have no statutory duty to explain to employees what their statutory rights are.[19]

Where appropriate, a conciliation officer is to 'have regard to the desirability of encouraging the use of other procedures available for the settlement of grievances' and anything communicated to a conciliation officer in connection with the performance of the above functions is not admissible in evidence in any proceedings before a tribunal except with the consent of the person who communicated it.[20] It should be noted that an agreement to refrain from lodging an unfair dismissal complaint is subject to all the qualifications by which an agreement can be avoided at common law, for example on grounds of economic duress.[21] Where a representative holds himself or herself out as having authority to reach a settlement, in the absence of any notice to the contrary, the other party is entitled to assume that the representative does in fact have such authority. In such circumstances the agreement is binding on the client whether or not the adviser had any authority to enter into it.[22] A conciliated settlement will be binding even though it is not in writing[23] and the employee will be prevented from bringing the case before a tribunal.[24]

Formerly an agreement purporting to preclude a person from bringing an industrial tribunal complaint was void unless action had been taken by a conciliation officer in accordance with the above provisions. However, since 30 August 1993 an agreement to refrain from bringing certain tribunal proceedings will not be void if it satisfies the conditions governing 'compromise agreements'. These conditions are that:

(i)   the agreement must be in writing and must relate to the particular complaint

(ii) the employee must have received independent legal advice from a qualified lawyer as to the terms and effect of the proposed agreement and, in particular, its effect on the employee's ability to pursue his or her rights before a tribunal

(iii) at the time the adviser gives the advice there must be in force an insurance policy covering the risk of a claim by the employee in respect of loss arising in consequence of the advice

(iv) the agreement must identify the adviser and state that the conditions regulating compromise agreements under the relevant Act are satisfied.[25]

The remedies for unfair dismissal

Re-employment

When applicants are found to have been unfairly dismissed tribunals must explain their power to order reinstatement or re-engagement and ask employees if they wish such an order to be made. Only if such a wish is expressed can an order be made and if no order is made the tribunal must turn to the question of compensation.[26] Where re-employment is sought, a tribunal must first consider whether reinstatement is appropriate and in so doing must take into account the following matters:

(i)   whether the complainant wishes to be reinstated
(ii) whether it is practicable for the employer to comply with an order for reinstatement
(iii) where the complainant caused or contributed to some extent to the dismissal, whether it would be just to order reinstatement.[27]

If reinstatement is not ordered the tribunal must then decide whether to make an order for re-engagement and, if so, on what terms. At this stage the tribunal must take into account the following considerations:

(i)   any wish expressed by the complainant as to the nature of the order to be made
(ii) whether it is practicable for the employer or, as the case may be, a successor or associated employer to comply with an order for re-engagement
(iii) where the complainant caused or contributed to some extent to the dismissal, whether it would be just to order re-engagement and, if so, on what terms.

Except in a case where the tribunal takes into account contributory fault under paragraph (iii) it shall, if it orders re-engagement, do so in terms which are, so far as is reasonably practicable, as favourable as an order for reinstatement.[28] According to the Court of Appeal, a tribunal could approach the question whether it would be practicable to order re-employment in two stages. The first stage would be before any order had been made, when a provisional decision could be taken. The second stage would arise if such an order was made but not complied with. At that point the tribunal would have to reach a final conclusion on practicability because it might affect the size of the special award (*see* page 220).[29]

If at least seven days before the hearing the employee has expressed a wish to be re-employed but it becomes necessary to postpone or adjourn the hearing because the employer does not, without special reason, adduce reasonable evidence about the availability of the job from which the employee was dismissed, the employer will be required to pay the costs of the adjournment or postponement.[30] In addition, section 70(1) EPCA 1978 provides that where an employer has taken on a permanent replacement this shall not be taken into account unless the employer shows either:

(i) that is was not practicable to arrange for the dismissed employee's work to be done without engaging a permanent replacement, or

(ii) that a replacement was engaged after the lapse of a reasonable period without having heard from the dismissed employee that he or she wished to be reinstated or re-engaged, and that when the employer engaged the replacement it was no longer reasonable to arrange for the dismissed employee's work to be done except by a permanent replacement.

Practicability is a question of fact for each tribunal and in *Boots PLC v Lees*[31] the EAT agreed that it was practicable to reinstate notwithstanding that the employee's ultimate superior remained convinced that he was guilty of theft. On the other hand, the following arguments have been used to prevent an order being made: that the employee was unable to perform the work; that a redundancy situation arose subsequent to the dismissal; and that other employees were hostile to the complainant's return to work. It has also been suggested by the EAT that in a small concern where a close personal relationship exists reinstatement will only be appropriate in exceptional circumstances.[32]

For these purposes reinstatement is defined as treating the complainant 'in all respects as if he had not been dismissed' and on making an order the tribunal must specify:

(i) any amount payable by the employer in respect of any benefit which the complainant might reasonably be expected to have had but for the dismissal, including arrears of pay, for the period between the date of termination and the date of reinstatement

(ii) any rights and privileges, including seniority and pension rights, which must be restored to the employee

(iii) the date by which the order must be complied with.[33]

The complainant also benefits from any improvements that have been made to the terms and conditions of employment since dismissal.[34]

An order for re-engagement may be on such terms as the tribunal decides and the complainant may be engaged by the employer, a successor or an associated employer in comparable or suitable employment. On making such an order the tribunal must set out the terms including: the identity of the employer, the nature of the employment and the remuneration payable, together with the matters listed above in relation to reinstatement.[35]

Where a person is reinstated or re-engaged as the result of a tribunal order but the terms are not fully complied with,[36] a tribunal must make an additional award of compensation of such amount as it thinks fit, having regard to the loss sustained by the complainant in consequence of the failure to comply fully with the terms of the order.[37] It is a matter for speculation how long re-employment must last for it to be said that an order has been complied with. If a complainant is not re-employed in accordance with a tribunal order he or she is entitled to enforce the monetary element in the industrial tribunal.[38] Compensation will be awarded together with an additional or special award unless the employer satisfies the tribunal that it was not practicable to comply with the order.[39] According to the Court of Appeal, a re-engagement order does not place a duty on an employer to search for a job for the dismissed employee irrespective of the vacancies that arise.[40]

The additional award will be of between 13 and 26 weeks' pay or of between 26 and 52 weeks' pay if the dismissal was the result of unlawful sex or race discrimination.[41] The industrial tribunal has a discretion as to where, within these ranges, the additional compensation should fall but it must be exercised on the basis of a proper assessment of the factors involved. One factor would ordinarily be the view taken of the employer's conduct in refusing to comply with the order.[42] It will also be material for the tribunal to take into account the extent to which the compensatory award (*see* pages 215–20) has met the actual loss suffered by the complainant.[43] Where the reason or principal reason for dismissal related to trade union membership (*see* chapter 18) or the employee had health and safety responsibilities (*see* (i) and (ii) on page 164) a special award amounting to 156 weeks' pay or £20,100, whichever is the greater, will be made.[44] Conversely, employees who unreasonably prevent an order being complied with will be regarded as having failed to mitigate their loss (*see* page 216).

Awards of compensation

Compensation for unfair dismissal will usually consist of a basic award and a compensatory award. However, where the reason or principal reason for a dismissal related to trade union membership or the employee had health and safety responsibilities (*see* (i) and (ii) on page 164) and the complainant requested the tribunal to order re-employment, a special award will be made. It should be noted that if an award is not paid within 42 days of the tribunal's decision being recorded it will attract interest at the rate of 8 per cent.[45]

Basic award
Normally this will be calculated in the same way as a redundancy payment and will be reduced by the amount of any redundancy payment received.[46] However, persons below the age of 20 will be entitled to a basic award and this will be reduced after the age of 64 for both men and women (*see* page 221). Where the reason or principal reason for dismissal is related to union membership or the employee had health and safety responsibilities (*see* (i) and (ii) on page 164) there is a minimum award of £2,700, subject to any deduction on the grounds stated below.[47] The basic award can be reduced by such proportion as the tribunal considers just and equitable on two grounds:[48]

(i)   the complainant unreasonably refused an offer of

reinstatement. Such an offer could have been made before any finding or unfairness

(ii) any conduct of the complainant before the dismissal, or before notice was given.[49] This does not apply where the reason for dismissal was redundancy unless the dismissal was regarded as unfair by virtue of section 59(1) (a) EPCA 1978. In that event the reduction will only apply to that part of the award which is payable because of section 73(6A) EPCA 1978.

Although the entitlement to an irreducible minimum award of two weeks' pay has now been removed, an award of two weeks' pay will be made to employees who were redundant but unable to obtain a redundancy payment in either of the following circumstances:

(i) they are not to be treated as dismissed by virtue of section 84(1) EPCA 1978, which deals with the renewal of a contract or re-engagement under a new one, or

(ii) they are not entitled to a payment because of the operation of section 82(5) or (6) EPCA 1978, which are concerned with offers of alternative employment.[50]

Finally, a tribunal is not required to make a basic award to an employee who has already received an *ex gratia* sum in excess of the total of the maximum compensatory and basic award.[51]

Compensatory award

The amount of this award is that which a tribunal 'considers just and equitable in all the circumstances having regard to the loss sustained by the complainant in consequence of the dismissal insofar as that loss is attributable to action taken by the employer'. However, the mere fact that the employer could have dismissed fairly on another ground arising out of the same factual situation does not render it unjust or inequitable to award compensation.[52] Similarly, loss of wages following dismissal from any new employment cannot be attributed to action taken by the original employer.[53]

Section 74(3) EPCA 1978 specifically mentions that an individual whose redundancy entitlement would have exceeded the basic award can be compensated for the difference, while a redundancy payment received in excess of the basic award payable goes to reduce the compensatory award.[54] The compensatory award can be reduced in two other circumstances: where the employee's action caused or contributed to the dismissal, and where the employee failed to mitigate his or her loss. Before reducing an award on the ground that the complainant caused or contributed to the dismissal, a tribunal must be satisfied that the employee's conduct was culpable or blameworthy, *i.e.* foolish, perverse or unreasonable in the circumstances.[55] Thus there could be a finding of contributory fault in a case of constructive dismissal on the basis that there was a causal link between the employee's conduct and the employer's repudiatory breach of contract.[56] In determining whether to reduce compensation the tribunal must take into account the conduct of the complainant and not what happened to some other employee, for example one who was treated more leniently.[57] Not all unreasonable conduct will necessarily be culpable or blameworthy; it will depend on the degree of unreasonableness. Although ill health cases will rarely give rise to a reduction in compensation on grounds of contributory fault, it is clear that an award may be reduced under the overriding 'just and equitable' provisions.[58] Having found that an employee was to blame, a tribunal must reduce the award to some extent, although the proportion of culpability is a matter for the tribunal.[59]

Clearly, complainants are obliged to look for work and should not unreasonably refuse an offer of reinstatement,[60] but failure to utilize an internal appeal procedure does not amount to a failure to mitigate.[61] The onus is on the employer to prove that there was such a failure. While acknowledging that the employee has a duty to act reasonably the EAT has concluded that this standard is not high in view of the fact that the employer is the wrongdoer.[62]

No account is to be taken of any pressure which was exercised on the employer to dismiss the employee[63] and according to section 155 TULRCA 1992 compensation cannot be reduced on the grounds that the complainant:

(i)   was in breach of or proposed to breach a requirement that he or she must be, or become, a member of a particular trade union or one of a number of trade unions; cease to be, or refrain from becoming a member of any trade union or of a particular trade union or of one of a number of

particular trade unions, or would not take part in the
activities of any trade union, of a particular trade union or
of one of a number of particular trade unions

(ii) refused, or proposed to refuse, to comply with a requirement
of a kind mentioned in section 152(3)(a) TULRCA 1992
(*see* page 274)

(iii) objected, or proposed to object, to the operation of a
provision of a kind mentioned in section 152(3)(b) (*see* page
274).

Nevertheless this section permits a distinction to be drawn
between what was done by the complainant and the way in which
it was done.[64]

The maximum compensatory award, in 1993 was £11,000 but
the Secretary of State may increase the limit by an order approved
by both Houses of Parliament. The limit applies only after credit
has been given for any payments made by the employer and any
reductions have been made.[65] As regards deductions, normally
an employer is to be given credit for all payments made to an
employee in respect of claims for wages and other benefits. Thus
payments in lieu of notice and *ex gratia* payments can be
deducted.[66] Where an employee has suffered sex or race discrimination as well as unfair dismissal, section 76 EPCA 1978 prevents
double compensation for the same loss.

It is the duty of tribunals to inquire into the various heads of
damage but it is the responsibility of the aggrieved person to
prove the loss. The legislation aims to reimburse the employee
rather than to punish the employer.[67] Hence employees who
appear to have lost nothing – for example, where it can be said
that, irrespective of the procedural unfairness which occurred,
they would have been dismissed anyway – do not qualify for a
compensatory award.[68] However, if the employee puts forward an
arguable case that dismissal was not inevitable the evidential
burden shifts to the employer to show that dismissal was likely to
have occurred in any event.[69] Additionally a nil or nominal award
may be thought just and equitable in a case where misconduct
was discovered subsequent to the dismissal.[70]

The possible heads of loss have been divided into the following
categories:

(i) *Loss incurred up to the date of the hearing.* Here attention focuses on the employee's actual loss of income, which makes it necessary to ascertain the employee's take home pay. Thus tax and national insurance contributions are to be deducted but overtime earnings and tips can be taken into account. It should also be noted that the loss sustained should be based on what the employee was entitled to, whether or not he or she was receiving it at the time of dismissal.[71] As well as lost wages section 74(2) EPCA 1978 enables an individual to claim compensation for the loss of other benefits, *e.g.* a company car or other perks. Similarly, 'expenses reasonably incurred' are mentioned in the statute so, for example, employees will be able to recover the cost of looking for a new job or setting up their own business. However, complainants cannot be reimbursed for the cost of pursuing their unfair dismissal claims.

(ii) *Loss flowing from the manner of dismissal.* Compensation can only be awarded if the manner of dismissal has made the individual less acceptable to potential employers. There is nothing for hurt feelings.

(iii) *Loss of accrued rights.* This head of loss is intended to compensate the employee for the loss of rights dependent on a period of continuous service but, since the basic award reflects lost redundancy entitlement, sums awarded on these grounds have tended to be nominal. Nevertheless, tribunals should include a sum to reflect the fact that dismissed employees lose the statutory minimum notice protection that they have built up (*see* chapter 10).[72]

(iv) *Loss of pension rights.* Undoubtedly this presents the most complex problems of computation. Basically, there are two types of loss: the loss of the present pension position and the loss of the opportunity to improve one's pension position with the dismissing employer. When an employee is close to retirement the cost of an annuity which will provide a sum equal to the likely pension can be calculated. In other cases the starting point will be the contributions already paid into the scheme and, in addition to having their own contributions returned, employees can claim an interest in their employer's contributions, except in cases of transferred or deferred pensions. However, in assessing future loss the tribunal must take into account a number of possibilities, for example, future dismissal or resignation, early death and the fact that a capital sum is being paid sooner than would have been expected. Although industrial tribunals have been given actuarial guidelines on loss of pension rights, in each case the factors must be evaluated to see what adjustment should be made or whether the guidelines are safe to use at all.[73]

(v) *Future loss.* Where no further employment has been secured tribunals will have to speculate how long the employee will remain unemployed. Here the tribunal must utilize its knowledge of local market conditions as well as considering personal circumstances. According to the EAT, employees who have become unfit for work wholly or partly as a result of unfair dismissal are entitled to compensation for loss of earnings, at least for a reasonable period following the dismissal, until they might reasonably have been expected to find other employment.[74] If another job has been obtained tribunals must compare the employee's salary prospects for the future in each job and see as best they can how long it will take the employee to reach in the new job the equivalent salary to that which would have been attained had he or she remained with the original employer.[75] Where the employee is earning a higher rate of pay at the time compensation is being assessed, the tribunal should decide whether the new employment is permanent and, if so, should calculate the loss as between the date of dismissal and the date the new job was secured.[76] Since employees are disqualified from receiving unemployment benefit or income support during the period in which they are compensated for their loss, the possibility of individuals claiming these benefits can be discounted.[77]

Finally, mention must be made of Employment Protection (Recoupment of Unemployment Benefit and Supplementary Benefit) Regulations 1977,[78] which were designed to remove the state subsidy to employers who dismissed unfairly. Such benefits had the effect of reducing the losses suffered by dismissed persons. These regulations provide that a tribunal must not deduct from the compensation awarded any sum which represents unemployment benefit or income support received and the employer is instructed not to pay immediately the amount of compensation which represents loss of income up to the hearing (known as the 'prescribed element'). The Department of Employment can then serve the employer with a recoupment notice which will require him or her to pay the Department from the prescribed element the amount which represents the unemployment benefit or income support paid to the employee prior to the hearing. When the amount has been refunded the remainder of the prescribed element becomes the employee's property. It is important to note that private settlements do not fall within the scope of these Regulations.

Special award

Where the reason or principal reason for dismissal related to trade union membership or the employee had health and safety responsibilities (*see* (i) and (ii) on page 164) and re-employment was sought but not ordered by the tribunal, an employee will be entitled to 104 weeks' pay subject to a minimum of £13,400 and a maximum of £26,800. If re-employment was ordered but not complied with, a higher special award will be made (*see* page 214). Special awards can be reduced by such proportion as a tribunal considers just and equitable on three grounds:

(i)   any conduct of the complainant before the dismissal, or before notice was given
(ii) the complainant unreasonably refused an offer of reinstatement
(iii) the complainant unreasonably prevented a re-employment order being complied with.[79]

Calculating a redundancy payment

The size of a redundancy payment depends on the employee's length of continuous service, his or her age and the amount of a week's pay. A week's pay is calculated in accordance with Schedule 14 EPCA 1978 (*see* chapter 15) and in this context means gross pay.[80] However, it does not take into account increased wage rates agreed subsequent to the employee's dismissal but backdated to a date prior to the dismissal.[81] Unless the contrary is shown employment is presumed to have been continuous (*see* chapter 15) but this only applies in relation to the dismissing employer (except when a business or undertaking has been transferred or an employee has been taken into employment by an associated employer). If continuity is not preserved on a transfer, an assurance given by one employer that the obligations of another will be met will not confer jurisdiction on a tribunal to award a payment based on overall service. However, an employee may be able to show that there was a contract to the effect that he or she would retain the benefit of previous employment.[82]

Redundancy payments are calculated according to the following formula, with a maximum of 20 years' service being taken into account. Starting at the end of the employee's period of service and calculating backwards:

(i)   one and a half weeks' pay is allowed for each year of employment in which the individual was between the ages of 41 and 64. Those who are aged 64 have their entitlement reduced by one-twelfth in respect of each month they remain in employment

(ii) a week's pay for each year of employment in which the individual was between the ages of 22 and 40

(iii) half a week's pay for each year of employment between the ages of 18 and 21.[83]

On making a redundancy payment the employer must give the employee a written statement indicating how the amount has been calculated. An employer who, without reasonable excuse, fails to do so can receive a fine not exceeding level 3 on the standard scale.[84]

Employee rights on insolvency

If an employer becomes insolvent or bankrupt an employee's wages in respect of the four months beforehand, up to a maximum of £800, become a preferential debt.[85] In addition, Schedule 6 of the Insolvency Act 1986 provides that the following shall be treated as wages for these purposes: a guarantee payment; statutory sick pay; remuneration payable during suspension on medical grounds; remuneration payable under a protective award; and a payment for time off for union duties, antenatal care or to look for work or make arrangements for training in a redundancy situation.

Section 122 EPCA 1978 gives employees the right to make a written request to the Secretary of State for a payment out of the National Insurance Fund to meet certain other debts which arise out of the employer's insolvency. These debts are:

(i)   arrears of pay up to a maximum of eight weeks. This includes any of the matters treated as wages for the purposes of the Insolvency Act 1986 (*see* previous paragraph)

(ii)   wages payable during the statutory notice period. It should be noted that employees are still required to mitigate their loss. Thus unemployment benefit received during the notice period will be deducted from the amount payable,[86] as well as an amount in respect of income tax.[87]

(iii)   holiday pay up to a maximum of six weeks, provided the entitlement accrued during the preceding 12 months

(iv)   a basic award of compensation for unfair dismissal

(v)   any reasonable sum by way of reimbursement of the whole or part of any fee or premium paid by an apprentice or articled clerk.

A financial limit is imposed on the amount that can be recovered in respect of any one week.[88] Under section 123 EPCA 1978 'persons competent to act', *e.g.* pension fund trustees, may request the Secretary of State to make up any contributions which an insolvent employer failed to make to an occupational or personal pension scheme.

Before reimbursing the employee the Secretary of State must be satisfied both that the employer has become insolvent and that the employee was entitled to be paid the whole or part of the debt claimed. Also, a payment cannot be made unless a 'relevant officer' appointed in connection with the insolvency, *e.g.* a liquidator, receiver or trustee in bankruptcy, has supplied a statement of the amount owed to the employee. However, this requirement may be waived if the Secretary of State is satisfied that the statement is not necessary to determine the amount owing.[89] If the Secretary of State fails to make a payment or if it is less than the amount which the employee thinks should have been made, a complaint may be presented to an industrial tribunal within three months of the Secretary of State's decision being communicated.[90] Where a tribunal finds that a payment ought to have been made under section 122 or 123 EPCA 1978 it must make a declaration to that effect and state the amount that ought to be paid. Finally, it should be noted that when the Secretary of State makes a payment to the employee the rights and remedies of the latter in relation to the employer's insolvency are transferred to the Secretary of State.[91]

Notes

1   Section 67(2) EPCA 1978 (*see* chapter 3, note 14).
2   Section 239(2) TULRCA 1992.
3   See *Swainston v Hetton Victory Club* [1983] IRLR 164.
4   Section 67(4) EPCA 1978.
5   See *Palmer v Southend BC* [1984] IRLR 119.
6   See *Palmer v Southend BC*, note 5.
7   [1978] IRLR 499.
8   [1983] IRLR 187. See *also MTIRA v Simpson* [1988] IRLR 212.
9   See *London International College v Sen* [1993] IRLR 333.
10   See *Pruden v Cunard Ltd* [1993] IRLR 317.
11   See *St Basil's Centre v McCrossan* [1991] IRLR 455.
12   See *Capital Foods Ltd v Corrigan* [1993] IRLR 430.
13   Section 101(1) EPCA 1978. See *Duffin v Secretary of State* [1983] ICR 766.
14   See *Price v Smithfield Group Ltd* [1978] IRLR 80.
15   See *Secretary of State v Banks* [1983] ICR 48 and *Swainston v Hetton Victory Club* (note 3 above).
16   Section 101(2) EPCA 1978.
17   [1982] IRLR 31.
18   Section 134(2). EPCA 1978.
19   See *Slack v Greenham Ltd* [1983] IRLR 271.
20   Section 134(4)(5) EPCA 1978.
21   See *Hennessy v Craigmyle Ltd* [1985] IRLR 446.
22   See *Freeman v Sovereign Chicken Ltd* [1991] IRLR 408.
23   See *Gilbert v Kembridge Fibres Ltd* [1984] IRLR 52.
24   Section 140(2)d EPCA 1978.
25   See section 140(3)(4) EPCA 1978 (as amended).
26   Section 68(1)(2) EPCA 1978.
27   Section 69(5) EPCA 1978.
28   Section 69(6) EPCA 1978. See *City and Hackney HA v Crisp* [1990] IRLR 47.
29   See *Port of London Authority v Payne* [1994] IRLR 9.
30   Schedule 9 paragraph 1(4) EPCA 1978.

31   [1986] IRLR 485.
32   See *Enessy Co. SA v Minoprio* [1978] IRLR 489.
33   Section 69(2) EPCA 1978.
34   Section 69(3) EPCA 1978, but see also section 70(2) EPCA 1978 on deductions of money received from the employer.
35   Section 69(4) EPCA 1978.
36   See *Artisan Press v Srawley* [1986] IRLR 126 on the difference between not re-employing and not fully complying with an order.
37   Section 71(1) EPCA 1978.
38   See section 30 TURERA 1993.
39   Section 71(2) EPCA 1978 (as amended).
40   See *Port of London Authority v Payne* [1994] IRLR 9.
41   Section 71(3) EPCA 1978. Except in the case of special awards a week's pay is limited by Schedule 14 paragraph 8 EPCA 1978 and the maximum calculable in 1993 was £205 (*see* chapter 15).
42   See *Motherwell Railway Club v McQueen* [1989] ICR 419.
43   See *Mabirizi v National Hospital for Nervous Diseases* [1990] IRLR 133.
44   Section 75(A)(2) EPCA 1978.
45   See Judgment Debts (Rate of Interest) order 1993 SI No 564.
46   Section 73(9) EPCA 1978.
47   Section 73(3)c and section 73(4A) EPCA 1978.
48   Section 73(6A)(7B)(7C) EPCA 1978.
49   See *RSPCA v Cruden* [1986] IRLR 83.
50   Section 73(2) EPCA 1978.
51   See *Chelsea FC v Heath* [1981] IRLR 73.
52   See *Devonshire v Trico-Folberth* [1989] IRLR 397.
53   See *Courtaulds Ltd v Moosa* [1984] IRLR 43.
54   Section 74(7) EPCA 1978.
55   See *Nelson v BBC (No 2)* [1979] IRLR 304; *Morrison v ATGWU* [1989] IRLR 361.
56   See *Polentarutti v Autokraft Ltd* [1991] IRLR 457.
57   See *Parker Foundry Ltd v Slack* [1992] IRLR 11.
58   See *Slaughter v Brewer Ltd* [1990] IRLR 426.
59   See *Warrilow v Walker Ltd* [1984] IRLR 304.
60   See *Sweetlove v Redbridge and Waltham Forest AHA* [1979] IRLR 195.
61   See *Muir Ltd v Lamb* [1985] IRLR 95.
62   See *Fyfe v Scientific Furnishings Ltd* [1989] IRLR 331.
63   Section 74(5) EPCA 1978.
64   See *TGWU v Howard* [1992] IRLR 170.
65   Section 75(3) EPCA 1978; see *Braund Ltd v Murray* [1991] IRLR 100.
66   See *Rushton v Harcros Timber* [1993] IRLR 254.
67   See *Morris v Acco Co. Ltd* [1984] TLR 10/84.
68   On the distinction between procedural and substantive unfairness see *Steel Stockholders Ltd v Kirkwood* [1993] IRLR 515.
69   See *Britool Ltd v Roberts* [1993] IRLR 481.

70 See *Tele-trading Ltd v Jenkins* [1990] IRLR 430.
71 See *Kinzley v Minories Finance Ltd* [1987] IRLR 490.
72 See *Guinness Ltd v Green* [1989] IRLR 289.
73 See *Bingham v Hobourn Engineering Ltd* [1992] IRLR 298.
74 See *Devine v Designer Flowers Ltd* [1993] IRLR 517.
75 See *Tradewind Airways Ltd v Fletcher* [1981] IRLR 272.
76 See *Fentiman v Fluid Engineering Ltd* [1991] IRLR 150.
77 See Social Security (Unemployment, Sickness and Invalidity) Regulations, 1983, Regulation 7(1)k.
78 SI 1977 No 674.
79 Section 75A(4)(5) EPCA 1978.
80 See *Secretary of State v Woodrow* [1983] IRLR 11.
81 See *Leyland Vehicles Ltd v Reston* [1981] IRLR 19.
82 See *Secretary of State v Globe Elastic Ltd* [1979] IRLR 327.
83 Schedule 4 EPCA 1978.
84 Section 102 EPCA 1978.
85 Section 386 Insolvency Act 1986.
86 See *Westwood v Secretary of State* [1984] IRLR 209.
87 See *Secretary of State v Cooper and Vinning* [1985] EAT 1335/83.
88 £205 in 1993. See *Morris v Secretary of State* [1985] IRLR 297.
89 Section 122(11) EPCA 1978. The 'time limit escape clause' (as amended) applies here (*see* chapter 3, note 14).
90 Section 124(1) EPCA 1978.
91 Section 125 EPCA 1978.

15   Calculating continuous service, normal working hours and a week's pay

Continuity of employment

Continuous employment is an important concept because many statutory rights are dependent on a minimum service qualification and certain benefits, for example redundancy payments, are calculated by reference to length of service. An individual's period of employment is to be computed in accordance with schedule 13 EPCA 1978 which applies retrospectively.[1] Paragraph 1(3) of this schedule provides that employment is presumed to have been continuous unless the contrary is shown, although this is not so where there are a succession of employers.[2] Apart from redundancy payment purposes, Schedule 13 also applies to periods of employment wholly or mainly outside Great Britain.[3] Continuity is normally assessed in relation to the particular contract on which a claim is based. However, if an employer deliberately subjects an employee to a combination of separate contracts which deal individually with different tasks or workplaces for the purpose of depriving the employee of statutory rights, a tribunal might conclude that the purported multiple contracts were in reality a single contract.[4]

A period of continuous employment, which begins with the day on which the employee 'starts work',[5] is to be computed in months and, except in so far as is otherwise provided, a week which does not count breaks the period of continuous employment. A person only accrues a period of continuous service if he or she is employed under a legal contract of employment. Thus if for a period of time the contract is illegal then for that period the contract cannot be relied on.[6] Where there is a dispute over continuity employees have to establish that there was a week which counted but in respect of subsequent weeks they can rely on the presumption contained in paragraph 1(3) of schedule 13 EPCA 1978 (unless there is evidence to the contrary).[7]

Weeks which count

Where there is a contract of employment in existence

(i) Paragraph 3 of schedule 13 EPCA 1978 focuses on hours actually worked by providing that any week[8] in which a person is employed for 16 hours or more counts.

(ii) According to paragraph 4 schedule 13 EPCA 1978, any week during the whole or part of which a person was governed by a contract of employment which normally involved employment for 16 hours or more weekly will count. Tribunals have to examine the express or implied terms of a contract to determine the length of the normal working week. Tea breaks and preparation time can count as hours of employment if the employee was clearly 'on duty' at these times,[9] although overtime is to be disregarded unless it is mandatory, *i.e.* the employee was obliged to work it and the employer to provide it.

The inclusion of the word 'normally' means that an employee does not have to work 16 hours in every single week. Thus holidays and periods of sickness where the contract is not terminated can count under this paragraph. According to the EAT, in deciding whether a contract under which an employee must work such hours as the employer reasonably requires is one which normally involves employment for sixteen hours or more weekly, the correct approach is to look at what in fact took place. However, tribunals are not required to examine each week as a separate entity to see whether paragraph 4 applies.[10] Nevertheless, a normal working week is to be distinguished from an average working week, so an employee who works $20\frac{1}{4}$ hours one week and $13\frac{1}{2}$ hours the next suffers repeated breaks in continuous service.[11]

(iii) Where a contract of 16 hours or more per week is reduced to less than 16 but more than eight hours, up to 26 weeks at the reduced hours will count.[12] In addition, if employees have already qualified for a statutory right, for example to claim unfair dismissal or a redundancy payment, that right is not lost unless their normal working hours fall below eight *and* they are actually employed for less than 16 hours in any week.[13]

(iv) Where employees have worked continuously for five years under a contract normally involving more than eight hours per week (but less than 16) then they are to be treated as if they had worked 16 hours or more weekly.[14]

Where there is no contract of employment in existence
A week counts if one of the following applies for the whole or part of that week:

(i) *An employee is incapable of work in consequence of sickness or injury.*[15] Clearly this deals with the situation where the employee's contract has been terminated, for if it had not been, the weeks of absence would count under paragraph 4 schedule 13 EPCA 1978 (page 227). Not more than 26 consecutive weeks can be counted under this head.

   In this context the expression 'incapable of work' does not mean incapable of work generally, nor does it refer to the particular work provided for in the contract which has ended. According to the Court of Appeal, where the work on offer by the employer differs from that for which the employee was previously employed, the tribunal must consider whether the work offered was of a kind which the employee was willing to accept or, even though the employee was unwilling, was suited to his or her particular circumstances.[16]

(ii) *An employee is absent from work on account of a temporary cessation of work.*[17] In this context the phrase 'absent from work' does not necessarily mean physical absence but means not performing in substance the contract that previously existed between the parties.[18] The words 'on account of' refer to the reason when the employer dismissed, and the fact that the unavailability of work was foreseen and the employee took another job will not prevent a tribunal holding that this provision applies. 'Cessation of work' denotes that a quantity of work has for the time being ceased to exist and was therefore no longer available to be given to the employee. Thus when a member of a pool of casual cleaners was not allocated work under a pool arrangement that absence was not on account of a temporary cessation of work.[19]

According to the House of Lords, 'temporary' means lasting a relatively short time and whether an interval can be so characterized is a question of fact for the industrial tribunal. Where there is a succession of fixed term contracts with intervals between them, continuity is not broken unless 'looking backwards from the date of expiry of the fixed term contract on which the claim is based, there is to be found between one fixed term contract and its immediate predecessor an interval that cannot be characterized as short relative to the combined duration of the two fixed term contracts'.[20] In *Flack v Kodak Ltd*[21] the EAT held that where an employee has worked intermittently over a period of years in an irregular pattern, tribunals ought to have regard to all the circumstances and should not confine themselves to the mathematical approach of looking at each gap and immediately adjoining periods of employment. The fact that cessation is not permanent does not mean that it must be temporary for these purposes.[22]

(iii) *An employee is absent from work in circumstances such that by arrangement or custom he or she is regarded as continuing in the employment of the employer for all or any purposes.* Although an arrangement must normally exist at the time the absence began, the EAT has held that the period between dismissal and voluntary reinstatement may be covered by this provision.[23] It should be noted that unfair dismissal complainants who are re-employed following a tribunal decision, a compromise agreement (*see* page 209–10), or action taken by a conciliation officer have their continuity preserved by special regulations.[24]

It would appear that the cause of the absence is immaterial. Thus employees who have been loaned to a third party may be protected as well as those given leave of absence for personal reasons. In *Lloyds Bank Ltd v Secretary of State*[25] the EAT held that employees who worked alternate weeks were to be regarded as being absent by arrangement on their weeks off rather than governed by a contract which normally involves work for less than 16 hours a week.

(iv) *The employee is absent from work wholly or partly because of pregnancy or childbirth.*[26] Not more than 26 consecutive weeks can be counted in these circumstances, although under paragraph 10 schedule 13 EPCA 1978 if a woman exercises her statutory right to return to work (*see* page 86) every week of her absence will count. It makes no difference that the employee has resigned or been dismissed.[27]

Strikes and lock-outs

Days on which an employee is on strike neither count nor break the employee's period of continuous service.[28] By virtue of paragraph 24(1) Schedule 13 EPCA 1978 for this purpose 'strike' means 'the cessation of work by a body of persons employed acting in combination, or a concerted refusal or a refusal under a common understanding of any number of persons employed to continue to work for an employer in consequence of a dispute, done as a means of compelling their employer or any person or body of persons employed, or to aid other employees in compelling their employer or any person or body of persons employed, to accept or not to accept terms and conditions of or affecting employment'. Thus time spent engaged in political strikes can count as part of a period of continuous service!

Where an employee is absent from work because of a lock-out, again continuity is not broken and, if the contract of employment subsists, the period of absence could be counted under paragraph 4 (page 227).[29] 'Lock-out' means 'the closing of a place of employment, or the suspension of work, or the refusal by an employer to continue to employ any number of persons employed by him in consequence of a dispute, done with a view to compelling those persons, or to aid another employer in compelling persons employed by him, to accept terms or conditions of or affecting employment'.[30]

It makes no difference that employees were dismissed during a strike or lock-out; as long as they were subsequently re-engaged their period of continuous employment will be preserved. Any attempt to provide otherwise, for example, by introducing a specific term relating to previous employment, will be construed as an attempt to exclude or limit the operation of this paragraph and will be ineffective as a result of section 140 EPCA 1978.[31]

Change of employer

Usually when an employee leaves one employer and starts working for another his or her period of continuous service will be broken. However, in certain circumstances a person will be regarded as having been employed by the new employer as from the date his or her previous employment commenced. Apart from the situation where an employer voluntarily agrees to give credit for service with a previous employer (which does not bind the Secretary of State),[32] there are five types of case in which employment is deemed to be continuous despite a change of employer:

(i)   if there is a transfer of a trade, undertaking, business or part of a business.[33] The words 'trade' and 'undertaking' are not defined in EPCA 1978, but 'business' includes a trade or profession and any activity carried on by a body of persons, whether corporate or incorporate.[34] In relation to business transfers the critical question is whether there has been the transfer of a 'going concern' which could be carried on without interruption or merely the disposal of assets. If the latter, continuity of employment is not maintained. Frequently, an important factor is the sale of goodwill (*see* chapter 13). It would seem that there could be a transfer of ownership without any written agreement and whether or not there has been a transfer must be decided as at the date when the act of which the employee complains occurred.[35]

(ii)   if an Act of Parliament results in one corporate body replacing another as employer[36]

(iii) if the employer dies and the employee is then re-employed by the personal representatives or trustees of the deceased[37]

(iv) if there is a change in the partners, personal representatives or trustees who employ the individual[38]

(v)   if the individual is taken into the employment of an

associated employer.[39] 'Associated employer' is defined in section 153(4) EPCA 1978 as follows: 'any two employers are to be treated as associated if one is a company of which the other (directly or indirectly) has control; or if both are companies of which a third person (directly or indirectly) has control'.[40] The Court of Appeal has ruled that this definition is exhaustive and since local government bodies and health authorities are not limited companies, consecutive periods of employment with them cannot be aggregated for statutory purposes.[41] However, by virtue of paragraph 18A schedule 13 EPCA 1978 if a teacher transfers between schools maintained by the same local education authority continuity is preserved.[42] The expression 'has control' is used in the company law sense of controlling 51 per cent or more of the shares. However, the register of shares does not conclusively establish the identity of the possessor of control since the person registered as owner might be a nominee.[43] While there must not be a gap between the employments (unless it is covered by the schedule) it is not necessary that the move to an associated employer be made with the acquiescence of either employer.

Normal working hours

Not only do normal working hours determine whether employment counts towards a period of continuous service but it is also necessary to know whether a person has normal working hours for the purpose of calculating a week's pay. For all statutory purposes normal working hours and a week's pay are to be ascertained by reference to Schedule 14 EPCA 1978.

Normal working hours are the number of hours employees are required to work by their contracts and where they are expressly stated this will usually be conclusive even if longer hours are actually worked.[44] Where the contractual terms have not been expressed by the parties, to determine the number of hours the contract normally involves it is necessary to look at the way the parties acted. If it was a term that employees should work the hours they were asked to then one looks at the hours actually worked.[45] Normal working hours will not include overtime unless that overtime is included in the minimum number of hours of employment.[46]

A week's pay

This concept is used for computing many payments under EPCA 1978, for example redundancy payments and the basic award of compensation for unfair dismissal.

Where there are normal working hours

(i)   If remuneration does not vary with the amount of work done a week's pay is the gross amount payable for a week's work under the contract of employment in force on the calculation date.[47] Calculation dates are laid down in paragraph 7 Schedule 14 EPCA 1978 and vary according to the particular statutory rights being enforced.

(ii) If the remuneration varies with the amount of work done a week's pay is the remuneration for the number of normal working hours payable at the average hourly rate.[48] The average hourly rate is ascertained by calculating the total number of hours actually worked in the 12 calendar weeks preceding the calculation date, the total amount of remuneration paid for these hours and then deducing the average hourly payment. The 12 calendar weeks preceding the calculation date consist of weeks during which the employee actually worked even though for some of this time he or she might have earned less than usual. However, a week in which no remuneration was required to be paid must be disregarded.[49] In *British Coal v Cheesbrough*[50] the average hourly rate was calculated by taking into account all remuneration paid in respect of all hours worked, including overtime, except that the premium element in respect of overtime was disregarded.

(iii) Where the normal working hours are worked at varying times and in varying amounts in different weeks, for example in the case of shift-workers, both the average rate of remuneration and the number of hours worked in a week will have to be computed, again in the 12 calendar weeks preceding the calculation date. In these circumstances, a week's pay is the average weekly number of normal working hours payable at the average hourly rate of remuneration.[51]

Where there are no normal working hours

Here a week's pay is the average weekly remuneration received over the period of 12 calendar weeks preceding the calculation date.[52]

If an employee has not been employed for a sufficient period to enable a calculation to be made under any of the above provisions a tribunal must decide what amount 'fairly represents a week's pay'. Paragraph 9 Schedule 14 EPCA 1978 sets out some matters for consideration in this respect. Finally, the word 'remuneration' has not been statutorily defined for these purposes but it has been held to include any payments made on a regular basis, *e.g.* commission, bonuses and attendance allowances. Payments in kind are excluded, for example free accommodation, as are payments received from a third party, such as tips.

Notes

1 See Schedule 13 paragraph 21 EPCA 1978.
2 See *Secretary of State v Cohen* [1987] IRLR 169.
3 See Schedule 13 paragraph 1(2) and *Weston v Vega Co-op Ltd* [1989] IRLR 429.
4 See *Lewis v Surrey County Council* [1987] IRLR 509.
5 See *General of the Salvation Army v Dewsbury* [1984] IRLR 222.
6 See *Hyland v J. Barker Ltd* [1985] IRLR 403.
7 See *Nicoll v Nocorrode Ltd* [1981] IRLR 163.
8 'Week' means a week ending with Saturday. See Schedule 13 paragraph 24(1) EPCA 1978. On the 16-hour threshold see *R v Secretary of State ex part EOC* (1994) TLR 4/3/94.
9 See *Turner v Sara Lou Ltd* (1984) EAT 513/84.
10 See *Green v Roberts* [1982] IRLR 499.
11 See *Opie v John Gubbins Ltd* [1978] IRLR 540.
12 Schedule 13 paragraph 5 EPCA 1978. On the thresholds see *R v Secretary of State ex parte EOC* (note 8).
13 Schedule 13 paragraph 7 EPCA 1978. See *Secretary of State v Deary* [1984] IRLR 180 and *R v Secretary of State ex parte EOC* (note 8).

14 Schedule 13 paragraph 6 EPCA 1978. See *Harber v North London Polytechnic* [1990] IRLR 198 and *R v Secretary of State ex part EOC* (note 8).

15 Schedule 13 paragraph 9(1)a EPCA 1978.

16 See *Pearson v Kent County Council* [1993] IRLR 165.

17 Schedule 13 paragraph 9(1)b EPCA 1978.

18 See *Stephens & Son v Fish* [1989] ICR 324.

19 *Byrne v City of Birmingham DC* [1987] IRLR 191.

20 *Ford v Warwickshire CC* [1983] IRLR 126.

21 [1986] IRLR 255.

22 See *Sillars v Charrington's Ltd* [1989] IRLR 152 on seasonal work.

23 *Ingram v Foxon* [1985] IRLR 5.

24 See Employment Protection (Continuity of Employment) Regulations 1993 SI 2165.

25 [1978] IRLR 41.

26 Schedule 13 paragraph 9(1)d EPCA 1978.

27 See *Mitchell v British Legion Club* [1980] IRLR 425.

28 Schedule 13 paragraph 15(1)(2) and section 151(5)(6)b EPCA 1978.

29 Schedule 13 paragraph 15(4) EPCA 1978.

30 Schedule 13 paragraph 24(1) EPCA 1978.

31 See *Hanson v Fashion Industries* [1980] IRLR 393.

32 See *Secretary of State v Globe Elastic Thread Co. Ltd* [1979] IRLR 327.

33 Schedule 13 paragraph 17(2) EPCA 1978. For a generous interpretation of this provision see *Macer v Abafast Ltd* [1990] IRLR 138. Note also the impact of the Transfer Regulations 1981 (page 17).

34 Section 153(1) EPCA 1978.

35 *Secretary of State v Cohen* (see note 2).

36 Schedule 13 paragraph 17(3) EPCA 1978.

37 Schedule 13 paragraph 17(4) EPCA 1978.

38 Schedule 13 paragraph 17(5) EPCA 1978. See *Jeetle v Elster* [1985] IRLR 227.

39 Schedule 13 paragraph 18 EPCA 1978.

40 An overseas company can be included if it can be likened to a company limited under the Companies Act 1985; see *Hancill v Marcon Ltd* [1990] IRLR 51. On companies trading as a partnership see *Pinkney v Sandpiper Drilling Ltd* [1989] IRLR 425.

41 See *Gardiner v London Borough of Merton* [1980] IRLR 61.

42 See Redundancy Payments (Local Government) (Modification) Order 1983 SI No 1160 (as amended), which covers certain educational institutions and 'relevant local government' services.

43 See *Payne v Secretary of State* [1989] IRLR 352 and *Strudwick v IBL* [1988] IRLR 457.

44 See *Gascol Conversions v Mercer* [1974] IRLR 155.

45 See *Dean v Eastbourne Fishermen's Club Ltd* [1977] IRLR 143.

46 Schedule 14 paragraph 2 EPCA 1978. See *Lotus Cars Ltd v Sutcliffe and Stratton* [1982] IRLR 381.

47 Schedule 14 paragraph 3(2) EPCA 1978; see *Keywest Club v Choud-hury* [1988] IRLR 51.
48 Schedule 14 paragraph 3(3) EPCA 1978.
49 Schedule 14 paragraphs 5(1) and 6(3) EPCA 1978; see *Secretary of State v Crane* [1988] IRLR 238.
50 [1990] IRLR 148.
51 Schedule 14 paragraph 4 EPCA 1978.
52 Schedule 14 paragraph 6 EPCA 1978.

16 The legal framework of collective bargaining

The general and specific duties of ACAS, the functions of the CAC and the role of the Certification Officer were all outlined in chapter 1. In this chapter we examine the legal definition of an employers' association and a trade union and describe the mechanism by which a union can obtain a certification of independence. We also consider the question of recognition and the duty placed upon employers to disclose information for the purpose of collective bargaining. Finally, the legal enforceability of collective agreements will be discussed.

Employers' associations

According to section 122 TULRCA 1992 an employers' association means an organization which consists either:

(i) wholly or mainly of employers or individual proprietors whose principal purposes include the regulation of relations between employers and workers (or trade unions), or

(ii) wholly or mainly of constituent or affiliated organizations with these purposes or representatives of such organizations, and in either case is an organization whose principal purposes include the regulation of relations between employers and workers (or trade unions) or between constituent and affiliated organizations.[1]

Thus whether a trade association is or is not to be legally regarded as an employers' association will depend on its particular objectives. The Certification Officer is responsible for maintaining a list of employers' associations containing the names of those organizations which are entitled to have their names entered on it.[2] Whether listed or not, employers' associations are granted immun-

237

ity in respect of the doctrine of restraint of trade, although the immunity of incorporated associations is only in connection with the regulation of relations between employers (or employers' associations) and workers (or trade unions).[3] Like trade unions, employers' associations are required to keep accounting records, to make annual returns and to have their accounts audited.[4] Part 1 Chapter 3 of TULRCA 1992 deals with the administrative provisions relating to employers' associations and trade unions.

Trade unions and certificates of independence

A trade union is an organization, whether permanent or temporary, which consists either:

(i)   wholly or mainly of workers whose principal purposes include the regulation of relations between workers and employers (or employers' associations), or

(ii) wholly or mainly of constituent or affiliated organizations with those purposes, or representatives of such organizations, and in either case is an organization whose principal purposes include the regulation of relations between workers and employers (or employers' associations) or include the regulation of relations between its constituent or affiliated organizations.[5]

This definition covers not only individual and confederated unions and the TUC, but also the union side of a joint negotiating committee. Section 10 TULRCA 1992 provides that a trade union 'shall not be, or be treated as if it were, a body corporate', yet it is capable of making contracts, suing and being sued in its own name, and being prosecuted.[6] However in *EETPU v Times Newspapers*[7] it was held that the union could not sue for libel, since it did not have the necessary legal personality to be protected by an action for defamation. All property belonging to a trade union must be vested in trustees and any judgment, order or award is enforceable against the property held in trust.[8] Trade unions are protected against the doctrine of restraint of trade, in respect of both their purposes and their rules.[9] (On immunity from certain actions in tort *see* chapter 20.)

The Certification Officer maintains a list of trade unions and a trade union which submits the appropriate fee, a copy of its rules, a list of officers, the address of its head office and the name under which it is known may apply for inclusion on this list.[10] A listed union is entitled to a certificate stating that its name is included on the list and such listing is a prerequisite for obtaining a certificate of independence. The Certification Officer makes copies of the lists of trade unions and employers' associations available for public inspection and must remove the name of an organization if requested to do so by that organization or he or she is satisfied that the organization has ceased to exist.[11] Any organization which is aggrieved by the refusal of the Certification Officer to enter its name on the relevant list, or by a decision to remove its name, may appeal to the EAT on a question of fact or law.[12]

A trade union whose name is on the relevant list can apply to the Certification Officer for a certificate that it is independent. The Certification Officer is responsible for keeping a record of all applications and must decide whether the applicant union is independent or not.[13] Section 5 TULRCA 1992 deems a trade union to be independent if:

(i) it is not under the domination or control of an employer or a group of employers or of one or more employers' associations, and

(ii) it is not liable to interference by an employer or any such group or association, arising out of the provision of financial or material support or by any other means whatsoever, tending towards such control.

The Certification Officer cannot make a determination until one month after the application has been entered on the record and, before making such a determination, 'he shall make such inquiries as he thinks fit and shall take into account any relevant information submitted to him by any person',[14] *e.g.* by a TUC-affiliated union opposed to a house union or staff association obtaining a certificate. If the Certification Officer concludes that the applicant is independent a certificate will be issued, yet only if the union is found not to be independent must reasons be given.[15] The Certification Officer may at any time withdraw a certificate if he or she is of the opinion that the union is no longer independent, in which case the procedure laid down in section 7 TULRCA 1992 must be complied with. A trade union aggrieved by a refusal to grant a certificate or by the withdrawal of its certificate may appeal to the EAT on a point of fact or law.[16] Of course, a union may choose not to appeal but to make any necessary changes and re-apply to the Certification Officer. A certificate constitutes conclusive evidence for all purposes that the union is independent. If a question arises in any proceedings as to whether a trade union is independent and there is no certificate in force and no refusal, withdrawal or cancellation of a certificate recorded, the body before whom the issue arose cannot decide the matter but may refer it to the Certification Officer.[17]

Over the years, certain criteria have evolved for assessing whether a union is under the domination or control of an employer. In *A. Monk Staff Association v Certification Officer and ASTMS*[18] the EAT confirmed that the following matters should be considered:

(i)   the union's history (was it originally the employer's creation?)
(ii)   its organization and structure (is it likely to be controlled by senior members of management?)
(iii)   its finance (to what extent is it subsidized by the employer?)
(iv)   the extent of employer provided facilities (are there free premises, etc?)
(v)   its collective bargaining record.

In this case it was also held that, on appeal against the Certification Officer's decision, the question of independence should be decided on all the evidence available and not confined to the material that was before the Certification Officer. Here there had been significant changes since the Certification Officer investigated the matter, including the appointment of an independent consultant/ negotiator. As regards 'liable to interference', the Court of Appeal has ruled that the Certification Officer is not required to assess the likelihood of interference by the employer. The Certification Officer's interpretation of the words as meaning 'vulnerable to interference' was the correct one, *i.e.* the degree of risk is irrelevant so long as it is recognizable and not insignificant.[19] Thus in *GCSF v Certification Officer*[20] the staff federation was denied a certificate because its continued existence depended on the approval of the GCHQ director.

Finally, it is worth documenting the major advantages that accrue to independent trade unions:

(i)   if recognized, they have the right to appoint safety representatives (*see* chapter 7)

(ii) if recognized, their representatives are entitled to receive information for collective bargaining purposes (*see* pages 243–6)

(iii) if recognized, their representatives must be consulted in respect of redundancies and transfers of undertakings (*see* chapter 13)

(iv) if recognized, their officials can take time off for union activities (*see* chapter 18)

(v)   they can make and apply for exemption for a 'dismissal procedures agreement' (*see* chapter 11)

(vi) they may obtain public funds for holding various ballots (*see* chapter 18)

(vii) employees cannot have action taken against them because they seek to join, have joined, or taken part in the activities of such a union. Interim relief is available to members who have been dismissed (*see* chapter 18).

Recognition

We have just seen that independent trade unions must be recognized by the employer in order to enjoy a number of statutory rights. The same definition applies in respect of each of these rights, namely, 'recognition in relation to a trade union means the recognition of the union by an employer, or two or more associated employers, to any extent for the purpose of collective bargaining'.[21]

Collective bargaining means negotiations relating to or connected with one or more of the matters specified in section 178(2) TULRCA 1992.[22] Although the question of recognition is one of fact for a court or industrial tribunal to decide, it is worth outlining some of the principles which have emerged to date.

First, it would appear that there must be an express or implied agreement between the union and the employer to negotiate on one or more of the matters listed in section 178(2) TULRCA 1992.

For agreement to be implied there must be clear and unequivocal conduct over a period of time.[23] Thus, while recognition has been inferred from consultations on discipline and facilities for union representatives despite the absence of formal agreement,[24] a discussion on wages which took place on a particular occasion was held to be insufficient to establish recognition, particularly when the employer's attitude was one of refusing to bargain.[25] Neither the fact that the union has a right of representation on a national body responsible for negotiating pay[26] nor that the employers' association to which the employer belongs recognizes the union will, by itself, constitute recognition by the employer.[27] It has also been confirmed that an agreement to permit the union to represent its members for grievance purposes is insufficient to establish that the union has been recognized at law.[28]

In practice, negotiating procedures have been established for handling recognition claims and the TUC Disputes Procedure can play a significant role where the question of recognition is tied in with an inter-union dispute, provided the disputants are affiliated to the TUC. However, if a dispute cannot be resolved within the normal negotiating machinery the parties may ask ACAS to conciliate. There has been no statutory procedure for achieving recognition since 1980, although even when statutory powers did exist the number of recognition cases submitted to voluntary conciliation exceeded the number of statutory references.

Finally, mention must be made of the Transfer Regulations 1981. According to Regulation 9, where the transferred undertaking retains a distinct identity, any trade union recognized by the transferor must be recognized by the transferee to the same extent.[29] There is no guidance as to what constitutes 'an identity distinct from the remainder of the transferee's undertaking', but it is clear that once a transfer has occurred the transferee can open negotiations about whether recognition should be continued. Similarly, Regulation 6 provides that collective agreement which exists at the time of the transfer continues in force after the transfer in relation to the employees transferred, as if it had been made with the new employer. This means that any provisions of a collective agreement which apply to individual employees will continue to operate and could include non-contractual disciplinary or grievance procedures.

Disclosure of information for collective bargaining

For the purposes of all the stages of collective bargaining between employers and representatives of recognized independent trade unions, employers have a duty to disclose to those representatives, on request, all such information relating to their undertakings as is in their possession or that of any associated employer which is both:[30]

(i)   information without which the union representatives would be to a material extent impeded in carrying on with them such collective bargaining,[31] and
(ii) information which it would be in accordance with good industrial relations practice that they should disclose.

An employer can insist that a request for information must be made in writing and likewise the information itself must be in written form if that is the wish of the union representatives.[32] According to section 181(1) TULRCA 1992, a 'representative' is an 'official or other person authorized by the trade union to carry on such collective bargaining'. However, an 'undertaking' is not defined for these purposes.

The phrase 'of all the stages' means that information can be sought in order to prepare a claim,[33] although it must relate to matters in respect of which the union is recognized. In *R v CAC ex parte BTP Tioxide*[34] the High Court held that the CAC had misdirected itself in concluding that the union was entitled to information relating to a job evaluation scheme in respect of which it had no bargaining rights but only the right to represent its members in re-evaluation appeals:

> there is no obstacle under the Act to an agreement which recognizes the union's right to collective bargaining, that is negotiating, in respect of one aspect of terms and conditions of employment and also recognizes a right to some form of dealings with employers, which does not answer to the description of collective bargaining, about another aspect.

In essence, for information to be disclosed under these provisions it must be both relevant and important.[35] Although each case must be judged on its merits, unions may be entitled to information about groups not covered for collective bargaining purposes. Thus

in Award 80/40 the CAC held that information about a productivity scheme for management, not covered by the union, was
relevant and important to negotiations over a scheme for technical
staff because of the similarity of the work of some employees
within both groups.

In determining what constitutes 'good industrial relations practice' attention must be paid to the ACAS Code of Practice,[36]
although other evidence is not to be excluded.[37] Thus unions may
seek to demonstrate good practice by referring to the approaches
taken by comparable employers.[38] To decide what information will
be relevant, negotiators are advised to take account of the subject
matter of the negotiations and the issues raised during them; the
level at which negotiations take place; the size of the company
and its type of business.[39] There is no list of items which should
be disclosed in all circumstances but the following examples of
information which could be relevant in certain situations are given
as a guide:[40]

(i)   pay and benefits
(ii) conditions of service
(iii) manpower
(iv) performance
(v)   financial

This is not an exhaustive list and other items may be relevant in
particular negotiations. The underlying philosophy of the code
is that employers and unions should endeavour to reach a
joint understanding on how the disclosure provisions
can be implemented most effectively: 'In particular, the parties
should endeavour to reach an understanding on what information could most appropriately be provided on a regular
basis.'[41]

The duty to disclose is subject to the exceptions detailed in
section 182 TULRCA 1992. Employers are not required to
disclose:

(i)   any information the disclosure of which would be against
      the interests of national security
(ii) any information which could not be disclosed without
      contravening other legislation

(iii) any information which has been communicated to the employer in confidence

(iv) any information relating specifically to an individual unless he or she has consented to its disclosure

(v) any information, the disclosure of which would cause substantial injury to the employer's undertaking for reasons other than its effect on collective bargaining

(vi) information obtained by the employer for the purpose of bringing or defending any legal proceedings.

While (iii) applies to standard form tenders headed 'In confidence',[42] it should be noted that it does not protect an employer who discloses information in confidence to lay union representatives and restricts them from communicating it to union members and full-time officials. Where a union seeks disclosure about individual salaries without the consent of the individuals concerned, in order to avoid the impact of (iv) it must be clear that the information relates to the posts involved and not to the individuals filling them.[43] As regards (v), paragraph 14 of the Code offers some examples of information which, if disclosed in particular circumstances, might cause substantial injury. This would cover such matters as cost information on individual products; detailed analysis of proposed investment; marketing or pricing policies; price quotas or the make-up of tender prices. Further guidance is offered in paragraph 15:

> ... substantial injury may occur if, for example, certain customers would be lost to competitors, or suppliers would refuse to supply necessary materials, or the ability to raise funds to finance the company would be seriously impaired as a result of disclosing certain information. The burden of establishing a claim that disclosure of certain information would cause substantial injury, lies with the employer.[44]

By virtue of section 182(2) TULRCA employers are not obliged to produce, allow inspection of, or copy, any document other than a document conveying or confirming the information disclosed,[45] and are not required to compile any information where to do so would involve an amount of work or expenditure out of reasonable proportion to the value of the information in the conduct of collective bargaining.[46]

A union which feels that its representatives have not received the information to which they are entitled can complain in writing to the CAC, and if the CAC is of the opinion that the complaint is 'reasonably likely to be settled by conciliation' it must refer it to ACAS. Where no reference to ACAS is made or no settlement or withdrawal is achieved, the CAC must hear the complaint, make a declaration stating whether it is well founded, wholly or in part, and give reasons for its finding. If the complaint is upheld the declaration will specify the information in respect of which the CAC believed the complaint to be well founded; the date on which the employer refused or failed to disclose information; and the period within which the employer ought to disclose the information specified.[47]

At any time after the expiry of this period the union may present a 'further complaint' that the employer has failed to disclose the required information. Again, the CAC must hear and determine the complaint and declare whether it holds it to be well founded.[48] On or after presenting the further complaint the union may submit a claim that the employees' contracts should be amended to include the terms and conditions detailed in the claim, *e.g.* for more pay. However, no such claim can be lodged, or if presented it will be treated as withdrawn, if the relevant information is disclosed at any time before the CAC has adjudicated on the further complaint. If the further complaint is well founded, the CAC may, after hearing the parties, award the terms and conditions detailed in the claim or others which it considers appropriate. Such an award will relate only to matters in respect of which the trade union is recognized. The terms and conditions awarded take effect as part of the contracts of employment of the employees covered, except in so far as they are superseded or varied by:

(i)   a subsequent award under these provisions
(ii) a collective agreement between the employer and the union
(iii) an individual agreement, express or implied, effecting an improvement in the terms and conditions laid down in the award.[49]

It should be observed that these statutory provisions do not enable a union to force the disclosure of information.

The directors' report on employee involvement

Schedule 7 paragraph 11 of the Companies Act 1985 requires companies with more than 250 employees working in the UK to include in their directors' report a statement describing the action that has been taken during the financial year to introduce, maintain or develop arrangements aimed at:

(i)   providing employees systematically with information on matters of concern to them

(ii) consulting employees or their representatives regularly so that employees' views can be taken into account in making decisions which are likely to affect their interests

(iii) encouraging employee involvement in the company's performance through an employee's share scheme or by some other means

(iv) achieving a common awareness on the part of all employees of the financial and economic factors affecting the company's performance.

It is worth noting that the Act does not actually oblige companies to take any measures to bring about involvement.

The legal enforceability of collective agreements

In this section we are concerned with the legal enforceability of collective agreements between employers and trade unions and not the effect of such agreements on individual contracts of employment. It is important to remember that the legal status of the arrangements made between the employer and the union has no bearing on the relationship between the employer and his or her workers. The mechanisms by which the terms of a collective agreement may be enforced between the parties to a contract of employment have been described in chapter 2.

A collective agreement is statutorily defined as any agreement or arrangement made by or on behalf of one or more trade unions and one or more employers, or employers' associations, which relates to one or more of the matters mentioned in section 178(2) TULRCA 1992.[50] A collective agreement is conclusively presumed not to have been intended by the parties to be a legally enforceable contract unless the agreement is in writing and contains a provision which states that the parties intend the agreement to be a legally enforceable contract.[51] Equally, the parties may declare that one or more parts of an agreement are intended to be legally enforceable.[52] Nevertheless, it should not be assumed that a collective agreement which declares the parties' intention to create legal relations is necessarily legally binding, since agreements exist which are too vague or uncertain to be enforced as contracts.

Notes

1. The words 'employee', 'employer' and 'worker' are defined in sections 295–6 TULRCA 1992. The expression 'associated employer' is defined in section 297 TULRCA 1992.
2. Section 123 TULRCA 1992.
3. Section 128 TULRCA 1992.
4. Section 131 TULRCA 1992.
5. Section 1 TULRCA 1992.
6. On the doctrine of *ultra vires* see *Thomas v NUM (South Wales)* [1985] IRLR 136.
7. [1980] 1 AER 1097.
8. Sections 12 and 13 TULRCA 1992.
9. Section 11 TULRCA 1992.
10. Section 3 TULRCA 1992.
11. Section 4 TULRCA 1992.
12. Section 9(1) TULRCA 1992.
13. Section 6(2)(5) TULRCA 1992.
14. Section 6(4) TULRCA 1992.
15. Section 6(6) TULRCA 1992.
16. Section 9(2) TULRCA 1992.
17. Section 8 TULRCA 1992.
18. [1980] IRLR 431.
19. See *Certification Officer v Squibb UK Staff Association* [1979] IRLR 75.
20. [1993] IRLR 260.
21. Section 178(3) TULRCA 1992.
22. Section 178(1) TULRCA 1992.
23. See *NUGSAT v Albury Bros* [1978] IRLR 504.
24. See *J. Wilson & Bros Ltd v USDAW* [1978] IRLR 20.
25. See *NUGSAT v Albury Bros* (note 23).
26. See *Cleveland CC v Springett* [1985] IRLR 131.
27. See *NUGSAT v Albury Bros* (note 23).
28. See *USDAW v Sketchley Ltd* [1981] IRLR 291.
29. On the meaning of a 'relevant transfer' see page 201.

30   Section 181(1)-(2) TULRCA 1992. Collective bargaining was defined
      on page 241.
31   See CAC Award No 88/3.
32   Section 181(3)(5) TULRCA 1992.
33   See CAC Award No 88/1 on disclosure in time to affect the progress
      of negotiations.
34   [1982] IRLR 61.
35   See CAC Award 78/353.
36   *Disclosure of Information to Trade Unions for Collective Bargaining
      Purposes,* HMSO, 1977.
37   Section 181(4) TULRCA 1992.
38   See CAC Award 80/107.
39   Paragraph 10 Code of Practice (note 36).
40   Paragraph 11 Code of Practice (note 36).
41   Paragraph 22 Code of Practice (note 36). See CAC Award 81/3.
42   See *CSU v CAC* [1980] IRLR 274.
43   See CAC Award 84/15.
44   See also CAC Award No 88/1.
45   See CAC Award 82/18.
46   CAC Awards 80/152 and 80/26.
47   Section 183 TULRCA 1992.
48   Section 184 TULRCA 1992.
49   Section 185(5) TULRCA 1992.
50   Section 178(1) TULRCA 1992.
51   Section 179(1)(2) TULRCA 1992.
52   Section 179(3) TULRCA 1992.

17 Data protection and access to medical reports

The Data Protection Act 1984

The Data Protection Act 1984 (DPA 1984) places obligations on employers as 'data users' or persons carrying on computer bureaux[1] and affords protection to employees as 'data subjects'[2] against the misuse of information held on computer. In particular, the Act gives employees access to data about themselves and, subject to exceptions, prohibits the unregistered disclosure of information. In terms of employment law, one outstanding feature of the DPA 1984 is that principles of good industrial relations practice are embodied in the statute itself rather than in an accompanying code of practice.

The scope of the legislation

The DPA 1984 applies to all 'personal data' which is 'recorded in a form in which it can be processed by equipment operating automatically in response to instructions given for the purpose'.[3] This means that manual records fall outside the scope of the legislation, provided opinions or codes which are computerized (*see* below) are not based on details which are held manually. Nevertheless, trade unions will be anxious to negotiate comprehensive data protection agreements which embrace both manual and computerized records. Most forms of electronic processing are caught by the DPA 1984. It makes no difference whether the processing is performed internally or subcontracted, since in either case the employer will control the content and use of the data. However, word processing is excluded if its sole purpose is preparing the text of documents.[4]

Even where the data does not identify an employee by name the DPA 1984 still applies if the individual can be identified from other information in the possession of the employer, for example, if employees are referred to by national insurance or works numbers. In addition to factual information 'personal data' includes 'any expression of opinion about the individual' although 'any indication of the intentions of the data user in respect of that individual are excluded'.[5] Thus the observation that an employee was inflexible falls within the ambit of this legislation, whereas a statement that the employer does not intend to promote need not be disclosed. Naturally, there will be occasions when it will be difficult to draw a dividing line between an opinion and an intention. However, the Data Protection Register (*see* below) has indicated that whether a statement is one of opinion or intention will be judged by looking at the way the information is used and recorded. Clearly, employers would be advised to assume that information derived from performance appraisals is covered by this statute. Indeed, the systematic disguising of opinion as intention may be an infringement of the data protection principles.

The Data Protection Principles

The following eight principles apply to all personal data covered by the DPA 1984:[6]

(i) 'The information to be contained in personal data shall be obtained, and personal data shall be processed, fairly and lawfully.'[7] This may mean that employers are expected to disclose the purposes for which information is sought at the time it is obtained, for example, when an application form is completed.

(ii) 'Personal data shall be held only for one or more specified and lawful purposes.' Specified purposes are those described on the Register (*see* pages 257–8).

(iii) 'Personal data held for any purpose or purposes shall not be used or disclosed in any manner incompatible with that purpose or those purposes.'

(iv) 'Personal data held for any purpose or purposes shall be adequate, relevant and not excessive in relation to that purpose or those purposes.'

(v) 'Personal data shall be accurate and, where necessary, kept up to date.' The best person to check whether this principle has been complied with is the employee, *e.g.* in relation to ethnic monitoring.

(vi) 'Personal data held for any purpose or purposes shall not be kept for longer than is necessary for that purpose or those purposes.'[8] Employers should pay particular attention to information relating to those who have left the organization.

(vii) 'An individual shall be entitled (a) at reasonable intervals and without undue delay or expense to be informed by any data user whether he holds personal data of which that individual is the subject; and to access to any such data of which that individual is the subject; and to access to any such data of which that individual is the subject; and to access to any such data held by a data user; and (b) where appropriate, to have such data corrected or erased.' What is a 'reasonable interval' will depend on the nature of the data, the purpose for which it is held and the frequency with which it is altered. Whilst the law places the initiative for data disclosure on the data subject, many organizations have adopted a policy of unprompted disclosure at regular intervals.

(viii) 'Appropriate security measures shall be taken against unauthorized access to or alteration, disclosure or destruction of, personal data.' In determining whether security measures are appropriate regard will be had to: the nature of the data, the harm that could result from unauthorized access, etc., the place where the data are stored, the security measures programmed into the equipment and the measures taken for ensuring the reliability of staff having access to the equipment.

The IPM *Code of Practice on Employee Data* (1988) makes a number of recommendations on what employers should be doing to comply with these principles. For example, that employees who want to see their computerized personnel records should not be charged (*see* below) and that in the interests of good employee relations access to manual records should also be provided where it is practical and realistic to do so. The Registrar has made it clear that the standards laid down in this code will be taken into account in deciding whether to take enforcement action against data users. Nevertheless, observance of the IPM code does not guarantee that the Registrar 'will in all cases and without qualification that data users have complied with the Act'.

The rights of data subjects

Data subjects or their agents who pay a specified fee (not exceeding £10 per file accessed) are entitled to be informed whether data users hold personal data about them and to be supplied with a copy of the data normally within 40 days of a request being made. While requests do not have to be made in a particular form there may be advantages to both parties if a standard form is used and assistance in form-filling is provided. Where any of the data is 'not intelligible without explanation the information shall be accompanied by an explanation'.[9] This means that employers will have to interpret any codes that have been used but the data may still contain technical terms which are not understandable by the data subject without outside help. The information to be supplied is that which is held at the time when the request is received, except where it can be shown that an amendment or deletion would have been made regardless of the request.[10]

Data users are not obliged to comply with a request unless they are supplied with such information as may reasonably be required to locate the information sought or satisfy themselves as to the identity of the person making the request. The Registrar's guidance suggests that for non-sensitive data being mailed to the subject's home address a signature will be sufficient proof. Where proof of identity is reasonably required the prescribed 40 day period does not start to run until that proof has been supplied to the data user. Access can also be denied where the information disclosed would identify another individual unless that other person has consented to the disclosure.[11] This will enable employers to protect their sources of information although the data user is still obliged to disclose 'so much of the information sought by the request as can be supplied without disclosing the identity of the individual concerned.'[12]

As regards health data, Regulation 4 of the Data Protection (Subject Access Modification) (Health) Order 1987[13] provides that an individual shall not have access to health data where its disclosure:

(i) would be likely to cause serious harm or injury to the physical or mental health of the data subject or any other person, or

(ii) would be likely to disclose the identity of another individual, other than the health professional who has been involved in the treatment of the data subject.

Nevertheless, data users must disclose as much of the information sought as can be supplied without causing serious harm, etc., to the data subject or enabling the third party to be identified. Before withholding or disclosing data the data user is obliged to consult an 'appropriate health professional'.[14] If a data user fails to comply with a request, a data subject can apply either to the Registrar or to a court.[15] The data user may be compelled to produce the information for a court's inspection and it it is found that the right of access has been infringed the data user will be ordered to comply with the request. However, a court cannot make an order if it considers it would be unreasonable to do so because of the frequency with which the applicant has made requests or for any other reason.[16]

Section 22 of the DPA 1984 enables individuals to claim compensation for the damage and distress caused by the inaccuracy of data. It should be noted that for these purposes data is only inaccurate if it is incorrect or misleading as to any matter of fact, *i.e.* not opinion. Nevertheless, a court is empowered to order rectification or erasure of data, including expressions of opinions which are based on inaccurate data, even though no damage has been or is likely to be caused.[17] It is a defence for data users to prove that they had taken such care as was reasonably required to ensure the accuracy of the data.[18] Similarly, where the data indicates that the information was supplied by either the data subject or a third party and there is also an indication included in the data that the data subject 'regards the information as incorrect or misleading' no remedy is available.[19]

Data subjects can claim compensation for damage and distress caused by the loss of personal data or its unauthorized disclosure and if there is a substantial risk of further disclosure a court may order the erasure of data.[20] Section 19 lists the penalties applicable to the statutory offences and provides that a prosecution can only be brought by the Registrar or by or with the consent of the

Director of Public Prosecutions. Where an offence is proved to have been committed with the consent or connivance of, or to be attributable to any neglect on the part of any director, manager or similar officer, that person as well as the body corporate can be found guilty of an offence.[21] Clearly, employers will need to consider whether breach of data protection principles should be made a disciplinary offence and whether special procedures should be provided for handling both subject access requests and data protection complaints.

General exemptions

From an employer's point of view perhaps the most important exemption is that which deals with payrolls and accounts. Section 32(1) exempts from registration and subject access data held for the following purposes:

(i) calculating amounts payable by way of remuneration or pensions in respect of service in any employment or office or making payments of, or of sums deducted from, such remuneration or pensions,[22] or

(ii) keeping accounts relating to any business or other activity carried on by the data user or keeping records of purchases, sales or other transactions for the purpose of ensuring that the requisite payments are made by or to him in respect of those transactions or for the purpose of making financial or management forecasts to assist him in the conduct of any such business or activity.

It would seem that data used to calculate statutory sick pay (*see* chapter 8) will fit within this exemption, although, subject to the health data exceptions (*see* pages 253–4), medical records are generally covered by the provisions of the DPA 1984. However, it should be observed that pay records will be exempt only if the data held is required for the exempt purpose and is not used for any other purpose, for example disciplinary matters.

Data held for the purposes of section 32(1) may be disclosed:[23]

(i) to any person, other than the data user, by whom the remuneration or pensions in question are payable

(ii) for the purpose of obtaining actuarial advice

(iii) for the purpose of giving information as to the persons in any employment or office for use in medical research into the health of, or injuries suffered by, persons engaged in particular occupations or working in particular places or areas

(iv) if the data subject, or a person acting on his or her behalf, has requested or consented to the disclosure of the data either generally or in the circumstances in which the disclosure in question is made

(v) if the person making the disclosure has reasonable grounds for believing that the disclosure falls within paragraph (iv) above.

Data held for the purposes mentioned in section 32(1) may also be disclosed for the purpose of audit or for giving information about the data user's financial affairs.[24]

Personal data held only for preparing statistics or carrying out research are exempt from the subject access provisions provided the data is not used or disclosed for any other purpose and the results are not made available in a form which identifies the data subjects.[25] Nevertheless, employers will have to register that they hold data for statistical and research purposes. Personal data held for taxation purposes and for discharging statutory functions are also exempt from the subject access provisions as is data to which legal professional privilege is claimed.[26] The most obvious exemption from the disclosure provisions is where the employee requests or consents to the disclosure, for example for the purpose of providing a reference. Difficulties may arise in relation to alleged implied consent, for example where information is disclosed to an employee's union representative. However, employers have a defence if they can show reasonable grounds for believing that the employee has consented.[27] Personal data are also exempt from the non-disclosure provisions if disclosure is urgently required for preventing damage to the health of any person. If challenged employers will have to demonstrate that they had reasonable grounds for believing that the disclosure was 'urgently required for that purpose'.[28]

Registration

Since May 1986 it has been a criminal offence to hold unregistered data or use if for purposes other than those specified in the Register.[29] Apparently, merely accessing data on a computer screen does not constitute 'use' for those purposes.[30]

According to section 4(3) of the DPA 1984 an entry in respect of a data user shall consist of the following particulars:

(i)   the name and address of the data user
(ii) a description of the personal data to be held by him or her and the purpose or purposes for which the data is to be held or used
(iii) a description of the source or sources from which he or she intends or may wish to obtain the data or the information to be contained within the data
(iv) a description of any person or persons to whom he or she intends or may wish to disclose the data. It is not necesary to register internal disclosures, since section 34(6) exempts disclosures to the employees or agents of a data user to enable them to carry out their function
(v)   the names or a description of any countries or territories outside the UK to which he or she intends or may wish directly or indirectly to transfer the data
(vi) one or more addresses for the receipt of requests from data subjects for access to the data.

Data users can amend the particulars specified in the registration and they must be renewed at least every three years.[31] Normally the Data Protection Registrar must notify data users whether their applications have been accepted or refused within six months of their receipt but this period can be extended if further time for consideration is needed.[32] Data users who have made applications in the required form are to be treated as if their applications had been accepted pending the Registrar's decision.[33] Applications for registration can be refused if the Registrar is satisfied that the applicant is likely to contravene any of the data protection principles or if this issue cannot be determined on the information available.[34] The Registrar must give reasons for refusing an application and inform the applicant of the rights of appeal (*see* page 259).[35]

Where employers intend to hold personal data for two or more purposes they may make separate applications for registration.[36] A fee (£75 in 1993) is payable for each application. Although many employers will have a choice as to whether to apply for single or multiple registration, separate legal entities, for example independent subsidiaries, are obliged to register separately. The major advantages of separate entries are administrative convenience and the ease of handling subject access requests. Multiple entries will be simpler to make and to amend and by registering for different periods of time (one, two or three years) employers can arrange for entries to be renewed at different times. When there are separate entries on the Register separate access requests must be made and fees paid in respect of each entry.

The Registrar's powers and the appeal process

Apart from the requirement to maintain a register of data users, and persons carrying on computer bureaux who provide services in respect of data, the Registrar has the following statutory duties:[37]

(i)   to provide facilities for the public inspection of the Register and to supply members of the public with a written copy of the particulars contained in an entry on the Register

(ii) to promote the observance of the data protection principles

(iii) to consider complaints which appear to raise a matter of substance and have been made without undue delay by a person directly affected

(iv) to disseminate information about the operation of the Act[38]

(v)   to encourage trade associations or other bodies representing data users to prepare, and to disseminate to their members, codes of practice for guidance in complying with data protection principles

(iv) to lay a general report on the performance of his or her functions before Parliament annually.

To ensure compliance with the data protection principles the Registrar is empowered to issue three types of notices. An enforcement notice will contain a statement of the principle, or principles, which the Registrar believes to have been contravened and the reasons why that belief is held. It will also specify the steps necessary to achieve compliance and will set a date by which those

steps must be taken.[39] As its name suggests, a deregistration notice
has the effect of removing an entry, or part of an entry, from the
Register at the expiration of a specified period. It can only be
used if the Registrar is satisfied that compliance with the data
protection principles cannot adequately be secured by serving an
enforcement notice. Indeed, the Registrar must state the reasons
for concluding that an enforcement notice would be inadequate
to ensure compliance.[40] A transfer prohibition notice may be
issued to prevent the transfer of data outside the UK if the Registrar is satisfied that there would be a contravention of any of the
data protection principles.[41]

Before imposing any of these notices the Registrar must consider the damage or distress caused or likely to be caused to
any person. Failure to comply with an enforcement or transfer
prohibition notice is an offence unless the accused proves that he
or she exercised 'all due diligence to comply with the notice'.[42]
Finally, it should be noted that the Registrar can apply to a judge
for a warrant to enter or search premises, inspect, examine, operate or test equipment, and to inspect or seize documents or other
material which may be evidence of an offence or breach of the
data protection principles.[43]

Appeals from a decision of the Registrar must normally be
served on the Data Protection Tribunal within 28 days of the date
on which notification of the disputed decision was given to the
appellant.[44] This tribunal consists of a legally qualified chairperson
appointed by the Lord Chancellor, and representatives of data
users and data subjects appointed by the Secretary of State.[45]
Where the Data Protection Tribunal considers either that a refusal
to register or a notice appealed against is unlawful, or that the
Registrar's discretion has been wrongly exercised, it may allow
the appeal or substitute its own decision or notice for that of the
Registrar.[46] There is a further right of appeal on a point of law to
the High Court (Court of Session in Scotland).[47]

The Access to Medical Reports Act 1988

Unlike the DPA 1984, this statute applies not only to reports
stored on computer but also to those stored manually. It provides
a right of access to any medical report relating to the individual

which is to be, or has been, supplied by a medical practitioner for employment or insurance purposes. The AMRA 1988 applies to 'medical reports' which are commissioned both before employment commences and during employment from 'a medical practitioner who is or has been responsible for the clinical care of the individual'.[48] Since reports prepared by independent medical advisers or company doctors seem to be excluded,[49] many employers will seek the contractual right to refer workers to a doctor nominated by the company.

An employer who wishes to apply for a medical report covered by this legislation is required to notify the individual that he or she proposes to make an application and must obtain that person's consent.[50] In addition, the employer must inform the individual in writing of the following rights created by the Act:

(i)   the right to withhold consent to such an application[51]
(ii)   if the individual does consent, the right to state that he or she wants access to the report. Where the individual so states, the employer must notify the medical practitioner of this fact at the time the report is sought[52]
(iii) the right of access to the report before it is supplied to the employer[53] and to any medical report relating to him or her that the practitioner has supplied during the previous six months.[54] A person who wants access to the report before it is supplied to the employer has 21 days to contact the medical practitioner about arrangements for access. For these purposes giving access to a report means supplying the individual with a copy of it or making the report (or a copy) available for inspection. A reasonable fee may be charged for the cost of supplying a report
(iv)   the right to request the amendment of, or record a difference of opinion over, any details contained in the report which the individual regards as misleading or incorrect. If the individual requests in writing that the medical practitioner should attach to the report a statement of that individual's views about any part of the report which the doctor refuses to amend, the doctor is obliged to do so[55]
(v)   the right to refuse consent to the disclosure of the report to the employer.[56]

An employer who applies for a medical report from a doctor must also inform that doctor of certain matters.[57] However, there is nothing to prevent employers using standard forms for notifying either employees or doctors.

Individuals can be denied access to the whole or part of a report if the medical practitioner thinks that its disclosure would be likely:

(i)   to cause serious physical or mental harm to the individual involved, or
(ii) to reveal information about another individual, or
(iii) to reveal the intentions of the practitioner in relation to the individual, or
(iv) to reveal the identity of another non-medical person who has supplied information to the medical practitioner.[58]

Where the medical practitioner decides that access to the report should be withheld (wholly or in part) because of one or more of the statutory exemptions, he or she must notify the individual of that fact. If a person is unhappy about the disclosure of information in these circumstances he or she may choose to refuse consent to the report being supplied to the employer. Obviously both job-seekers and job-holders will think hard about the conclusions employers might draw from the withholding of consent to a medical report.

People who feel that their rights under this Act have been infringed can complain to the County Court.[59] If the court is satisfied that a person has failed (or is likely to fail) to comply with a requirement relating to the complainant, it may order compliance. Thus, if a medical report has already been supplied without the individual's consent or access to it, all that can be enforced is the right of access to the report and to have a statement of views attached to it.

Notes

1   Defined in section 1(5)(6).
2   Defined in section 1(4); the DPA 1984 does not cover information relating to corporate bodies.
3   Section 1(2); this Act does not apply to data held outside the UK: section 39.
4   Section 1(8).

5   Section 1(3).
6   See Schedule 1 Parts I and II.
7   See Schedule 1 Part II paragraph 7 on data held for historical, statistical or research purposes.
8   See note 7.
9   Section 21(1).
10 Section 21(7).
11 Section 21(4).
12 Section 21(5).
13 SI 1987 No 1903.
14 Regulation 4(6).
15 It is the Registrar's view that a data user must always reply to a subject access request. However, the reply need do not more than make it clear that the data held 'do not include personal data which I am required to reveal to you' (Guideline 5).
16 Section 21(8).
17 Section 24(1).
18 Section 22(3).
19 Section 22(2).
20 Sections 23(1), 24(3).
21 Section 20(1).
22 See *Rowley v Liverpool City Council* (1989) TLR 26/10/89. 'Remuneration' includes remuneration in kind and 'pensions', and includes gratuities or similar benefits: section 32(5).
23 Section 32(3).
24 Section 32(4). See *Rowley v Liverpool City Council* (note 22).
25 Section 33(6).
26 Sections 28(1)(2), 31.
27 Section 34(6).
28 Section 34(8); see section 27 on safeguarding national security and section 28(3) on the prevention or detection of crime and collection of taxes, etc.
29 Section 5(5).
30 See *R v Brown* (1993) TLR 4/6/93.
31 Sections 6(3), 8(2).
32 Sections 7(1)(5).
33 Sections 6, 7(6).
34 Section 7(2).
35 Section 7(4).
36 Section 6(2).
37 Section 6(2).
38 The Registrar has produced Guidelines which aim to inform individuals of their rights under the Act and to help employers understand their obligations. In addition 'Guidance Notes' are available which deal with specific issues in more detail.
39 Section 10.
40 Section 11.
41 Section 12.

42 Sections 10(8), 12(10).
43 See Schedule 4.
44 See section 13 and the Data Protection Tribunal Rules 1985 SI No 1568.
45 See sections 3 and 13.
46 Section 14(1).
47 Section 15(5).
48 Section 2(1).
49 The situation is slightly ambiguous because 'care' is defined to include 'examination, investigation or diagnosis for the purposes of, or in connection with, any form of medical treatment'. Thus company doctors will be covered by the Act when they provide treatment.
50 Section 3(1).
51 Section 3(2).
52 Section 4(1).
53 Section 4(2).
54 Section 6(2).
55 Section 5(2).
56 Section 5(1).
57 Section 4(1)(2).
58 Section 7.
59 Section 8.

18 The trade union rights of employees

It was observed in chapter 4 that it was unlawful to refuse employment to a person on the ground that she or he was a union member or non-member. In this chapter we will be considering time off for trade union duties and activities, action short of dismissal and dismissals relating to trade union membership and activities. Finally, reference will be made to the prohibition of certain union membership requirements in commercial contracts.

Time off for trade union duties and activities

No minimum period of service is required before trade unionists can claim time off.

Duties

According to section 168 TULRCA 1992 employers must permit employees who are officials of independent trade unions recognized by them to take reasonable time off with pay during working hours to enable them:

(i) to carry out

- their duties which are concerned with negotiations with the employer that are related to or connected with any of the matters specified in section 178(2) TULRCA 1992 (also set out in section 244, *see* page 297) and in relation to which the employer recognizes the union, or
- any other duties which are concerned with the performance of any functions that are related to or connected with any matters listed in section 178(2) TULRCA 1992 and that the employer has agreed may be performed by the union, or

(ii) to undergo training in aspects of industrial relations which is both relevant to the carrying out of any of the duties mentioned in (i) and approved by their trade union or the TUC.

An official is defined as someone who is an officer of the union or branch of it, or someone who is elected or appointed in accordance with the rules to be a representative of its members or some of them.[1] (*See* chapter 7 on time off for safety representatives, and *see* chapter 16 on the meaning of 'independence' and recognition.)

The amount of time off allowed, together with the purposes for which, the occasions on which, and any conditions subject to which, time off may be taken, depends on what is reasonable in all the circumstances having regard to any relevant provisions in the ACAS Code of Practice.[2] The code does not lay down any fixed amount of time that employers should permit officials to take off, its main theme being that employers and trade unions should reach agreements on arrangements for handling time off in ways appropriate to their situations.

Officials who are permitted time off should receive normal remuneration as if they had worked or, where the remuneration varies with the work done, average hourly earnings should be paid.[3] No claim can be made for overtime which would normally have been worked unless that overtime was contractually required, and there is no entitlement to be paid for time spent on trade union duties outside working hours.[4] It follows that an employee on the night shift who attends works committee meetings during the day will not be entitled to a payment whereas a day shift worker would. Nevertheless, employees may reasonably require paid time off during working hours to enable them to undertake the relevant duties or training, for example to travel to or return from a training course.[5] Two further points should be noted. First, the 'set-off formula' applies here.[6] Second, employers who give their part-time employees paid time off only up to the limit of their normal working hours may be in breach of Article 119 of the Treaty of Rome (on sex discrimination).[7]   ·

The Code of Practice recommends that officials of recognized trade unions should be allowed reasonable time off for duties concerned with negotiations related to or connected with:[8]

(i) terms and conditions of employment, or the conditions in which employees are required to work, *e.g.*:

- pay
- hours of work
- holiday pay and entitlement
- sick pay arrangements
- pensions
- vocational training
- equal opportunities
- notice periods
- the working environment
- utilization of machinery and other equipment

(ii) engagement or non-engagement, or termination or suspension of employment or the duties of employment, of one or more workers, *e.g.*:

- recruitment and selection policies
- human resource planning
- redundancy and dismissal arrangements.

(iii) allocation of work, or the duties of employment as between workers or groups of workers, *e.g.*:

- job grading
- job evaluation
- job descriptions
- flexible working practices.

(iv) matters of discipline, *e.g.*:

- disciplinary procedures
- arrangements for representing trade union members at internal interviews
- arrangements for appearing on behalf of trade union members, or as witnesses, before agreed outside appeal bodies or industrial tribunals.

(v) trade union membership or non-membership, *e.g.*:

- representational agreements
- any union involvement in the induction of new workers.

(vi) facilities for officials of trade unions, *e.g.*:

- accommodation
- equipment
- names of new workers to the union.

(vii) machinery for negotiation and consultation and other procedures, *e.g.* arrangements for:

- collective bargaining
- grievance procedures
- joint consultation
- communicating with members
- communicating with other union officials also concerned with collective bargaining with the employer.

The code states that where an officials is not taking part in industrial action but represents members who are, normal arrangements for time off with pay should apply. Additionally, the code suggests that management should make available the facilities necessary for officials to perform their duties efficiently and to communicate effectively with members. The items mentioned are accommodation for meetings, access to a telephone, notice boards and the use of office facilities.[9]

Preparatory and explanatory work by officials may well be in fulfilment of duties concerned with any of the matters listed in section 178(2) TULRCA 1992.[10] What has to be demonstrated is that there is a sufficient nexus between the collective bargaining and the duty for which leave is sought.[11] Industrial tribunals will have to decide whether the preparatory work is directly relevant to one of the matters specified in section 178(2) and, if the employer does not negotiate on the issue, the employer's agreement to the performance of the duty will have to be demonstrated.[12] It also seems that the recognized union must expressly or impliedly require the performance of the duty, otherwise it would be impossible to hold that the individual was 'carrying out those duties . . . as such an official'[13] If no agreement on time off is reached in advance of a meeting, a sensible approach might be to determine claims for payment on the basis of what the minutes disclosed. Where only a proportion of the time was spent on section 168 TULRCA 1992 matters a tribunal will probably find that only a proportion of the time should reasonably be paid for.

As regards industrial relations training, again no fixed amount is specified but the code recommends that officials should be permitted paid time off for initial basic training as soon as possible after their election or appointment. Time off should be allowed for further training where the official has special responsibilities or where it is necessary to meet changed industrial relations circumstances.[14] In determining whether a course meets the requirement of relevance to the specified duties, the description of people attending the course by those responsible for it will be pertinent.[15] Indeed, as a general principle it would seem wise for employers to insist on being shown a copy of course prospectuses.

Activities

An employer must permit a member of a recognized independent trade union to take reasonable time off during working hours for trade union activities and to represent the union. However, in the absence of any contractual term to the contrary, an employer does not have to pay for such time off. Trade union activities are not statutorily defined, although the code gives the following examples of the activities of a member:

(i)   attending workplace meetings to discuss and vote on the outcome of negotiations with the employer
(ii) meeting full-time officials to discuss issues relevant to the workplace
(iii) voting in properly conducted ballots on industrial action
(iv) voting in union elections.[16]

Paragraph 22 of the code gives examples of activities where the member is acting as a representative of a union:

(i)   branch, area or regional meetings of the union where the business of the union is under discussion
(ii) meetings of official policy-making bodies such as the executive committee or annual conference
(iii) meetings with full-time officials to discuss issues relevant to the workplace.

Section 170(2) TULRCA expressly excludes activities which consist of industrial action, although paragraph 39 of the code recommends that time off should be provided for the use of agreed procedures. Finally, in *Wignall v British Gas*[17] the EAT rejected the argument that the statute requires every proposed activity on the part of the employee in the service of his or her union to be weighed and tested on its own merits without regard to any other activities or duties on the union's behalf for which the employee might be taking time off. Thus every application for time off under section 170 should be looked at on its merits in the particular circumstances.

Employees wishing to complain of failure to permit time off or to pay the amount required by section 169 TULRCA 1992 must apply to an industrial tribunal within three months of the date when the failure occurred.[18] If the tribunal finds that the complaint is well founded it must make a declaration to that effect and may make an award of compensation of such amount as it considers 'just and equitable in all the circumstances having regard to the employer's default . . . and to any loss sustained by the employee which is attributable to the matters complained of'.[19]

Action short of dismissal

Section 146 TULRCA 1992 gives employees the right not to have action short of dismissal taken against them as individuals by their employer for the purpose of:

(i)   preventing or deterring them from being or seeking to become a member of an independent trade union or penalizing them for doing so

(ii) preventing or deterring them from taking part in the activities of an independent trade union at any appropriate time, or penalizing them for doing so

(iii) compelling them to become a member of any trade union or of a particular trade union or of one of a number of particular trade unions

(iv) enforcing a requirement that, in the event of their failure to become, or their ceasing to remain a member of any trade union or a particular trade union or one of a number of particular trade unions, they must make one or more payments. For this purpose, any deduction from remuneration which is attributable to the employee's failure to become, or his or her ceasing to be a trade union

member will be treated as a breach of section 146
TULRCA 1992.

Action is defined as including omissions[20] so failure to promote as
well as more positive acts, like segregation, are covered. There
was some doubt as to whether a threat constituted 'action' for
these purposes but in *Grogan v British Railways Board*[21] it was
held that a threat of disciplinary measures amounted to action
taken for the purpose of preventing or deterring the applicant
from joining an independent trade union. As regards the requirement that the action must be taken against an employee as an
individual, the Court of Appeal has offered the following guidance: 'if an employee is selected for discrimination because of
some characteristic which he shares with others, such as membership of a particular trade union, then the action is . . . taken against
him as an individual'.[22]

It is clear that employees have the right to join any independent
trade union of their choice.[23] Thus in *Carlson*'s case[24] the EAT
decided that the denial of a car park permit to a member of a
non-recognized independent trade union constituted a form of
penalization outlawed by this section. In this context 'penalizing'
was held to mean 'subjecting to a disadvantage'. Similarly, refusing
to allow an individual to be represented by an official of his or
her trade union at a meeting with the employer could be a breach
of the statute. For these purposes the EAT has acknowledged that
there is no genuine distinction between membership of a union
on the one hand and making use of the services of a union
official on the other.[25]

As there is no statutory definition tribunals have the task of
determining what are 'activities of an independent trade union'.
The following have been accepted as such: attempting to recruit
new members or form a workplace union branch, taking part in
union meetings and consulting a union official. Thus those claiming
that they have suffered because of their activities do not have to
show that they were authorized union representatives, although
individual complaints or group meetings which have no union connection will not be protected. It is not conclusive that workers did
not get together at a committee or formal branch meeting; it would
appear sufficient that union members have discussed matters with
which an independent trade union is concerned.[26] However, in

Therm-a-Stor v Atkins[27] the Court of Appeal drew a distinction between the employer's reaction to a trade union's activities and reaction to an individual employee's activities in a trade union context. Thus where a union district secretary's letter asking for recognition led to dismissal it was held that the reason for dismissal had nothing to do with anything which the employee concerned had personally done or proposed to do. It is clear that the 'activities of an independent trade union' refers to the activities of a specific trade union rather than the activities of unions generally.

According to the EAT, an industrial tribunal must establish:

(i)   the belief held by the employer upon which the decision was taken
(ii) that such belief was genuinely held
(iii) whether the facts upon which the belief was based, judged objectively, fell within the 'activities of an independent trade union'.[28]

Can industrial action be regarded as such an activity? In *Rasool's* case[29] the EAT was prepared to accept that attendance at an unauthorized meeting for the purpose of considering the view of employees in relation to impending wage negotiations was such an activity. Nevertheless, such activity is not normally taken at an 'appropriate time' since this is defined as being outside working hours or within working hours in accordance with arrangements agreed with, or consent given by the employer. Such consent may be express, for example in a collective agreement, or may be implied from the conduct of the parties. However, unless there is an arrangement which covers the situation, it would seem that a shop steward who is unaccredited by management at the relevant time cannot be taken to have implied permission to call a meeting during working hours.[30] So employers who wish to restrict union activities during working hours should state clearly in the contracts of employment or statement of particulars they issue that they do not consent to such activity. Activities carried out at an 'appropriate time' means activities occurring during the period of employment and excludes activities during a prior period. Nevertheless the statute is infringed if the employee suffers action short of dismissal (or dismissal) on the basis of previous trade union activities, when the only rational basis for his doing so is the fear that those activities will be repeated in the present employment.[31]

The phrase 'working hours' is defined as meaning any time when an employee is required to be at work but, in order to protect union activities carried out during paid tea breaks, it has been construed as meaning the time when work is actually performed.[32] It would appear that employees are free to use their employer's premises outside working hours, which means that non-recognized unions will normally be afforded organizing rights. However, any contractual right which an employee has to be on the employer's premises cannot survive the suspension or termination of his or her contract of employment.[33]

A claim that there has been action short of dismissal must be presented within three months of the date on which the action complained of occurred, or if there is a series of similar actions, the last of those actions.[34] Where a complainant alleges that disciplinary proceedings were wrongly taken against him or her on the grounds of union membership or activities the 'relevant' action is the entire disciplinary proceedings up to and including receipt by the complainant of notification that his or her final appeal has been dismissed.[55] However, the EAT has also held that the implementation of an agreement which penalizes union members constituted one act rather than a series of actions, so that the time limit runs from the date the agreement takes effect.[36]

Normally the burden is on the employer to show the purpose for which the action was taken against the employee. But a different approach is taken 'where (a) there is evidence that the employer's purpose was to further a change in his relationship with all or any class of his employees, and (b) there is also evidence that his purpose was one falling within section 146'. In these circumstances a tribunal must regard only the intended change in the employment relationship as the purpose of the employer's actions 'unless it considers that the action was such as no reasonable employer would take' having regard to that purpose.[37] This approach is clearly designed to assist employers who wish to derecognize a trade union and/or introduce personally bargained contracts of employment.

No account can be taken of any pressure which was exercised on the employer by way of industrial action or threat of it. Nevertheless, if employees complain that action has been taken against them in order to compel them to become union members and the employer claims that he or she was induced to take action by such pressure, either the employer or the complainants can request that the person who applied the pressure be joined as a party to the proceedings. Such a request must be granted if it is made before the hearing begins but may be refused if it is made after that time.[38] If the complainant is awarded compensation the tribunal may order the person exercising the pressure to pay the whole or part of it. Of course, it is very doubtful whether seeking a contribution from a trade union in these circumstances would be conducive to good industrial relations. Indeed, in many cases it could have the effect of prolonging or rekindling a bitter dispute.

Where an industrial tribunal finds an employee's complaint to be well founded it must make a declaration to that effect and may make an award of compensation. The amount awarded must be such as the tribunal considers 'just and equitable in all the circumstances having regard to the infringement of the complainant's right' and 'to any loss sustained by the complainant which is attributable to that action.[39] In this context 'loss' is taken to include any expenses reasonably incurred and any benefit which the applicant might have received but for the unlawful action. Compensation can be reduced if employees fail to mitigate their loss, or cause or contribute to the action taken against them. In *Brassington*'s case[40] the EAT ruled that the statute did not impose a quasi-fine, so that compensation could only be awarded if the employee could show that an injury resulted. Yet this injury is not restricted to pecuniary loss The stress engendered by the situation may have caused injury to the employee's health, or a sincere desire to join a union, with all the benefits of help and advice which that might entail, could have been frustrated.

Dismissals relating to trade union membership

According to section 152(1) TULRCA 1992 a dismissal is unfair if the reason for it (or if more than one, the principal reason) was that the employee:

(i)   was or proposed to become a member of an independent trade union, or

(ii) had taken, or proposed to take part in the activities of an independent trade union at any appropriate time,[41] or

(iii) was not a member of any trade union or of a particular trade union, or had refused or proposed to refuse to become or remain a member.

Section 152(3) TULRCA 1992 provides that dismissals are to be treated as falling within (iii) above if one of the reasons for them was that employees:

(i) refused (or proposed to refuse) to comply with a requirement that in the event of their failure to become, or their ceasing to remain a trade union member they must make some kind of payment, or

(ii) objected, or proposed to object to the operation of a provision under which their employer is entitled to deduct sums from their remuneration if they fail to become or remain a trade union member.

It would seem that if an employee is dismissed because of her or his proposal to leave an independent trade union that will be unfair, even though the proposal is conditional on something occurring or not occurring.[42]

The usual qualifying period and upper age limit for claiming unfair dismissal do not apply if the reason, or principal reason, for dismissal was one of those specified in section 152 TULRCA 1992.[43] This being so, the burden is on employees to prove that their dismissal related to trade union membership. However, where the question of jurisdiction does not arise, the only burden on the employee is to produce some evidence which casts doubt on the employer's reason.[44]

Although the normal remedies are available to those who have been unfairly dismissed (*see* chapter 14) the desirability of reinstating or re-engaging in this type of case is emphasized in two ways. First, an employer who fails to satisfy a tribunal that it was not practicable to comply with an order for re-employment will be obliged to pay a higher special award if the dismissal was unfair by virtue of section 152 or 153 TULRCA 1992.[45] Secondly, where employees allege that their dismissals were unfair by virtue of section 152 TULRCA or section 57A (1)(a) or (b) EPCA 1978 they can seek 'interim relief'.[46] This is available where employees present their claims within seven days of the effective date of termination and, where sections 152(1)(a) or (b) TULRCA 1992 are relied on, they submit written certificates signed by an authorized union official which state that there appears to be reasonable grounds for supposing that the reason for dismissal was the one alleged in the complaints. The tribunal must hear such an application as soon as practicable[47] and, if it thinks it 'likely' (*i.e.* there is a pretty good chance) that the complainant will be found to have been unfairly dismissed by virtue of section 152 TULRCA 1992 or section 57A(1)(a) or 6 EPCA 1978, it must ask whether the employer is willing to reinstate or (if not) to re-engage the employee pending the determination of the complaint. If the employer is willing to reinstate or the employee is willing to accept re-engagement, the tribunal shall make an order to that effect. Where the employer fails to attend the hearing or is unwilling to re-employ, the tribunal must make an order for the continuation of the employee's contract of employment. In essence, such an order amounts to suspension on full pay.[48]

Where there has been pressure to dismiss on the grounds of non-membership of a trade union, section 160 TULRCA 1992 enables the person who applied the pressure to be joined (by either the employer or the employee) as a party to the unfair dismissal proceedings. A request that a person be joined must be acceded to if it is made before the hearing but can be refused if it is made after that time. No such request can be entertained after a remedy has been awarded and the tribunal is empowered to apportion compensation in a 'just and equitable' manner.

Union membership or recognition requirements in contracts

Section 144 TULRCA 1992 renders void any term or condition in a contract for the supply of goods or services which requires that the whole or part of the work to be done under the contract is performed only by trade unionists or members of a particular trade union, or only by non-union members or non-members of a particular trade union. Additionally, section 145 TULRCA 1992 prohibits a refusal to deal on union membership grounds. For these purposes there is a refusal to deal where:

(i)   a contract for the supply of goods or services is terminated
(ii) a person is excluded from a list of approved suppliers
(iii) a person is not invited to tender or is not considered on the grounds that the persons likely to be employed to perform the contract are, or are not, members of a trade union (or a particular trade union).

It should be noted that a list of approved suppliers can take any form and might even be maintained by a union.

Similarly, section 186 TULRCA 1992 states that any term or condition of a contract for the supply of goods or services is void in so far as it purports to require the employer to recognize one or more trade unions for negotiating purposes or to negotiate or consult any trade union official. Section 187 TULRCA 1992 makes it unlawful to commit any of the acts mentioned in (i)-(iii) above if one of the grounds for doing so is that the person against whom it is taken does not, or is not likely to recognize, negotiate or consult as mentioned in section 186 TULRCA 1992.

Anyone adversely affected by a failure to comply with sections 145 and 187 TULRCA 1992 – for example, an employer or employee deprived of work – can seek damages from the employer concerned for breach of statutory duty and can sue the union involved or its officials in tort. To establish a breach of statutory duty it will be sufficient to show that one of the grounds for not being included on the tender list (or having a contract of supply terminated, etc.) was a union membership or recognition requirement prohibited by section 145 and 187 TULRCA 1992. Sections 222(3) and 225 TULRCA 1992 provide that there will be no immunity from liability in tort (*see* chapter 20) for inducing or attempting to induce a person to contravene section 145 and 187 TULRCA 1992, or for boycotting the work of non-union (or union) members.[49]

Notes

1   Section 119 TULRCA 1992.
2   *Time off for Trade Union Duties and Activities*, Department of Employment, HMSO, 1991.
3   Section 169(3) TULRCA 1992.

4 'Working hours' are defined in the same way as section 146(2) TULRCA 1992 (see page 272).

5 See *Hairsine v Hull City Council* [1992 IRLR 211.

6 Section 169(4) TULRCA 1992. (see chapter 6, note 3).

7 See *Arbeiterwohlfahrt der Stadt Berlin v Botel* [1992] IRLR 423.

8 Paragraph 12.

9 Pararaph 28.

10 See paragraph 13.

11 See *London Ambulance Service v Charlton* [1992] IRLR 510.

12 See *British Bakeries v Adlington* [1989] IRLR 218.

13 See *Ashley v Ministry of Defence* [1984] IRLR 57.

14 Paragraph 18.

15 See *Ministry of Defence v Crook* [1982] IRLR 488.

16 Paragraph 21.

17 [1984] IRLR 493.

18 Unless the 'time limit escape clause' applies (see chapter 3 note 14): section 171 TULRCA 1992.

19 Section 172 TULRCA 1992.

20 Section 298 TULRCA 1992.

21 [1978] Unreported EAT decision.

22 *Ridgway v NCB* [1987] IRLR 80.

23 See *Ridgway v NCB* (note 22).

24 *Carlson v Post Office* [1981] IRLR 158.

25 See *Discount Tobacco Ltd v Armitage* [1981] IRLR 15.

26 See *British Airways v Francis* [1981] IRLR 9.

27 [1983] IRLR 78.

28 See *Port of London Authority v Payne* [1992] IRLR 447.

29 *Rasool v Hepworth Pipe Ltd* (No 2) [1980] IRLR 135.

30 See *Marley Tile Co. v Shaw* [1980] IRLR 25.

31 See *Fitzpatrick v British Rail* [1991] IRLR 376.

32 See *Zucker v Astrid Jewels Ltd* [1978] IRLR 385.

33 See *City and Hackney Health Authority v NUPE* [1985] IRLR 252.

34 Unless the 'time limit escape clause' applies (see chapter 3, note 14): section 147 TULRCA 1992.

35 See *British Airways Board v Clark and Havill* [1982] IRLR 238.

36 See *Adlam v Salisbury and Wells Theological College* [1985] ICR 786.

37 Section 148(3)TULRCA 1992.

38 Section 150 TULRCA 1992.

39 Section 149 TULRCA 1992.

40 See *Brassington v Cauldon Wholesale Ltd* [1977] IRLR 479.

41 'Appropriate time' has the same meaning as in section 146(2) TULRCA 1992 (see page 271–2).

42 See *Crosville Motor Ltd v Ashfield* [1986] IRLR 475.

43 Section 54(1) TULRCA 1992.

44 See *Maund v Penwith District Council* [1984] IRLR 24.

45 Section 158 TULRCA 1992. See chapter 14

46 Section 161 TULRCA 1992 and section 77 EPCA 1978 (as amended).

47 See section 162 TULRCA 1992 and section 77 EPCA (as amended).
48 See section 164 TULRCA 1992.
49 See *Messenger News Group v NGA* [1984] IRLR 397.

19 Trade unions and their members

Admission

A union is entitled to stipulate the descriptions of persons who are eligible for membership but provided it observes its own rules no court can order a union to admit a particular applicant. However, the Sex Discrimination Act 1975 and the Race Relations Act 1976 make it unlawful for an organization of workers to discriminate in the terms on which it is prepared to admit into membership, or by refusing or deliberately omitting to accept an application for membership. Equally, it is unlawful for an organization of workers to discriminate on the prohibited grounds against a member in the way it affords access to any benefits, facilities or services, or subjects to any detriment including deprivation of membership.[1]

Section 174 TULRCA 1992 gives employees the right to join the union of their choice. It provides that an individual may not be excluded (or expelled) from a union unless the reason is one of the following:

(i)   the individual fails to satisfy an enforceable membership requirement in the union's rules. A requirement is 'enforceable' if it restricts membership solely by reference to one or more of the following criteria:

  • employment in a specified trade, industry or profession
  • occupational description (including grade, level or category)
  • possession of specified qualifications or work experience[2]

(ii) the individual does not qualify for membership by reason of the union operating only in particular parts of Great Britain

(iii) where the union operates only in relation to one employer or a number of associated employers and the individual is not employed by that employer or one of those employers

(iv) the exclusion (or expulsion) is entirely attributable to the individual's conduct. For these purposes 'conduct' does not include being or ceasing to be:

- a member of another trade union
- employed by a particular employer or at a particular place
- a member of a political party.

Nor does it include any conduct for which an individual may not be disciplined by a trade union (*see* page 282).[3]

A person excluded (or expelled) in contravention of these provisions can complain to an industrial tribunal. This must normally be done within six months of the date of exclusion (or expulsion). However, where a tribunal finds that it was not reasonably practicable to comply with this time limit, the period may be extended by such amount as is considered reasonable.[4] If the claim is upheld the tribunal will make a declaration to that effect. Complainants who are admitted or readmitted to the union can apply to the tribunal for compensation after a four-week period but must do so before six months have elapsed from the date of the declaration. If there is no admission or readmission, applications for compensation must be made to the EAT. The industrial tribunal and EAT will award such compensation as is considered 'just and equitable in all the circumstances' up to a maximum of £17,150 (at 1993 compensation levels). However, compensation fixed by the EAT must be at least £5,000.[5]

Check-off arrangements

Section 68 TULRCA 1992 gives workers the right not to suffer deductions of unauthorized or excessive union subscriptions. Where a 'subscription deduction arrangement' exists, the employer must ensure that no subscription deduction is made from wages unless it is authorized. A deduction will be authorized if:

- the worker has signed and dated a document authorizing the deduction

- the authorization was given within three years of the deduction being made
- the authorization has not been withdrawn in writing.

It should be noted that a worker's authorization of a deduction does not in itself oblige the employer to continue to the check-off arrangement.[6]

The amount deducted must not exceed the 'permitted amount' *i.e.* the amount fixed under the check-off arrangement. If the subscription rate rises the employer cannot deduct a larger sum until the worker has been given at least a month's notice of the increase and the new subscription rate. In addition, this notice must remind the worker that she or he may withdraw from the deduction arrangement at any time by giving written notice to the employer. No notice is necessary if the larger deduction results from a pay rise but any change in the percentage figure by reference to which deductions are made must be notified.[7]

An individual who suffers a deduction in breach of these provisions can complain to an industrial tribunal. If the claim is upheld the tribunal must make a declaration and order the employer to repay the amount unlawfully deducted. Where a deduction results in a contravention of section 68 and a contravention of other specified statutory rights, the tribunal can only make an award for whichever represents the greatest loss.[8] Finally, readers should be aware that deductions are to be regarded as having been authorized until 28 August 1994, unless the employee has given written notice withdrawing authorization.

Discipline, expulsion and resignation

The rules of a trade union constitute a contract between the union and its members and must be strictly adhered to. A trade union wishing to take disciplinary action must, therefore, ensure that its rule book contains the necessary powers.[9] Section 64 TULRCA 1992 gives members the right not to be unjustifiably disciplined by the union and section 65 deems disciplinary action by a union to be unjustifiable for the following types of conduct:

(i) failing to participate in industrial action or criticizing such action

(ii) alleging that the union or an official is acting unlawfully. This protects members who bring legal proceedings against the union

(iii) encouraging or assisting others to perform their contracts of employment (for example, during industrial action) or encouraging others to make an allegation of the type mentioned in (ii)

(iv) asking the Commissioner for the Rights of Trade Union Members or the Certification Officer for advice or assistance on any matter, or consulting another person about an allegation against the union or its officers

(v) refusing to comply with a requirement imposed by a union (for example, during disciplinary proceedings) which amounts to an infringement of the above rights

(vi) proposing or preparing to engage in any conduct mentioned above

(vii) failing to agree, or withdrawing agreement, to a check-off arrangement (*see* pages 280–1)

(viii) resigning or proposing to resign from the union or another union, joining or proposing to join another union, refusing to join another union or being a member of another union

(ix) working with, or proposing to work with, individuals who are not members of the union or who are not members of another union

(x) working for, or proposing to work for, an employer who employs or has employed individuals who are not members of the union, or who are or are not members of another union

(xi) requiring the union to do an act which it is required to do under TULRCA 1992 when requested to do so by a member.

In this context disciplinary action covers virtually all forms of detrimental treatment.[10] Thus in *NALGO v Killorn*[11] a member was subjected to a detriment when suspension deprived her of the benefits of membership and she was named as a strike-breaker in a branch circular with the intention of causing her embarrassment.

Those wishing to complain about unjustifiable discipline must normally apply to an industrial tribunal within three months of the relevant union decision.[12] Not surprisingly, individuals cannot be prevented from complaining by their union rule book and any settlement will be binding only if ACAS has been involved or the conditions regulating compromise agreements are satisfied.[13] If a tribunal upholds a complaint it will make a declaration to that effect. Compensation is available if a separate application is lodged not earlier than four weeks and not later than six months from the date of the tribunal's declaration.[14] If the union has revoked its disciplinary action compensation will be assessed by an industrial tribunal, otherwise applications must go to the EAT.[15] Both tribunals are empowered to award such compensation as is just and equitable in the circumstances. The maximum in 1993 is £17,150 and at the EAT there is a £2,700 minimum irrespective of the merits of the case. As with unfair dismissal, compensation can be reduced on the grounds of contributory fault or a failure to mitigate loss.[16] The remedies for unjustifiable discipline are not available where the complainant could bring an action under section 174 TULRCA 1992 (*see* pages 279–80). However, if the exclusion or expulsion is for any of the reasons listed under (i)-(xi) on page 282 it is not to be attributed to the conduct of the individual.[17]

If the rules specify the grounds on which disciplinary action may be taken it will be unlawful for the union to rely on any other grounds, and where the rules provide for a procedure to be adopted that procedure must be rigidly followed. Ultimately, a court's interpretation of the rules will take precedence over that of the union, although occasionally the judges have acknowledged that union rules should not be construed literally but should be given a reasonable interpretation which accords with their intended meaning.[18] The court's jurisdiction as final arbiters on questions of law cannot be ousted. Thus a rule which purports to make a decision of a union appeal body 'final and binding' will be of no effect if challenged.[19] Even where there is an express provision that internal remedies must be exhausted before a member goes to law, a court will not be bound by such a requirement. Indeed, section 63 TULRCA 1992 gives union members a right to start legal proceedings in connection with any matter which can be dealt with under the rule book so long as a valid application to resolve the matter within the union's rules has previously been made. However, the court proceedings must be commenced at least six months after the date of the application to the union and this period can be extended if a court is satisfied that any delay in operating the internal procedure resulted from the applicant's unreasonable conduct. If these conditions are met the court is bound to deal with the matter, but if they are not the burden will be on complainants to show why they should not first exhaust the internal procedures.[20]

At one time, judges were of the opinion that the essential fairness or otherwise of union rules was not for them to decide, although more recently they have taken the view that if such rules are contrary to natural justice they should be declared invalid. In this context natural justice requires that a member should be given notice of the charge and a reasonable opportunity of meeting it. However, there is no legal obligation on a union to give notice of a decision to terminate membership or grant an opportunity of being heard if there is nothing the member could say which would affect the outcome.[21] Where hearings are granted they must be fairly conducted and *bona fide* decisions reached on their merits; in other words, without even the appearance of bias.[22] However, unless contained in the rule book, there would appear to be no right to legal representation. As regards appeals, the courts have decided that since they do not constitute a rehearing appeals cannot correct defects at the initial hearing.

Under common law a person who is wrongfully expelled may seek a declaration that he or she is still a union member, an injunction to prevent the expulsion being put into effect and damages for breach of contract. In addition, section 174 TULRCA 1992 establishes a right not to be expelled from a trade union unless there is a statutorily permitted reason for expulsion.[23] This precisely parallels the right not to be excluded and the method of enforcement is as described in relation to a refusal to admit (*see* page 280). It should be noted that although the industrial tribunal procedure will be cheaper, the common law remedies may prove more attractive. There are three main reasons for this: firstly, an injunction may be obtained to compel the union to treat the plaintiff as still being a member; secondly, damages cannot be reduced on the grounds of contributory fault; thirdly, a court is unlikely to condone breaches of the union's rules and procedures.

As regards resignation, section 69 TULRCA 1992 implies into every contract of membership of a trade union (whether made before or after the passing of this Act) a term conferring a right on the member, on giving reasonable notice and complying with reasonable conditions, to terminate his or her membership of the union.

Elections

Section 46 TULRCA 1992 stipulates that, irrespective of its rule book, every trade union must elect its president, general secretary and members of its executive by ballot at least every five years.[24] The election results must be given effect within a reasonable period (not exceeding six months), although the actions of the principal executive committee remain valid even if that body is not elected in accordance with the statute.[25] In conducting such elections unions must satisfy the following conditions:

(i)   members must be given equal entitlement to vote unless they belong to a specified class which is excluded from voting by the union rules

(ii) members who are entitled to vote must be allowed to do so in secret by marking a voting paper without interference from the union (or any of its members, officials or employees) and, so far as is reasonably practicable, they should do so without incurring any direct cost to themselves[26]

(iii) ballot papers and a list of candidates must be sent by post to a member's address and each member must be given an opportunity to vote by post

(iv) votes must be fairly and accurately counted, although any inaccuracy can be disregarded if it is 'accidental and on a scale which could not affect the result of the election', and the result of the election must be determined solely by counting the number of votes cast directly for each candidate[27]

(v)   no member must be unreasonably excluded from standing as a candidate, unless she or he belongs to a class which has been excluded by the union rules, and no candidate can be required to be a member of a political party[28]

Section 48 TULRCA 1992 gives candidates in union elections the right to prepare an election address and to have it distributed with the ballot papers. Unions cannot impose a word limit of less than a hundred words and the address can only be edited with the permission of the candidate. There is also a duty to ensure, so far as is practicable, that the same facilities apply equally to all candidates. Section 24 TULRCA obliges trade unions to compile and maintain a register of the names and addresses of their members and to secure, so far is reasonably practicable, that entries in the register are accurate and kept up to date.

Prior to an election being held a trade union must appoint a qualified independent person (a 'scrutineer').[29] The scrutineer must supervise the production and distribution of voting papers; make a detailed report on the conduct of an election, indicating any matters about which he or she is dissatisfied; and retain custody of the returned voting papers for at least a year after the ballot result was announced. Before the scrutineer begins performing his or her functions, a trade union must either personally inform all its members, so far as is reasonably practicable, of the scrutineer's name or notify the members of the name in such other way as is in keeping with the union's practice. A trade union must supply the scrutineer with a copy of the register of members' names and addresses as it applies to the particular election. The scrutineer must inspect the register (*see* above) whenever it appears appropriate to do so and, in particular, when requested to do so by a member who suspects that the register is not accurate or up-to-date. The latter requirement does not apply where the scrutineer considers that the suspicion is ill founded.[30]

The storage and distribution of the voting papers and the counting of votes must be undertaken by 'independent persons' appointed by the union. Such a person may be the scrutineer or a person whom the union believes will carry out his or her functions competently, and whose independence cannot reasonably be called into question.[31] Finally, in addition to the detailed statutory provisions, the Secretary of State is empowered to issue codes of practice on union elections.[32]

If a trade union fails to comply with any of the above provisions, within a year from the date the election result was announced a member may apply to the Certification Officer or the High Court for a declaration. The High Court can also make an enforcement order requiring the union to take remedial action. The period for ensuring compliance with an enforcement order will be specified by the court, and any person who was a member when the order was made is entitled to enforce obedience to it.[33] Where an application is lodged with the Certification Officer that person is empowered to make enquiries and, where it is considered appropriate, both the applicant and the trade union will be given an opportunity to be heard. Whether or not a declaration is made, the Certification Officer must give written reasons for his or her decision and such reasons may be accompanied by written observations. The making of an application to the Certification Officer does not prevent the applicant, or any other person, from making an application to the High Court in respect of the same matter and, where this occurs, the court will have due regard to the Certification Officer's findings.[34]

Political funds

Contribution to a union's political fund cannot be made a condition of admission to a union and members who wish to contract out of a political levy must be free to do so. Similarly, contracted-out members cannot be excluded from any benefit or disqualified from holding any office, except for a position connected with the management of a political fund.[35] According to sections 73–8 TULRCA 1992, unions wishing to maintain political funds must ballot their members at least every 10 years and observe the same conditions as apply to elections (*see* pages 285–6). Where a political fund resolution has ceased to have effect, members who were exempt from the obligation to contribute must not be excluded from any benefits or placed in any respect, either directly or indirectly, under any disadvantage compared with other union members by reason of being so exempt.[36] Similarly, where a resolution has lapsed but the union has continued to collect contributions, it must pay a refund of any contribution made after the date of cessation to any member who applies for one.[37]

Union members can apply to the High Court for a declaration that the union has failed to take such steps as are necessary to ensure that the collection of political levies was discontinued as soon as reasonably practicable. The court may make an order specifying the steps that the union must take within a stipulated period of time in order to ensure the ending of the political levy. If such an order is made, any member of the union who was also a member when the order was made can enforce obedience to the order.[38]

Section 86 TULRCA 1992 imposes a duty on employers not to deduct contributions to a political fund from the emoluments payable to a member who has either informed the employer in writing that he or she is exempt from paying the political levy or has given written notification to the union of his or her objection to paying it. Employers must comply as soon as is reasonably practicable and will be in breach of the Act if they simply refuse to deduct any union dues from the pay of the person who submitted a certificate under this section. Aggrieved employees may apply to the county court for a declaration that the employer has failed to comply and the court can make an order requiring the employer to take remedial action within a specified period.[39]

Ballot funding and facilities

By virtue of section 115 TULRCA 1992 the Secretary of State 'may by regulations make a scheme providing for payments by the Certification Officer towards expenditure incurred by independent trade unions in respect of certain ballots. The Funds for Trade Union Ballots Regulations 1984 (as amended) are now in force and pamphlets have been published by the Certification Office offering guidance on these provisions. The present scheme covers secret ballots if they are held for one of the following purposes:[40]

(i) obtaining a decision or ascertaining the views of members as to the calling or ending of a strike or other industrial action

(ii) carrying out an election in accordance with Part 1 Chapter IV of TULRCA 1992 (*see* pages 285–6) or one provided for by the union rules

(iii) electing a member to be a representative of other members also employed by the employer

(iv) amending the rules of a union[41]

(v) voting on a decision to amalgamate with another union[42]

(vi) obtaining a decision on a resolution for the continuation of a political fund (*see* page 287)

(vii) obtaining a decision or ascertaining the views of members as to the acceptance or rejection of a proposal made by an employer relating to contractual terms and conditions.

The current scheme for funding ballots is being phased out over a three-year period and section 115 TULRCA 1992 will be repealed on 31 March 1996. In the financial year 1993/4 public funds will cover only 75 per cent of each valid claim; 50 per cent in 1994/5 and 25 per cent in 1995/6.

According to section 116 TULRCA 1992, if employers, together with any associated employers, employ more than 20 people, recognized independent trade unions may request that they permit their premises to be used for the purpose of giving workers who are members of a union a 'convenient opportunity of voting' in a 'relevant ballot' (unless the ballot is one in which every person who votes must be given a convenient opportunity to vote by post). A 'relevant ballot' is one which is held for the purpose of one of the matters listed (i)-(vii) above and is secret. A trade union can complain to an industrial tribunal that it was reasonably practicable for the employer to comply with the request but that there was a failure to do so. Such a complaint must be lodged before the end of a period of three months, beginning with the date of the failure.[43] If it is well founded, the tribunal must make a declaration to that effect and may make an award of compensation of such amount as is 'just and equitable in all the circumstances having regard to the employer's default in failing to comply with the request and to any expenses incurred by the union in consequence of the failure'.[44] An appeal can be made to the EAT only on a question of law.

This provision is also due to be repealed on 31 March 1996. To some extent this can be explained by the fact that TULRCA 1992 requires most union ballots to be postal. Nevertheless section 116 applies to a larger range of ballots than those currently required by statute.

Inter-union disputes

There is no legal machinery for handling inter-union disputes and relations between TUC-affiliated unions are regulated by the

Bridlington Principles.[45] These deal with problems of recognition, demarcation and wages and conditions, as well as competition for members. An affiliated union should not recruit among a grade of workers where another union already has a majority of such workers and negotiates for them, unless it has the permission of that union. More generally, an affiliated union should not accept a member of another affiliated union without inquiry, and if it emerges that the applicant is engaged in a trade dispute, is in arrears, or is under discipline, he or she should be rejected. Clearly the application of these principles has been undermined by sections 174–6 TULRCA 1992, which gives individuals the right to join the union of their choice (*see* page 279).

If a dispute cannot be resolved informally the TUC will set up a Disputes Committee, which is empowered to make an award. Where an award is not complied with the General Council may refer the matter to the annual Congress, which may choose to expel a recalcitrant union. Principles 7 and 8 declare that a union should not take official strike action over an inter-union dispute before the TUC has examined the issue and unions should take 'immediate and energetic' steps to end any unofficial stoppage connected with such a dispute. An employer who is affected by an inter-union problem may seek assistance from ACAS (*see* page 10).

Notes

1   Section 12 SDA 1975, section 11 RRA 1976. See also EOC Code of Practice, paragraphs 6–8, and CRE Code of Practice, part 3.
2   Section 174(3) TULRCA 1992.
3   Section 174(4) TULRCA 1992.
4   Section 175 TULRCA 1992. Complainants can appeal to the EAT on a question of law only: section 291 TULRCA 1992.
5   Section 176 TULRCA 1992.
6   Section 68(9) TULRCA 1992.
7   Section 68(6–8) TULRCA 1992.
8   Section 68A TULRCA 1992.
9   See *Clarke v Chadburn* [1984] IRLR 350.
10 Section 64(2) TULRCA 1992.
11 [1990] IRLR 464.
12 Section 66(2) TULRCA 1992.
13 Section 288 TULRCA 1992.

14 Section 67(3) TULRCA 1992.
15 On the requirement to take all necessary steps to secure the reversal of an expulsion see *NALGO v Courtney* [1992] IRLR 114.
16 Section 67(6–7) TULRCA 1992.
17 Section 174(4) TULRCA 1992.
18 See *Jacques v AUEW* [1986] ICR 683.
19 See *Leigh v NUR* [1970] 2 WLR 60.
20 See *Longley v NUJ* [1987] IRLR 109.
21 *Cheall v APEX* [1983] IRLR 215.
22 See *Roebuck v NUM* [1976] ICR 573 and *Hamlet v GMBATU* [1986] IRLR 293.
23 See *McGhee v TGWU* [1985] IRLR 199 on the meaning of expulsion.
24 Section 46(3) TULRCA 1992 defines a 'member of the executive'. On exemptions for certain presidents and general secretaries see section 46(4) TULRCA 1992.
25 Sections 59 and 61 TULRCA 1992.
26 See *Paul v NALGO* [1987] IRLR 43.
27 See *R v Certification Officer ex parte EPEA* [1990] IRLR 98.
28 Section 47 TULRCA 1992.
29 Defined by section 49(2) TULRCA 1992 and the Trade Union Ballots and Elections (Independent Scrutineer Qualifications) Order 1993. SI No 1909.
30 See sections 49 and 52 TULRCA 1992. On the confidentiality of the register see section 24A TULRCA 1992.
31 Section 51A TULRCA 1992.
32 Section 203 TULRCA 1992.
33 Section 54 TULRCA 1992.
34 Section 56(2) TULRCA 1992. See *Lenahan v UCATT* [1991] IRLR 79.
35 Section 82 TULRCA 1992.
36 Section 91(4) TULRCA 1992.
37 Section 90 TULRCA 1992.
38 Section 81 TULRCA 1992.
39 Section 87 TULRCA 1992.
40 Regulations 5, 6 FTUB Regulations 1984 SI No 1654 (as amended by SI 1988 No 1123 and SI 1988 No 2116)
41 See *R v Certification Office ex parte RCN* [1991] IRLR 258.
42 See Part 1 Chapter VII TULRCA 1992.
43 Unless the 'time limit escape clause' applies (see chapter 3, note 14): section 116(5) TULRCA 1992.
44 Section 116(6) TULRCA 1992.
45 See TUC Booklet *TUC Disputes, Principles and Procedures.*

20 Liability for industrial action

It has already been explained that all forms of industrial action are likely to constitute a breach of an individual's contract of employment and that industrial tribunals have no jurisdiction to consider the complaints of those who have been dismissed while engaged in a strike or other industrial action.[1] In this chapter we will be concentrating more on the liability of those who organize industrial action than those who participate in it. In this respect we will be examining the nature of the common law liabilities and the extent to which statutory provisions can be used to negate their effect. We shall be focusing mainly on the civil law but it will also be necessary to deal with the possibility of criminal prosecutions.

The 'economic' torts

Inducing a breach of contract

There are two forms of inducement, direct and indirect:

Direct
This form of inducement may occur when a union official puts direct pressure on an employer to breach a commercial contract. Thus if A induces B to break the contract of supply with C and C suffers loss as a result, C could sue B for breaking the contract (but is unlikely to in the circumstances), or could sue A if the following matters are shown:

(i)   that A knew of the contract which would be broken or was 'recklessly indifferent' as to its existence
(ii) that A's conduct was intentional. Here, once sufficient

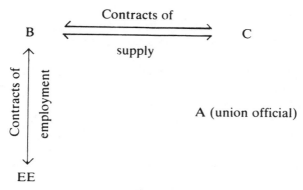

Figure 2

knowledge has been established, the intention to produce a breach will be presumed

(iii) that there was clear evidence of inducement. In this context inducement means pressure, persuasion or procuration and must be distinguished from the giving of advice, information or a warning.[2]

Indirect

Here A induces union members to break their contracts of employment so that B is forced to break the contract with C. C can sue A if the requirements of knowledge, intention and inducement are met and the use of unlawful means is proved. It makes no difference that A believed that the functions performed by the members were voluntary rather than contractual.[3] For the purposes of all the economic torts unlawful means may be either tortious *e.g.* breaking a contract, inducing a breach of statutory duty, or criminal acts *e.g.* the use of violence.

Thus the essential difference between direct and indirect inducement is one of causation. Where the person immediately responsible for bringing the pressure to bear was the defendant or someone for whose acts he or she was legally responsible, the inducement is direct. If it was a third party responding to the defendant's inducement or persuasion but exercising his or her choice (and not being a person for whom the defendant was legally responsible) the inducement is indirect.[4]

Section 219(1)(a) TULRCA 1992 provides that an act done in

contemplation or furtherance of a trade dispute – the so called 'golden formula' (*see* pages 296–9) – will not be actionable in tort on the ground only that it induces another to break a contract. In *Norbrook Ltd v King*[5] it was pointed out that the effect of the phrase 'on the ground only' is that the use of unlawful means to induce a breach of contract deprives the user of statutory protection. That is not the same as saying that the immunity is lost when the breach is caused by immune methods while in the course of trespassing (although the actor is liable for the tort of trespass). However, it is clear the section 219 does not provide immunity against prosecution in respect of acts which are in themselves criminal.[6]

Intimidation

This tort is committed where C suffers as a result of action taken by B in response to an unlawful threat made to B by A. In this situation C or B can sue A at common law, whether the threat is of tortious or criminal conduct.[7] However, section 219(1)(b) TULRCA 1992 now provides that an act done in contemplation or furtherance of a trade dispute shall not be actionable in tort on the ground only that it consists of a person 'threatening that a contract (whether one to which he is a party or not) will be broken or its performance interfered with, or that he will induce another person to break a contract or interfere with its performance'.

Conspiracy

Again, this tort could take one of two forms:

(i)   A combination to injure with illegitimate objectives. This is where two or more persons combine in order to harm the plaintiff by use of means which are lawful in themselves but with a predominant purpose other than that of advancing their own legitimate interests. Thus if those combining can show a genuine trade union reason behind their action (for example, protecting jobs) the conspiracy will not be actionable despite any loss caused to an employer.[8]

(ii) Where people combine in order to harm the plaintiff by using unlawful means a tort is committed irrespective of the purpose of the combination. The use of unlawful means eliminates the justification of self-interest.

Since almost all strikes involve combinations of workers inflicting loss on employers, section 219(2) TULRCA 1992 provides that a combination to do any act in contemplation or furtherance of a trade dispute is not actionable in tort if the act is one which, if done by one person alone, would not be actionable.

Interference with business by unlawful means

This tort was developed to take account of the practice of inserting *force majeure* clauses into commercial contracts. The effect of such a clause is to exempt a party from liability where a breach of contract would otherwise have arisen as a result of industrial action. To meet the argument that those participating in the industrial action could not be held liable for causing a breach of contract, since none occurred, Lord Denning insisted that interference, in the sense of conduct which impedes or prevents a party performing contractual obligations, is enough if it is deliberate and done with knowledge of the existence of the contract. It is now clear that, whether the interference is direct or indirect, both an intention to injure and unlawful means must be shown to establish liability.[9]

Statutory immunity is provided by section 219(1)(a) TULRCA 1992, which states that, so long as the 'golden formula' applies, an act is not to be actionable in tort on the ground only that it 'interferes or induces any other person to interfere' with the performance of a contract. In *Hadmor Productions v Hamilton*[10] the House of Lords held that inducing or threatening to induce a breach of contract could not be regarded as unlawful means for the purpose of establishing liability for interference with the business of a third person.

Inducing a breach of statutory duty

In *Meade v Haringey LBC*[11] two Court of Appeal judges expressed the opinion that persons inducing a public body to act in breach of its statutory duty would be committing a tort for which there would be no statutory immunity. If this view is adopted it will be relatively easy to restrain action taken by workers in the public sector.

Economic duress

If the financial consequences to an employer of not acceding to the request of a trade union or another person are catastrophic, it could be argued that there was such coercion of the employer's will as to vitiate consent to any agreements made with, or payments made to, the union (or person) applying the pressure. Contracts made in these circumstances will be voidable and it will be possible to claim restitution of money paid under them. The rationale is that the employer's apparent consent was induced by pressure exercised by that other party which the law does not regard as legitimate. In *Universe Tankships Inc of Monrovia v ITWF*[12] the House of Lords accepted that sections 219 and 244 TULRCA 1992 afforded an indication of where public policy requires the line to be drawn between the kind of commercial pressure by a trade union which ought to be treated as legitimized and the kind which amounts to economic duress. The events which gave rise to this case occurred in 1978 and it is safe to say that subsequent legislation will have encouraged the judiciary to take a narrower view of what is regarded as legitimate pressure.

The 'golden formula'

We have observed that statutory immunity in tort for various types of industrial action depends on that action taking place in contemplation or furtherance of a trade dispute. Although we will be outlining later the requirement to conduct a ballot before industrial action (*see* page 302), it should be noted that so long as the action taken is in contemplation or furtherance of a trade dispute the TULRCA 1992 immunities apply irrespective of whether or not the action is in breach of a disputes procedure. However, if the 'golden formula' does not apply it will be relatively easy for an employer to show that one of the economic torts is being committed and obtain an interlocutory injunction on that basis (*see* pages 305–8 on injunctions).

The meaning of 'trade dispute'

Section 244 TULRCA 1992 defines a trade dispute as a dispute between workers and their employer which relates wholly or mainly to one or more of the following:

(i)   terms and conditions of employment, or the physical conditions in which any workers are required to work. These are not confined to contractual terms and conditions[13]

(ii) engagement or non-engagement, or termination or suspension of employment, or the duties of employment of one or more workers. However, if the reason or one of the reasons for calling industrial action is 'the fact or belief that the employer has dismissed one or more employees in circumstances such that by virtue of Section 237 TULRCA 1992 (dismissal in connection with unofficial industrial action) they have no right to complain of unfair dismissal' the immunity provided by section 219 TULRCA 1992 is lost[14]

(iii) allocation of work or the duties of employment as between workers or groups of workers

(iv) matters of discipline

(v)   the membership or non-membership of a trade union on the part of a worker. Nevertheless, there will be no immunity from liability in tort where the purpose of the industrial action is to enforce union membership or persuade employers to insert recognition or consultation requirements in contracts for the supply of goods or services[15]

(vi) facilities for officials of trade unions

(vii) the machinery for negotiation or consultation and other procedures, relating to any of the foregoing matters, including the recognition by employers or employers' associations of the right of a trade union to represent workers in any such negotiation, or consultation, or in the carrying out of such procedures.

Clearly where there is a dispute between a union and an employer there is a dispute between those workers on whose behalf the union was acting and that employer.[16] In addition, section 244(2) TULRCA 1992 provides that in certain circumstances a dispute between a Minister of the Crown and any workers is to be treated as a dispute between those workers and their employers.[17]

A 'worker' is defined to cover only those employed by the employer in dispute.[18] However, the 'golden formula' will not apply if the dispute concerns a former employee unless either the employment was terminated in connection with the dispute or the termination was one of the circumstances giving rise to the dispute. A realistic view of who is an employer was taken in *Examite Ltd v Whittaker* where it was stated that 'the Act applies to employers whatever particular hat these particular employers may wear from time to time'.[19]

A trade dispute can exist even though it relates to matters occurring outside the UK:

> so long as the person or persons whose actions in the UK are said to be in contemplation or furtherance of a trade dispute relating to matters occurring outside the UK are likely to be affected in respect of one or more of the matters specified in section 244(1) TULRCA by the outcome of that dispute'.[20]

It is also provided that an act, threat or demand done or made by a person or organization against another which, if resisted, would have led to a trade dispute with that other, shall, notwithstanding that because that other submits to the act or threat or accedes to the demand no dispute arises, be treated as being done or made in contemplation or furtherance of a trade dispute.[21]

What would the legal position be if the dispute has a political or personal element? It is at this point that the significance of the words 'relates wholly or mainly to' can be appreciated. Prior to the EA 1982, to be classed as a trade dispute all that was required was that the dispute be 'connected with' one or more of the matters now mentioned in Section 244(1) TULRCA. If it was connected, it was immaterial whether the dispute also related to other matters or had a political or personal motive. Now, however, the courts are required to identify the predominant purpose and in the docks strike of 1989 the TGWU established that its concern was with the industrial consequences of the repeal of the dock labour scheme rather than the legislation itself.[22]

Contemplation or furtherance

The word 'contemplation' refers to something imminent or likely to occur, so the 'golden formula' cannot be invoked if the action was taken too far in advance of any dispute. 'Furtherance' assumes the existence of a dispute and an act will not be protected if it is not for the purpose of promoting the interests of a party to the dispute (for example, if it is in pursuit of a personal vendetta) or occurs after its conclusion.[23] In *MacShane and Ashton v Express Newspapers*[24] the House of Lords held that while the existence of a trade dispute had to be determined objectively, the test for deciding whether an act is in furtherance of such a dispute is a subjective one: 'If the person doing the act honestly thinks at the time he does it that it may help one of the parties to the dispute to achieve their objective and does it for that reason, he is protected'. Apparently there is no requirement that a union should act exclusively in furtherance of a trade dispute; it is sufficient if the furtherance of a trade dispute is one of its purposes. Indeed, the presence of an improper motive is relevant only where it is so overriding that it negates any genuine intention to advance the trade dispute.[25]

Secondary action

In this book 'primary action' refers to action taken directly against the employer in dispute and 'secondary action' is that taken against the employer's suppliers and customers. Section 244 defines secondary action as being an inducement to break or interfere with a contract of employment or a contract for personal services, or a threat to do so, where the employer under that contract is not party to the dispute. For these purposes an employer is not to be regarded as a party to a dispute between another employer and its workers. Similarly, where more than one employer is in dispute, the dispute between each employer and its workers is to be treated as a separate dispute.[26]

The protection afforded against certain tort liabilities by section 219 TULRCA 1992 will not be available unless the secondary action satisfies the requirements of section 224. These can only be met if the secondary action is taken in the course of such attendance as is declared lawful by section 220 TULRCA 1992

(i) by a worker employed (or last employed) by the employer who is party to the dispute, or
(ii) by a union official whose attendance is lawful by virtue of section 220(1)(6) TULRCA 1992. (On peaceful picketing and section 220 TULRCA 1992 *see* page 309).

Unions' responsibility for the acts of their members and officials

Trade unions are to be treated in law as ordinary persons. This means that they get the benefit of the immunities conferred by section 219 TULRCA 1992 but can be sued if they are responsible for unlawful industrial action. However, a union will only be held liable for the torts mentioned in section 20(1) TULRCA 1992 if the acts in question were authorized or endorsed by the union. Where other torts are committed the ordinary principles of vicarious liability apply.[27] Irrespective of union rules, acts are to be regarded as authorized or endorsed if there was authorization or endorsement by:[28]

(i) any person empowered by the rules to do, authorize or endorse acts of the kind in question, or
(ii) the principal executive committee or the president or general secretary, or
(iii) any other committee of the union or any other official of the union (whether employed by it or not).

In this context 'rules' means the 'written rules of the union and any other written provisions forming part of the contract between a member and other members'. 'President' and 'general secretary' are defined to include, where there is no such office in the union, the person who holds the 'nearest equivalent' office.[29] For these purposes any group of persons constituted in accordance with the rules of the union is a committee of the union and 'an act shall be taken to have been done, authorized or endorsed by an official if it was done, etc.' by any member of a group whose purposes include organizing or co-ordinating industrial action.[30] These provisions apply irrespective of anything in the union rules which prevents particular officials or committees calling industrial action.

A union can avoid liability for the actions of union committees and officials if those actions are repudiated by the principal executive committee or the president or general secretary 'as soon as reasonably practicable after coming to the knowledge of any of them'. However, a repudiation will only be effective if:

(i)   written notice of the repudiation is given to the official or committee in question without delay; and

(ii) the union has done its best to give individual written notice of the fact and date of repudiation without delay to:

- every member who the union has reason to believe is taking part, or might otherwise take part, in the industrial action. The notice to members must contain the following statement: 'Your union has repudiated any call for industrial action to which this notice relates and will give no support to such action. If you are dismissed while taking unofficial industrial action, you will have no right to complain of unfair dismissal.'
- the employer of every such member.[31]

An act shall not be treated as repudiated if the union's principal executive committee, president or general secretary subsequently behave in a manner inconsistent with that repudiation. Additionally, if a request is made to any of these bodies within three months by a person who is a party to a commercial contract that has been, or may be, interfered with and who has not been given notice of the repudiation, that body must immediately confirm the repudiation in writing.[32] Finally, in any injunction proceedings arising out of this section, the courts are empowered to require unions to take such steps as are considered appropriate for ensuring that:

(i)   there is no inducement of persons to take part in industrial action, and

(ii) no person engages in any conduct after the grant of the injunction by virtue of having been induced before it was granted to take part in industrial action.[33]

Ballots and notice of industrial action

Trade unions and their officials can benefit from the immunity provided by section 219 TULRCA 1992 only if the union has authorized or endorsed the industrial action, having gained majority support in a ballot of the members concerned not more than four weeks before the start of the action.[34] It is the Court of Appeal's view that once industrial action has begun it should continue 'without substantial interruption' if reliance is to be placed on the result of the original ballot. Whether the original action has come to an end is a matter of fact and degree.[35]

For section 219 TULRCA 1992 immunity to be available the following requirements must be met:[36]

(i)   trade unions must take such steps as are reasonably necessary to ensure that, at least seven days before the start of the ballot, a written notice is received by 'every person who it is reasonable for the union to believe . . . will be the employer of persons who will be entitled to vote in the ballot'. This notice must:

- state that the union intends to hold a ballot
- specify the date which the union reasonably believes will be the opening day of the ballot
- describe (so that the employer can readily ascertain them) the employees who the union reasonably believes will be entitled to vote.

Additionally, at least three days before the opening of the ballot, the union must take such steps as are reasonably necessary to ensure that the same employer receives a sample voting paper.[37]

(ii)   conditions (ii) and (iv) on union elections must be satisfied (*see* page 285).

(iii)   entitlement to vote must be given equally to those, and only those, whom the union reasonably believes will be called upon to take strike or other industrial action. Immunity is lost if any member who was called on to take part on the industrial action was denied entitlement to vote.[38] The Court of Appeal has suggested that any call for industrial action should be limited to those who were employed and given the opportunity of voting at the time of the ballot.[39]

(iv) there must be a separate ballot at each workplace unless the union reasonably believes that in relation to each of its members there is some factor which:

- relates to the terms and conditions of that member's employment or occupational description
- is a factor which that member has in common with one or more of the other members who are voting, and
- where there are members employed by the same employer who are not entitled to vote, is neither a factor which that member has in common with any of those non-voting members nor a factor which individuals employed by that employer have in common as a consequence of having the same place of work.[40]

(v) so far as is reasonably practicable, all members entitled to vote must be sent a voting paper at his or her registered address, and be given a convenient opportunity to vote by post.[41]

(vi) the voting paper must:

- state the name of the independent scrutineer appointed to carry out the functions described on page 286[42]
- specify the address to which, and the date by which, it is to be returned
- be marked with a number which is one of a series of consecutive whole numbers
- contain the following statement: 'If you take part in a strike or other industrial action you may be in breach of your contract of employment'
- invite a 'yes' or 'no' answer to the question whether members are prepared to participate in a strike or other industrial action. According to the Court of Appeal, the questions on the ballot must be framed so that members can draw a distinction between their willingness to take strike action and their willingness to take action short of a strike[43]
- identify the person(s) authorized to call industrial action

and that person must be one of those specified in (i)–(iii) on page 300

(vii) as soon as is reasonably practicable after the ballot, the union must take such steps as are reasonably necessary to ensure that all those entitled to vote and every relevant employer are informed of the number of votes cast, the numbers voting 'yes' and those voting 'no' and the number of spoiled ballot papers[44]

(viii) trade unions must take all reasonably necessary steps to ensure that the employer of those to be called upon to take industrial action receives written notice of the action. This notice must be received after the employer has been informed of the ballot result and at least seven days prior to the date on which the action is to commence. The notice must include the following:

- a description (which enables the employer to readily ascertain them) of the employees whom the union intends to call to take part in, or continue with industrial action
- a statement of whether the industrial action is intended to be continuous or discontinuous
- where there is continuous action, the date on which it is intended to start; where the action is discontinuous, the dates on which it is intended to take place
- a statement that the notice is given for the purposes of section 234A TULRCA 1992

Not surprisingly, this notice provides immunity from legal proceedings only if the employees induced to take part in the action are specified in the notice and they participate in the specified action on the specified date(s). Equally, where industrial action ceases to be authorized or endorsed (other than in compliance with a court order or undertaking), and is subsequently re-authorized or re-endorsed, the union must give another notice to the employer before the industrial action is resumed.

Finally, where a member has been (or is likely to be) induced by the union to take part in any industrial action which does not satisfy the ballot requirements of Part V TULRCA 1992 he or she can apply to the High Court for an order requiring the union to stop authorizing or endorsing the industrial action without the support of a valid ballot.[45] Two points should be noted in relation to this right. First, although a court can order the union to ensure that there is no further inducement it has no power to compel the union to conduct a valid ballot. Secondly, the Commissioner for the Rights of Trade Union Members is empowered to offer assistance to the member taking such proceedings (*see* page 308 on an individual's rights where industrial action affects the supply of goods or services).

Remedies

Damages

Section 22(2) TULRCA 1992 limits the amount of damages that can be awarded 'in any proceedings in tort' against a trade union which is deemed liable for industrial action.[46] The words 'in any proceedings' are crucial, since separate proceedings may be brought by all those who have suffered from the industrial action. The limits set are:

(i)   £10,000, if the union has fewer than 5,000 members
(ii) £50,000, if the union has 5,000 or more members but fewer than 25,000
(iii) £125,000 if the union has 25,000 or more members but fewer than 100,000
(iv) £250,000 if the union has 100,000 or more members

It should be noted that interest on such damages may be available.[47] Finally, it should be noted that damages, costs or expenses cannot be recovered from certain 'protected property'. This includes union provident funds and political funds, which cannot be used for financing industrial action.[48]

Injunctions

If an employer is suffering economic harm as a result of unlawful industrial action the logical remedy is to seek an injunction so as to prevent further loss being incurred. An injunction may be sought against a trade union or some other person, although section 236 TULRCA 1992 prevents a court from compelling an employee to do any work. The general principle that if damages would provide an adequate remedy an injunction must be refused will not apply in this context: 'where it is clear that the defendants were acting unlawfully it would require wholly exceptional circumstances to be a proper exercise of discretion to allow such a conduct to continue'.[49]

There are three basic types of injunction which need to be mentioned:

(i)   In situations of extreme urgency an *interim* injunction can be sought. This is a temporary measure which endures until a named day and can be obtained on the basis of affidavits (sworn statements) submitted by the applicant alone. If the respondent is absent this is known as an *ex parte* (one party) injunction. According to section 221 TULRCA 1992, a court shall not grant an application if the party against whom the injunction is sought claims (or in the court's opinion might claim) that the act was done in contemplation or furtherance of a trade dispute unless all reasonable steps have been taken to give that party notice of the application and an opportunity of being heard.

(ii) An *interlocutory* injunction restrains the commission of an act until the issue comes to trial. Again, no witnesses will be called but there will be legal argument and affidavits from both sides.

(iii) A *permanent* injunction is one which is granted at the end of the trial.

Before granting an interlocutory injunction, a judge will have to consider the following questions:

(i)   Is there a serious questions to be tried?
(ii) Does the balance of convenience lie with the plaintiff? In *NWL v Nelson*[50] Lord Diplock argued that judges should not blind themselves to the practical realities by pretending that an injunction merely preserves the *status quo* until the trial is heard: 'It is the nature of industrial action that it can be promoted effectively only so long as it is possible to strike while the iron is hot; once postponed it is unlikely

that it can be revived . . . the grant or refusal of an interlocutory injunction generally disposes finally of the action.' In such a case the court has to balance the risk of doing an injustice to either party and evaluate the public interest.[51]

(iii) Where the party against whom the injunction is sought claims that the action was in contemplation or furtherance of a trade dispute, is there a likelihood of the defendant establishing a defence to the action under section 219 or 220 TULRCA 1992?[52] It has been held by the House of Lords that the effect of section 221(2) TULRCA 1992 is that in exercising its discretion a court should put into the balance of convenience the degree of likelihood of the defendant succeeding in establishing a trade dispute defence.[53] Thus in *Health Computing v Meek*[54] no injunction was granted because there was a 'substantial probability' that the defendants would establish that they were acting in contemplation or furtherance of a trade dispute. However, that it is likely that a trade dispute defence would be established should not be regarded as an overriding or paramount factor precluding the granting of an injunction. There may be cases where the consequences to the plaintiff or to others may be so serious that the court feels it necessary to grant this form of remedy. In the *Duport Steels* case[55] the Law Lords confirmed that there is a residual discretion to grant an injunction notwithstanding the likelihood of a trade dispute defence succeeding at trial. Nevertheless the opinion was expressed that it required an exceptional case where the consequences of the threatened act might be disastrous.

(iv) What good will be done to the plaintiff by the grant of the injunction sought? In *Hadmor Productions v Hamilton*[56] the House of Lords held that the High Court judge had been entitled to attach great weight to the view that an injunction would not have been of practical use to the plaintiff. It is not sufficient ground for granting an injunction to argue that if the defendants had no intention of engaging in unlawful conduct the injunction would do them no harm![57]

Failure by union officials to comply with an injunction may amount to contempt of court, for which the union is vicariously liable. Indeed, it would appear that a delay in complying with a court order cannot be justified by reference to the union's internal constitution.[58] Where there is deliberate defiance of a court order a substantial fine may be imposed.[59] In this context it should be observed that section 15 TULRCA 1992 makes it unlawful for a union to use its property to indemnify an individual on whom a penalty has been imposed for contempt or a criminal offence. Additionally, where it is alleged that a union's trustees have unlawfully applied union property or complied with an unlawful direction given under the union rules, a member can seek a High Court order to remove the trustees, recover the property or appoint a receiver.[60]

Industrial action affecting the supply of goods or services to an individual

Section 235A TULRCA 1992 gives an individual the right to apply to the High Court for an order if:

(i)   a trade union or other person has done, or is likely to do, an unlawful act to induce a person to take part in or continue with industrial action, and

(ii) an effect, or likely effect, of the industrial action is, or will be, to prevent or delay the supply of goods or services, or to reduce the quality of goods or services supplied to the claimant.

For these purposes an act is unlawful if it is actionable in tort by anyone, or if it could form the basis of an application by a union member under section 62 TULRCA 1992 (*see* above, pages 304–5). It is immaterial whether or not the individual concerned is entitled to be supplied with the goods or services in question.

If a court is satisfied that the claim is well founded, it must make an order restraining the industrial action. To assist individuals to bring proceedings, section 235B TULRCA 1992 creates a Commissioner for Protection against Unlawful Industrial Action. This person can fund, or make arrangements for, legal advice and representation. In deciding whether, and to what extent, assistance should be granted, the commissioner may have regard to: whether the case is so complex that it is unreasonable to expect the applicant to handle it unaided; and whether the case involves a matter of substantial public interest or concern. It remains to be seen how this 'citizen's right' will contribute to the resolution of industrial disputes.

Picketing

Civil law aspects

According to section 220 TULRCA 1992:

> it shall be lawful for a person in contemplation or furtherance of a trade dispute to attend:
>
> (a) at or near his own place of work,
>   *or*
> (b) if he is an official of a trade union, at or near the place of work of a member of that union whom he is accompanying and whom he represents,
>
> for the purpose only of peacefully obtaining or communicating information, or peacefully persuading any person to work or abstain from working.

'Place of work' is not statutorily defined but it would seem to refer to a person's principal place of work or base.[61] As regards the words 'at or near', the Court of Appeal has confirmed that a geographical approach should be taken and that the matter will be one of fact and degree in each case.[62] If people normally work at more than one place or at a place where it is impracticable to picket, their place of work shall be any of their employer's premises from which they work or from which their work is administered.[63] Unemployed workers whose last employment was terminated in connection with a trade dispute, or whose dismissal was one of the circumstances giving rise to a trade dispute, are entitled to picket at their former place of work. It should be observed that section 220 TULRCA 1992 does not necessarily provide employees with a place that they can effectively picket, for example, if their place of work is closed down. A trade union official who has been elected or appointed to represent some of the members is to be regarded for the purposes of picketing as representing only those members; otherwise, a union official is regarded as representing all the union's members.[64]

Section 220 TULRCA 1992 protects mere attendance only for one of the designated purposes. If an act is done in the course of picketing which is not lawful by virtue of section 220 then section 219 TULRCA 1992 will not prevent an action in tort being brought. Thus pickets acting within the scope of section 220 TULRCA 1992 may be liable for conspiracy to use unlawful means if they are accompanied by pickets who are not so acting. Equally, a person who is not picketing at a permitted place may be sued for trespass to the highway as well as all the economic torts. This is so even if the employer at the premises picketed has accepted the work of the primary employer in dispute. Peaceful picketing at one's own place of work may also result in civil liability, for example, if it is in support of workers in dispute with another employer.

In *Thomas v NUM (South Wales)*,[65] Scott J refused to distinguish between 'so-called pickets who are stationed close to the gates of the colliery and the rest, so-called demonstrators, who stand near by'. The judge held that whether the presence or conduct of pickets represents a tortious interference with the right of those who wish to go to work depends on the particular circumstances of the case. In his view, where feelings run high substantial numbers of pickets are almost bound to have an intimidatory effect on those going to work. Thus while picketing *per se* is not a common law nuisance, mass picketing is, *i.e.* picketing so as by sheer weight of numbers to block the entrance to premises or prevent the entry of vehicles or people.[66]

An employer whose contracts are interfered with by picketing which falls outside section 220 TULRCA 1992, as amended, may bring an action for damages against those responsible and ask a court to make an order stopping the unlawful picketing (*see* pages 305–8 on injunctions). An injunction will normally be sought against the person or union on whose instructions or advice the picketing is taking place, but it will also restrict the activities of any others who act on behalf of that person or union (*see* pages 300–1 on a union's responsibility for the acts of its officials). While the police are not obliged to help an employer identify pickets, a court can ask the police to assist its officers in enforcing injunctions.

The impact of the criminal law

The immunity provided by the civil law cannot protect a picket who commits a criminal offence and even peaceful picketing can lead to criminal proceedings if it is not lawful by virtue of section 220 TULRCA 1992:

> The criminal law protects the right of every person to go about his lawful daily business free from interference by others. No one is under any obligation to stop when a picket asks him to do so, or if he does stop, to comply with the picket's request, for example, not to go into work. Everyone has the right, if he wants to do so, to cross a picket line to go into his place of work or to deliver or collect goods. A picket may exercise peaceful persuasion, but if he goes beyond that and tries by means other than peaceful persuasion to deter another person from exercising those rights, he may commit a criminal offence.[67]

Paragraph 43 of the Department of Employment *Code of Practice on Picketing* lists a range of criminal offences that may be committed by pickets:

(i)   to use threatening, abusive or insulting words or behaviour, or disorderly behaviour within the sight or hearing of any person . . . likely to be caused harassment, alarm or distress by such conduct

(ii)   to use threatening, abusive or insulting words or behaviour towards any person with intent to cause fear of violence or to provoke violence

(iii) to use or threaten unlawful violence

(iv)   to obstruct the highway or the entrance to premises or to seek physically to bar the passage of vehicles or persons, etc.

(v)   to be in possession of an offensive weapon

(vi)   intentionally or recklessly to damage property

(vii) to engage in violent, disorderly or unruly behaviour or take any action which is likely to lead to a breach of the peace

(viii) to obstruct a police officer in the execution of his duty.[68]

Although it is not the function of the police to take a view of the merits of a particular trade dispute, the law gives them the discretion to take whatever measures may reasonably be considered necessary to ensure that picketing remains peaceful and orderly. Hence the police are entitled to limit the number of pickets at any one place where they have reasonable cause to fear disorder.[69] Having identified the main cause of violence and disorder on the picket line as excessive numbers, the Code of Practice exhorts pickets and their organizers to ensure that 'in general the number of pickets does not exceed six at any entrance to, or exit from a workplace; frequently a smaller number will be appropriate'.[70] The code also has paragraphs dealing with the functions of a picket organizer and the safeguarding of essential supplies and services.[71]

Other criminal activities

Apart from the law relating to picketing the criminal law does not generally play an important role in regulating industrial conflict. However, if employees occupy their employer's premises they become trespassers under the civil law and the employer may invoke a specified procedure to regain possession. In addition, persons occupying a workplace may be charged under the Criminal Law Act 1977 with using violence to secure entry and trespassing with a weapon of offence, *e.g.* ordinary working tools if they are intended to be used offensively.[72] Of the remaining statutory provisions which could give rise to criminal liability, the most important today are probably sections 240–1 TULRCA 1992.

According to section 240:

> a person commits an offence who wilfully and maliciously breaks a contract of service or hiring, knowing or having reasonable cause to believe that the probable consequence of his so doing, either alone or in combination with others, will be (a) to endanger human life, or cause serious bodily injury, or (b) to expose valuable property whether real or personal to destruction or serious injury . . .

Anyone found guilty of such an offence is liable to pay a fine not exceeding level 2 on the standard scale or to be imprisoned for up to three months or both. This provision is less likely to form the basis of a prosecution than an action for an injunction to prevent a breach of it by someone who anticipates that serious injury will result from industrial action.

Section 241 TULRCA 1992 provides that:

> A person commits an offence who, with a view to compelling another person to abstain from doing or to do any act which that person has a legal right to do or abstain from doing, wrongfully and without legal authority:
>
> 1 uses violence to or intimidates such other person or his wife or children, or injures his property; *or*
> 2 persistently follows such other person about from place to place; *or*
> 3 hides any tools, clothes or property owned or used by such other person, or deprives him of or hinders him in the use thereof; or
> 4 watches or besets the house or other place where such other person resides, or works, or carries on business, or happens to be, or the approach to such house or place; *or*
> 5 follows such other person with two or more other persons in a disorderly manner in or through any street or road.
>
> A person found guilty of this offence is liable to imprisonment for a term not exceeding six months or a fine not exceeding level 5 on the standard scale, or both.

To establish guilt under this section it must be provided that the conduct relied on was wrongful and that the intention with which it was done was, at least in part, to compel others from doing specified acts which they had a legal right to do.[73] In *Galt v Philp*[74] it was held that employees who locked and barricaded the entrance to the premises where they were employed so as to prevent others from working were guilty of 'besetting' within heading 4 above.

Notes

1 See chapters 3 and 12 respectively.
2 See *Camellia Tanker Ltd v ITWF* [1976] IRLR 183.
3 See *Metropolitan Borough of Solihull v NUT* [1985] IRLR 211.
4 See *Middlebrook Mushrooms v TGWU* [1993] IRLR 232.
5 [1984] IRLR 200.
6 See *Galt v Philp* [1984] IRLR 156.
7 See *Messenger News Group v NGA* [1984] IRLR 397.

8   See *Crofter Harris Tweed Co. v Veitch* [1942] AC 435.
9   See *ABP v TGWU* [1989] IRLR 305 (C/A).
10 [1982] IRLR 103.
11 [1979] ICR 494. See also *Barretts & Baird Ltd v IPCS* [1987] IRLR 3.
12 [1982] IRLR 200. See also *Dimskal Shipping v ITWF* [1992] IRLR 78.
13 See *Hadmor Productions v Hamilton* (note 10).
14 Section 223 TULRCA 1992. *See* page 166 on dismissal during industrial action.
15 Sections 222 and 225 TULRCA 1992 respectively.
16 *ABP v TGWU* [1989] IRLR 291.
17 See *London Borough of Wandsworth v NAS-UWT* [1993] IRLR 344.
18 Section 244(5) TULRCA 1992.
19 [1977] IRLR 312. Compare *Dimbleby & Sons v NUJ* [1984] IRLR 161.
20 Section 244(3) TULRCA 1992.
21 Section 244(4) TULRCA 1992.
22 See *ABP v TGWU* (note 9 above).
23 See *Huntley v Thornton* [1957] 1 WLR 321 and *Stratford v Lindley* [1965] AC 307.
24 [1980] IRLR 35.
25 See *ABP v TGWU* (note 9 above).
26 Section 224(4) TULRCA 1992.
27 See *News Group v SOGAT* [1986] IRLR 227.
28 Section 20(2) TULRCA 1992.
29 Section 119 TULRCA 1992.
30 Section 20(3)(b) TULRCA 1992.
31 Section 21(1)–(3) TULRCA 1992.
32 Section 21(5)–(6) TULRCA 1992.
33 Section 20(6) TULRCA 1992.
34 Section 234 TULRCA 1992.
35 *Post Office v UCW* [1990] IRLR 143.
36 See, generally, *Code of Practice on Trade Union Ballots and Industrial Action* (first revision, 1991) but note that this precedes some legislative changes.
37 Section 226A TULRCA 1992.
38 Section 227 TULRCA 1992.
39 *Post Office v UCW* (note 35).
40 Section 228(3).
41 Section 230(2) TULRCA 1992.
42 See sections 226B and 231B TULRCA 1992.
43 *Post Office v UCW* (note 35).
44 See sections 231 and 231A TULRCA 1992.
45 Section 62 TULRCA 1992.
46 For exceptions see section 22(1) TULRCA 1992.
47 See *Boxfoldia Ltd v NGA* [1988] IRLR 383. On aggravated and exemplary damages see *Messenger News Group v NGA* (note 7).
48 Section 23 TULRCA 1992.
49 *Express Newspapers v Keys* [1980] IRLR 247 per Griffiths, J.

50   [1979] IRLR 478.
51   *ABP v TGWU* (note 9).
52   See section 221(2) TULRCA 1992.
53   See *NWL v Nelson* (note 50).
54   [1980] IRLR 437.
55   *Duport Steels v Sirs* [1980] IRLR 112.
56   See note 10.
57   See *Shipping Company Uniform Inc v ITWF* [1985] IRLR 71.
58   See *Kent Free Press v NGA* [1987] IRLR 267.
59   See *Read Transport v NUM* (South Wales) [1985] IRLR 67.
60   Section 16 TULRCA 1992.
61   See *Union Traffic v TGWU* [1989] IRLR 127.
62   See *Rayware Ltd v TGWU* [1989] IRLR 134.
63   Section 220(2) TULRCA 1992.
64   Section 220(4) TULRCA 1992.
65   [1985] IRLR 136.
66   See also *News Group v SOGAT* (note 27), where the torts of nuisance
     and intimidation were committed.
67   Paragraph 42 Department of Employment *Code of Practice on Pick-
     eting* (first revision 1992).
68   See also the Public Order Act 1986, which created the offences
     of disorderly conduct, riot, violent disorder, affray and threatening
     behaviour.
69   See *Moss v McLaughlan* [1985] IRLR 76.
70   Paragraph 51 Department of Employment *Code* (note 67); see
     Thomas v NUM (note 65).
71   Paragraphs 54–7 and 62–4 Department of Employment *Code* (note
     67).
72   See sections 6, 8 Criminal Law Act 1977.
73   See *Elsey v Smith* [1983] IRLR 293.
74   See note 6.

Appendix

Industrial tribunal jurisdictions: service requirements and time limits

Type of claim	Service required[1]	Time limit[2]	Chapter references
Written particulars of contract of employment	2 months	3 months after employment ceased	2
Itemized pay statement	–	3 months after employment ceased	2
Unlawful deduction from wages	–	3 months after deduction or non-payment	3
Unlawful refusal of employment on union grounds	–	3 months after date of conduct complained of	4
Sex or race discrimination	–	3 months after the act complained of	5
Equal pay	–	6 months after employment ceased	5
Time off for ante-natal care	–	3 months after day of appointment	6
Failure to permit return after pregnancy (*i.e.* unfair dismissal or redundancy)	2 years at the beginning of the 11th week before the expected week of confinement	3 months (or 6 months if redundant) after employment ceased	6
Time off for safety representatives	–	3 months after failure to permit or pay	7
Medical suspension pay	1 month	3 months after day payment owed	8

cont'd

Type of claim	Service required[1]	Time limit[2]	Chapter references
Dismissal connected with medical suspension	1 month	3 months after employment ceased	8+11
Guarantee payment	1 month	3 months after day payment is owed	9
Redundancy payment	2 years (over the age of 18)	6 months after employment ceased	9, 11, 13, 14
Time off for public duties	–	3 months after failure to permit	9
Unfair dismissal	2 years. None if reason for dismissal is inadmissible	3 months after employment ceased	11, 12, 14
Interim relief (union grounds only)	–	7 days after employment ceased	18
Written statement of reasons for dismissal	2 years. None if on the grounds of pregnancy/ maternity	3 months after employment ceased	12
Breach of redundancy or transfer of undertaking consultation procedure	–	3 months after employment ceased	13
Remuneration under protective award	–	3 months after employment ceased	13
Time off for redundant employee to look for work	2 years at date notice expired	3 months after failure to permit or pay	13
Payment from Secretary of State where employer insolvent	–	3 months after Secretary of State's decision	14
Time off for trade union duties and activities	–	3 months after failure to permit (or pay in the case of duties)	18

cont'd

Type of claim	Service required[1]	Time limit[2]	Chapter references
Action short of dismissal on union membership grounds	–	3 months after the action complained of	18
Exclusion or expulsion from a trade union	–	6 months after refusal or expulsion	19
Compensation for exclusion or expulsion from a trade union	–	6 months after tribunal declaration	19
Unjustifiable discipline by a trade union	–	3 months after union determination	19

Notes:

1 The 'service required' means the period of continuous employment needed for an employee to make a claim (*see* chapter 15).

2 Time limits can be extended in specified circumstances so reference should always be made to the relevant parts of this book or the statute concerned

Bibliography

General textbooks

Anderman, S: *Labour Law – Management decisions and workers' rights*. London, Butterworth. 1993.
Bowers, J. & Honeyball, S: *Textbook on Labour Law*. 3rd edition. London, Blackstone Press. 1993.
Osman, C (ed.) *Butterworths Employment Law Guide*. 2nd edition. London, Butterworth. 1993.
Pitt, G: *Employment Law*. London, Sweet & Maxwell. 1992.
Smith, I & Wood, J: *Industrial Law*. 5th edition. London, Butterworth. 1993.

Specialist books

Aikin, O: *Contracts*. London, IPM. 1992.
Barrett, B & Howells, R: *Health and Safety Law*. London, Pitman. 1993.
Bourn, C & Whitmore, J: *Discrimination and Equal Pay*. London, Sweet & Maxwell. 1993.
Fowler, A: *Redundancy*. London, IPM. 1993.
Greenhalgh, R: *Industrial Tribunals*. London, IPM. 1992.
James, P & Lewis, D: *Discipline*. London, IPM. 1992.
McMullen, J: *Business Transfers and Employee Rights*. 2nd edition. London, Longman. 1992.
Smith, I, Goddard, C & Randall, N: *Health and Safety: the New Legal Framework*. London, Butterworth. 1993.

Statute book

Wallington, P (editor): *Butterworths Employment Law Handbook*. London, Butterworth. 1993.

Reference books

The following works are updated periodically.
Encyclopedia of Labour Relations Law. London, Sweet & Maxwell.

Harvey on Industrial Relations and Employment Law. London, Butterworth.

Journals

Industrial Relations Services publish the *Industrial Relations Law Bulletin*, and Incomes Data Services produce *Incomes Data Briefs*. Both publications are issued twice monthly, focus on current developments in the field and provide explanations and comment. The *Industrial Law Journal* is published quarterly and is the main academic journal.

Law reports

The main series of specialist law reports are the *Industrial Relations Law Reports* and the *Industrial Cases Reports.*

Other publications

ACAS produces a number of booklets on employment law topics which are available free of charge from ACAS and local offices of the Department of Employment. The CRE and EOC publish material on the anti-discrimination laws and the Health and Safety Commission and Executive provide information within their own area.

Index

Law and Employment Series

For many managers the law relating to employment can seem labyrinthine – but with today's escalating number of legal claims, they ignore it at their peril.

Managers must be able to construct sound yet flexible and progressive policies built on firm legal foundations. This important series will enable them to meet the challenge. It forms a superbly practical and, above all, accessible source of reference on employment practice and the law.

The IPM has specially commissioned Olga Aikin – one of the country's foremost authorities on employment law, a qualified barrister and well-known legal writer – to steer the project.

Individual titles have been written by leading employment law experts and human resource practitioners. Together, they provide a unique combination of up-to-date legal guidance with in-depth advice on current employment issues.

Redundancy

Alan Fowler

Making redundancies is always unpleasant. This book aims to give practical guidance on good management practice to avoid redundancy as well as detailed advice on how to handle it – legally and fairly. In addition to the statutory minimum obligations, it covers:

- long-term measures to avoid redundancy: effective planning, training, flexible working arrangements etc.
- short-term action – recruitment freezes, redeployment, early retirement etc.; lay off and short-time working
- handling redundancies – criteria for selection, employee and union communication, consultation, involvement and notification
- compensation – including examples of good practice beyond the statutory limits, outplacement provision, counselling etc.
- redundancy implications of business failure.

208 pp Royal pbk 0 85292 497 6 £14.95

Industrial Tribunals

Roger Greenhalgh

Industrial tribunal cases present managers with a host of dilemmas – not simply whether to fight or settle, but when and how to use tribunal procedures and how best to conduct their response at hearing. This book provides clear guidance on identifying and implementing the best strategy to serve overall business objectives. It covers:

- the role and nature of tribunals
- rules of procedure from the originating application to the decision and beyond
- the decision to defend, settlement and avoiding appearance at tribunals
- preparing the case
- production of documents, witness statements, proofs of evidence etc.
- presenting the case – examining witnesses, oral presentation, challenging procedural points, use of documentary evidence etc.
- after the hearing – the decision, appeal, costs, enforcement of awards.

200 pp Royal pbk 0 85292 496 8 £14.95

Pay and Benefits

Joan Keogh

Getting the reward package right is a crucial element in recruitment and retention. But although employers enjoy considerable freedom in formulating their strategies, the law lays many traps for the unwary. This clear and practical guide sets out:

- the legal constraints on payment systems
- how to put together the package – bonus schemes, incentives, profit-related pay
- how to avoid discrimination
- fringe benefits – share options, permanent health insurance, company cars – and their tax implications
- the rules on Sick Pay, Maternity Pay and pensions
- how to deal with termination
- statutory requirements and recommended good practice.

August 1994 216 pp approx Royal pbk
ISBN 0 85292 534 4 £14.95

Discrimination

Linda Clarke

Many employers still regard non-discrimination as a matter of looking for loopholes to avoid falling foul of the law. Yet the case, both moral and commercial, for recruiting and promoting the best people is overwhelming. This clear and comprehensive guide explains:

* the law on sexual discrimination (harassment, maternity rights and equal pay)
* how to avoid discrimination on grounds of race, disability and medical condition, trade union status and age
* how to eliminate prejudice from the recruitment process (advertising, application forms, interviews and job offers)
* how to ensure fair treatment for all employees (appraisal, discipline, promotion and performance-related pay)
* the distinction between positive action and positive discrimination
* legal requirements and good personnel practice.

144 pp Royal pbk
ISBN 0 85292 528 X £14.95

Working with the Unions

Colin Pope

Recent legislation and competitive pressures have swept aside many industrial relations traditions. Yet working effectively with the unions is a continuing and crucial challenge for most organisations. So, although employers should always seek co-operation rather than conflict, it is also essential that they understand the legal framework and establish machinery for dealing with disputes. This clear and comprehensive guide considers:

* recognition, derecognition and single-union agreements
* effective bargaining strategies for the 1990s
* consultation on equal opportunities, training, technological change, and health and safety
* arbitration, conciliation and the role of ACAS
* disputes, strike ballots and termination of contracts
* likely union responses – and the best countermeasures.

August 1994 216 pp approx Royal pbk
ISBN 0 85292 529 8 £14.95